A WORLD BANK COUNTRY STUDY

Public Expenditure Review of Armenia

THE WORLD BANK
Washington, D.C.

ISBN: 0-8213-5584-8
eISBN: 0-8213-5585-6
ISSN: 0253-2123

Library of Congress Cataloging-in-Publication Data has been requested.

Contents

TABLES

FIGURES

BOXES

ABSTRACT

This is the first full scale World Bank Public Expenditure Review (PER) for Armenia, which reviews the main fiscal trends in Armenia for the period of 1997–2001 and develop recommendations with respect to further fiscal adjustment, expenditure prioritization, and budget consolidation. The analysis in the Report is focused on the following core issues:

- Quality of fiscal adjustment: How sustainable have been the recent Government achievements to reduce fiscal deficits and budget arrears?
- Other sustainability concerns: How much potential risk for the fiscal system is associated with off-budget Government activities, including operations of the Pension Fund, quasi-fiscal subsidies provided by the energy sector, and Government guarantees.
- Fiscal transparency: How reliable are the fiscal data in Armenia? What are the main directions for improvements in reporting on fiscal operations of the public sector?
- Expenditure priorities: What are the priorities for strategic re-allocation of public spending, both at the inter-sectoral and intra-sectoral level, to maximize growth and welfare effects within fiscally sustainable limits?
- Expenditure management: What should be the short-term priorities for upgrading standards of fiscal management, given the existing economy-wide institutional constraints?

The report has the following structure. Chapter 1 reviews the main features of the Government's fiscal adjustment effort, initiated in the mid 1990s. It is focused on the analysis of aggregated indicators of fiscal performance such as deficit, public debt, budget arrears, and tax revenues. Chapter 2 looks at the main expenditure trends in the Armenia consolidated budget for 1997–2001 and makes an assessment of the quality and depth of expenditure restructuring. Chapter 3 looks at the public sector's activities that remain non-reflected in the regular Government budget, which includes extra-budgetary funds, in-kind external grants, subsidies provided by the state-owned companies in the energy and utility sectors, and operations of the Social Insurance Fund.

Chapter 4 presents in-depth analysis of progress made to date in the area of expenditure management and suggests a draft medium-term action plan to address identified weaknesses in budget preparation, presentation, execution, and reporting. Chapters 5–7 review expenditure policies in the main social sectors (health, education, social protection and insurance) and provide recommendations on: (i) how current expenditures could be made more efficient; (ii) what should be the main direction for intra-sectoral expenditure reallocation; and (iii) what should be medium-term targets for an increase in public expenditures in these sectors. Chapter 8 estimates a minimum level of budget support in core public infrastructure, which would stop deterioration of existing core assets in respective sectors and prevent the further accumulation of arrears. Chapter 9 presents an analysis of Armenia's public investment program.

ACKNOWLEDGMENTS

The report is a joint product of the World Bank and the Ministry of Finance and Economy of Armenia. The Bank team was led by Lev Freinkman, Senior Country Economist for Armenia, while the Government team was led by Pavel Safaryan, First Deputy Minister.

The following individuals were responsible for drafting the chapters of the main report:

Lev Freinkman (Chapters 1, 2, and 3), Gohar Gyulumyan (Chapters 3 and 9), Mary Betley (Chapter 4), Sue Ellen Berryman (Chapter 5), Edmundo Murrugarra (Chapter 6), Aleksandra Posarac (Chapter 7), and Robert H. Nooter (Chapter 8).

The core Government team included Pavel Safaryan, Karlen Antonyan, Jora Asatryan, Vladimir Astvatsaturyan, Karine Harutyunyan, Atom Janjoughazyan, Tigran Khachatryan, Arshalouys Margaryan, Victor Martirosyan and Ashot Yesayan.

The background papers were prepared by the team of local consultants consisting of Vahram Avanesyan, Levon Barkhudaryan, and Armen Yeghiazaryan. The team also benefited from advice and comments of John Zohrab, IMF Treasury Adviser in Armenia.

Artsvi Khachatryan provided research assistance. Lala Ananikyan, David Hambartsumyan, Gayane Harutyunyan, Anahit Hovhannisyan, Marine Hovhannessyan, Emilia Hovhannisyan, Mourad Mouradyan, and Susanna Onanian helped with the data collection.

Zakia Nekaien-Nowrouz processed the report, while Usha Rani Khanna edited various versions of the text.

Comments and suggestions were provided by Konstantin Atanesyan, Ani Balabanyan, David Davtian, Mohammad Reza Ghasimi, Karen Grigorian, Susanna Hayrapetyan, Artak Kyurumyan, Heath McDonald, Naira Melkumyan, Gayane Minasyan, Allister Moon, Gevorg Sargsyan, Antti P. Talvitie, Bagrat Tunyan, Evgeny Polyakov, Aleksandra Posarac, and Brian Steven Smith.

Philippe Le Houerou and Charles Humphreys were the peer reviewers.

Samuel K. E. Otoo is the Sector Manager. Cheryl Gray is the Department Director. Judy M. O'Connor was the Country Director for Armenia.

The team is grateful to the Department for International Development (UK) for an important contribution to project implementation.

ABBREVIATIONS AND ACRONYMS

AMD	Armenian Dram
ASYCUDA	Automated System for Customs Data
BBP	Basic Benefit Package
BOP	Balance of Payment
CBA	Central Bank of Armenia
CEE	Central and Eastern Europe
CIS	Commonwealth of Independent States
CPA	Central Procurement Agency
CPIA	Country Policy and Institutional Assessment
CPI	Consumer Price Index
DFID	Department for International Development
EBF	Extra-Budgetary Fund
EBRD	European Bank for Reconstruction and Development
ECA	Europe and Central Asia
EQZ	Earthquake Zone
EU	European Union
FDI	Foreign Direct Investment
FMIS	Financial Management Information System
FSU	Former Soviet Union
GCHA	Government Commission on Humanitarian Assistance
GFS	Government Financial Statistics
GOA	Government of Armenia
GDP	Gross Domestic Product
IAS	International Accounting Standards
IBRD	International Bank for Reconstruction and Development
IDA	International Development Association
IGR	Institutional and Governance Review
IMF	International Monetary Fund
ISLC	Integrated Survey of Living Conditions
IT	Information and Telecommunication
MOFE	Ministry of Finance and Economy
MOSR	Ministry of State Revenues
MSS	Ministry of Social Security
MTED	Ministry of Trade and Economic Development
MTEF	Medium Term Expenditure Framework
NEHAP	National Environmental Health Action Plan
NGO	Non-Government Organization
NPV	Net Present Value
NSS	National Statistical Service
OECD	Organization of Economic Cooperation and Development
OFB	Overall Fiscal Balance
PEM	Public Expenditure Management
PER	Public Expenditure Review
PIU	Project Implementation Unit
PISA	Program for International Student Assessment
PPP	Purchasing Power Parity
PRSP	Poverty Reduction Strategy Paper
PSD	Private Sector Development

R&D	Research and Development
SAC5	Fifth Structural Adjustment Credit
SHA	State Health Agency
SIF	Social Insurance Fund
SME	Small and Medium Enterprises
SOE	State-Owned Enterprise
TA	Technician Assistance
TB	Treasury Bill
USAID	United States Agency for International Development
VAT	Value Added Tax
WHO	World Health Organization

CURRENCY AND EQUIVALENT UNITS
Exchange Rate Effective February 20, 2003
Currency Unit = Dram
Dram = US$0.0017
US$1.0 = 582 Dram

WEIGHTS AND MEASURES
Metric System

FISCAL YEAR
January 1 to December 31

EXECUTIVE SUMMARY

Over the last several years, Armenia's economic performance has been rather strong. Since 1994, annual growth has exceeded 5 percent—a remarkably resilient performance in the face of the Russian financial crisis of 1998 and political assassinations in October 1999. Since the second half of 2000, the economy has shown an additional improvement in performance, supported by export expansion.

Fiscal adjustment and budget reforms played an important role in attaining macroeconomic stability and therefore creating the economic environment supportive for economic growth. After 1997, the macroeconomic situation has remained mostly stable, with low inflation, a stable exchange rate, and a sufficient level of international reserves. Table A below reflects that the Government undertook a major adjustment effort in 1997 that resulted in a reduction of the consolidated deficit of the public sector from more than 11 percent of GDP in 1995–96 to about 10 percent of GDP. The Government provided for further fiscal adjustment in 1999–2000, and it reduced the consolidated deficit to the level of about 7.5 percent of GDP. Preliminary results for 2001 suggest an additional improvement.

The available data point out, however, that despite quite a comfortable macro picture and considerable recent fiscal adjustment, the sustainability of fiscal performance remains a major concern. It is primarily due to revenue collection, which, although improved since 1995–96, is still low and unstable and reflects persistent weaknesses in tax and customs administration as well as the sizable share of the informal economy. The performance of the energy sector and other public utilities also remains a source of significant fiscal risks.

In addition, there are also major problems related to expenditure management that result in low efficiency of budget spending. The introduction of institutional reforms in the budget sphere has followed fiscal adjustment; this has resulted in gaps between announced government policies and approved budget allocations, weak correlation between approved budgets and actual disbursements, and in the imbalanced structure of actual expenditures that continue to reflect in part the pre-reform legacy. In addition, regular accumulation of budget arrears undermines credibility of the budget process.

TABLE A: THE PACE OF FISCAL ADJUSTMENT (percent of GDP)							
	1995	1996	1997	1998	1999	2000	2001
A. Fiscal Deficit, consolidated budget, cash	−8.9	−8.3	−4.7	−3.7	−5.2	−4.8	−4.2
B. "Off-budget" deficit (budget arrears + deficit of the energy sector)	−2.4	−4.7	−5.4	−6.9	−2.6	−2.5	−1.0
C. Government deficit, accrual (budgeted and off-budget, =A+B)	−11.3	−13.0	−10.1	−10.5	−7.8	−7.3	−5.2

Given that this is the first full scale Public Expenditure Review (PER) for Armenia, the initial objective of the Report is to clarify the basic facts about the fiscal performance of Armenia's public sector, based on both more accurate interpretation of available budget data and more systematic review of the off-budget financial flows. Assembling a more accurate fiscal database for 1997–2001 was a foundation for pursuing other more substantive objectives of the Report such as in-depth analysis of the main fiscal trends in Armenia, identification of the remaining major weaknesses in the fiscal framework, and development of recommendations for further fiscal adjustment, expenditure prioritization, and budget consolidation.

Summary of the Proposed Fiscal Strategy

The core of the fiscal strategy, recommended by the PER, could be summarized as follows:

■ Improve revenue performance by at least 2 percent of GDP in the medium term;
· ■ Provide for major improvements in budget accountability that would ensure that incremental resources are spent in a transparent and efficient way;
■ Ensure an additional reduction in budget deficit relative to the 2001 level and full elimination of quasi-fiscal deficit;
■ Channel a large chunk of incremental revenues to increase expenditures on basic health and education as well as on old-age pensions;
■ Accelerate sectoral and civil service reforms to ensure much more efficient use of budget resources, primarily in social sectors and public administration.

Table B provides a summary of policy recommendations of the Report.

Depth and Quality of Fiscal Adjustment

The level of public expenditures in Armenia decreased by about 3 times in real terms between 1990 and the mid-90s. This resulted from a simultaneous decline in both real output (by more than 50 percent) and in the relative size of the Government (consolidated budget expenditures declined from 35 percent to about 25 percent of GDP). This dramatic budget compression, however, took place in an environment, which was not supportive for comprehensive restructuring and re-prioritization of budget spending. Making budget cuts proved to be much easier than enforcing a radical expenditure restructuring.

Overall, by early 1999, Armenia demonstrated (relative to the period of 1992–96) a considerable fiscal adjustment and rather advanced budget consolidation, which included the following distinguishing features:

■ modest successes in advancing reforms in the energy sector, reducing the volume of energy-related subsidies and incorporating a relatively large part of what remains into the regular budget;

TABLE B: MAIN RECOMMENDATIONS

Advance fiscal adjustment and budget consolidation	▪ Reduce budget deficit to 3.5 percent of GDP in the medium term. ▪ Expand budget coverage to include all existing sectoral extra-budgetary funds, non-cash grants from official donors, and quasi-fiscal subsidies. ▪ Reduce losses and improve monitoring of state-owned enterprises to avoid uncontrolled accumulation of debts and other liabilities.
Improve tax collection	▪ Establish a target of increasing tax collection by 2 percent of GDP. ▪ Strengthen tax administration in the areas of excisable goods, VAT, personal income and payroll taxes.
Improve budget transparency and accountability	▪ Introduce the new budget classification (GFS2001). ▪ Ensure that budgets are appropriated by the administrative classification. ▪ Improve quality of budget presentation and reporting, including reports on public debts, budget arrears, non-cash external grants, and activities of the Reserve Fund. ▪ Accelerate introduction of international accounting standards in budget institutions. ▪ Establish a modern consolidated system of financial reporting by state enterprises, including public sector entities in education and health. ▪ Increase accountability of respective managers for compliance with appropriations, established by the Budget Law.
Advance expenditure rationalization and reallocation	▪ Reduce the level of budgeted and quasi-fiscal subsidies as well as the level of budget credits. ▪ Based on additional review, close down some elements of public infrastructure to reduce budget liabilities. ▪ Potential savings and incremental tax revenues should be primarily channeled to social sectors (general education and primary health, old age pensions) and financing in basic infrastructure (transport, including roads, water, irrigation). ▪ Advance implementation of the civil service reform to ensure reductions in public employment and increase budget wages.
Strengthen strategic approach to budgeting	▪ Strengthen institutional and legal framework and capabilities to make the regular MTEF preparation/update a part of the annual budget cycle. ▪ Use MTEF as an instrument of development of strategic priorities for resource allocation. ▪ Provide a gradual switch from line-based and norm-based budget to program budgeting. ▪ Broaden public debate on expenditure strategy as a part of the PRSP process.
Streamline budget execution	▪ Initiate the second stage of Treasury reforms to strengthen commitment controls, information systems, and internal audit.
Advance sectoral reforms to ensure more effective utilization of funds at the sectoral level	▪ Expand the role of line ministries in budgeting and their responsibility for outcomes. ▪ Advance restructuring of school and hospital networks to ensure reduction of excessive capacity and improved quality of public services. ▪ Initiate a comprehensive reform of financing of university education. ▪ Increase the level of old age pensions by improving tax collections and transferring non-insurance liabilities of the SIF to the budget. ▪ Restructure the system of unemployment benefits and services.

- ▪ consistency in enforcing a tight monetary policy and avoiding quasi-fiscal financing of the real sector through directed credit programs;
- ▪ avoiding any systematic usage of non-cash payment schemes and thus escaping a trap of money substitutes;
- ▪ lower than the regional average incidence of tax expenditures (both tax arrears and tax exemptions).

This resulted in relatively robust macroeconomic outcomes, such as stable exchange rate trends and the manageable level of external public debt. Cross-country comparisons also suggest that Armenia has been less affected by uncontrolled growth of contingent public liabilities, including off-budget quasi-public borrowing.

Despite this progress, Armenia's fiscal *adjustment is still incomplete*. To ensure sustainability of economic recovery, it is critical to make an additional adjustment effort and address the existing fiscal risks. Some deterioration in the revenue performance in 1999–2000 confirms vulnerability of earlier adjustments. While the outcomes for 2001 appear as a substantial improvement, the 2001 consolidated deficit of the public sector still remained above its sustainable medium-term level, which was estimated by this Report to be about 3.5 percent of GDP.[1] The level of quasi-fiscal deficit, primarily in the energy sector (power, gas, heating), while reduced, is still significant (2.3 percent of GDP in 2000).

Budget consolidation also remains incomplete, with a considerable part of public expenditures being uncovered by the official budget and formal budget process. Main elements of the fiscal system which should be moved to the budget include non-cash external grants (estimated to amount to 2 percent of GDP a year), sectoral extra-budgetary funds (0.4 percent of GDP in 2000 and probably more than 1 percent of GDP in 2001), and quasi-fiscal subsidies that are funded by state-owned companies in the energy sector (between to 2 and 3 percent of GDP in 1999–2000). Thus, total expenditures of the public sector, when fully consolidated, amounted to 30 percent of GDP in 2000.

Most quasi-fiscal financing and in addition a substantial chunk of budget resources is used to provide large non-transparent, regressive and highly inefficient subsidies to the population and some large SOEs. Total annual subsidies—including accumulated debts to utilities and tax arrears—are estimated to have been 6–7.5 percent of GDP in 1996–2000.[2] At least half of these subsidies are still provided through quasi-fiscal channels. These implicit subsidies consume scarce public resources, which alternatively could be used more efficiently by providing targeted social assistance for the most needy.

While more than 100 (almost 50 percent of their total remaining number) of medium and large SOEs reported losses in 2000, the Government system of monitoring the financial performance of state enterprises remains weak and segmented. Total annual losses of SOEs outside of the power sector are close to 1 percent of GDP. All this poses an additional risk for sustainability of recent fiscal improvements. The Government should accelerate *liquidation and/or forced restructuring* of the largest loss-making firms, which would have a beneficial impact on both the fiscal system and the entire enterprise sector. It should also revitalize its privatization program, implementation of which slowed down considerably in 2000–01.

Fiscal uncertainties, associated with the unstable revenue performance and excessive budget dependence on donor funding, depress expectations of the private sector and thus further delay new investments and entry of strategic foreign investors. Persisting fiscal problems delay a phase-out of quasi-fiscal financing in public utilities and infrastructure as well as improvements in financing core social services. The recovery of infrastructure and social services is especially important for improving the longer-term growth prospects of the country and reducing the risk of social tensions.

The important policy priority is to improve *revenue performance* by at least 2 percentage points of GDP over the next few years, which would provide for attaining a 20 percent of GDP mark." A major current expenditure problem in Armenia relates to the small size of the existing budget envelope. Given the expenditure cuts that have already taken place, the scope for further aggregate

---

1. It is believed that Armenia could afford relatively high deficit levels for the next several years because its good access to highly concessional financing, including IDA, bilateral donors, and Diaspora's sources, in a combination with high growth rates keeps its debt profile sustainable.

2. The preliminary data for 2001 suggest a significant reduction in the level of subsidization but this needs an additional analysis and re-confirmation.

expenditure compression is quite limited. While some additional reduction in budget deficit is desirable, most incremental resources should go to increase expenditures, including clearance of arrears and replacement of quasi-fiscal financing with explicit budget support.

The Government has been addressing the revenue problem by accelerating capacity building in tax and customs administration with assistance from the IMF and bilateral donors. However, the developments in the last three years suggest that a radical improvement in revenue performance requires, in addition to the reforms in administration, a much stronger Government's ownership of the reform process that would allow address the problem of powerful vested interests. Also, surprisingly little was done recently for strengthening compliance with personal income and payroll tax legislation by the wealthiest quintile of the population, especially by business managers and business owners. For instance, based on conservative estimates, less than 60 percent of the wage bill in the formal sector is taxed by payroll taxation.

Therefore, in Armenia, as in many other developing countries, tax collection could be treated as the informative indicator of Government's commitment to fight vested interests and address broader problems of governance and unfair competition. The initial steps to boost collections should be concentrated in the areas that are known as the worst offenders. They include:

- Improved revenue flow from taxation of main excisable goods (such as petrol and tobacco) by reducing their under-reporting and smuggling;
- Improved car registration and budget revenues from car importation;
- Increased revenue yield from a limited number of the largest retail markets in Yerevan to ensure a level playing field in the sector;
- Improved administration of the personal income tax and payroll tax by introducing Personal Identification Numbers/Tax Identification Numbers (PINs/TINs) and expanding coverage of mandatory tax declarations to include entrepreneurs and business owners;
- Making progress in the administration of VAT refund for exporters;
- Ultimately transferring responsibility for payroll tax collection from the Pension Fund to the Ministry of State Revenues, as soon as the latter demonstrates an improved efficiency in collection of personal income tax.

Fiscal Transparency and Accountability

Government accountability for budget outcomes as well as rational spending of available resources are the main pre-conditions for expanding the budget envelope, including the one in social sectors. Therefore, the immediate top priority for the Government is to improve both transparency and efficiency of existing spending. The Government has to demonstrate its real commitment to higher standards of expenditure policy before making an additional tax collection effort. In other words, it is critical to ensure proper balance and sequencing between future improvements in tax administration, expenditure rationalization and quality of public sector accounts.

Strengthening the quality of fiscal data is a necessary initial step to improve expenditure analysis and to design an adequate expenditure rationalization strategy, including proper reallocation of resources between sectors. This would require a major improvement in the quality of budget reporting at all levels?budgetary organizations, line ministries, and the central Treasury to be supported by switching to the new GFS (2001) budget classification and gradual transition to the new accounting standards. Specific priorities in this area include:

- Better budget presentation and reporting, including full consistency in presentation between annual budget Laws and budget execution reports;
- Annual budget appropriations based on the administrative classification, with presentation also by economic and functional classifications. Basing the appropriations on the administrative classification would reflect the increased roles and responsibilities of sectoral ministries to prepare and implement their expenditure programs within the approved budget ceilings;

- Improvements in accuracy of reporting on budget arrears and budget guarantees, and on activities funded under multi-sectoral donor projects as well as from non-cash external grants;
- Improvements in reporting on salaries in the budgetary sector as well as in statistics of public employment, including establishment of a database on all budgetary-funded staff positions;
- Improvements in transparency of operations of the Reserve Fund;
- Making budgetary support for public utilities more transparent: stop calling subsidies "budget credits", stop the practice of offsetting budgetary debts to utilities, make sure that any future debt-for-equity deals are properly accounted for and reported;
- Improvements in statistics on public investments;
- Establishment of a modern consolidated system of financial reporting by state enterprises, including public sector entities in education and health;
- A general improvement in availability of statistics for the public sector that is important for budgetary planning, including items such as number of students in public schools and universities, public housing, length of publicly funded roads, etc.;
- Increased accountability of respective managers for compliance with appropriations, established by the Budget Law.

Strategic Focus of the Budget Process and the MTEF

Because reforms necessary to restructure public expenditure policy have followed budget compression, there is a major need for updating (and in some cases, clearly formulating) expenditure priorities. This has to be followed by an additional reallocation of funds to concentrate limited resources in the most critical areas, especially those related to support of primary social services and basic infrastructure. Without such a shift, the country's human capital base will continue to erode, raising the price of future broad-based growth.

This shift would be difficult to implement, however, without major reforms in the current budget processes. While the Government achieved considerable success in implementing aggregate expenditure controls, the underlying budget process and procedures needs a significant change in order to reflect the reforms that are under way and are planned, including the Medium Term Expenditure Framework (MTEF). Without the ability to link Government policies explicitly to expenditure allocations through the budget process, the MOFE will find it difficult to establish a closer link between budgets and Government policies, and it would delay the process of expenditure rationalization.

The main changes in budget formulation should include:

- Moving away gradually from line-item budgeting to program-based budgets;
- Greater involvement of sector ministries in the budget process; sector ministries, not the MOFE, should have the primary role in programming and implementing sector policies and budgets, as well as be responsible for attaining objectives of agreed sectoral programs;
- Expansion in the role of sectoral ministries in the budgetary process should be conditioned on the improvement in their accountability for utilization of public resources in respective sectors, which would require a major upgrade in accounting and reporting practices as described in the previous section;
- More budget authority to be given to budget managers for flexible utilization of their allocations based on global budgeting, whilst ensuring appropriate budget controls and accountability arrangements are in place;
- Refocusing the role of the MOFE on setting overall budget policy, on determining the size of sectoral expenditure programs (annual sectoral ceilings), and analysis of consistency between adopted sectoral policies and sectoral budgetary submissions.

At the same time, the Government plans to continue to develop a more strategic medium-term approach to budgeting based on the PRSP document, which would identify the strategic priorities for public spending. This would require strengthening the institutional and legal framework for the MTEF and capabilities for making the regular MTEF preparation/update a part of the annual budget cycle. Starting from the MTEF for 2003–2005, the Government should progressively rely on the MTEF to guide the preparation of annual budgets. The next MTEF update should project the total budgetary framework for the medium term and spell out sectoral priorities, which provide a basis for realistic sector resource ceilings for the 2003 Budget.

At the same time, as part of the PRSP process, the Government has to broaden public debate on expenditure strategy and available strategic options. It is important to raise public awareness of strategic public expenditure issues such as revenue potential and sustainable levels of aggregate public expenditure, pension and social welfare issues, costs of basic education and health provision, civil service size and remuneration.

Fiscal Planning and Management

This report emphasizes the importance of making the budget credible in order to ensure that planned Government policies can be achieved. Budget credibility requires actual budgetary releases to be similar to budget plans and calls for appropriate fiscal discipline to be in place. Also, frequent changes in authorized budget amounts should be avoided.

In Armenia, actual budget outcomes do not correspond well to the adopted budget laws, especially at the disaggregated level. Moreover, the analysis indicates that the deviations between the approved and executed budgets were significant, and the deviations increased in 1999–2000 compared to 1998.

This budget uncertainty and associated loss of credibility derives from several factors. Its primary source, however, reflects failure to resolve the underlying imbalance between expenditure commitments and resources available. The Armenian budget is over-committed: the Government has not been able to concentrate spending in a fewer number of functions/institutions, it struggles to support too many pieces of the traditional expenditure structure but in many cases provides funding at unsustainable low levels. Chronic underfunding across the board keeps the fiscal pressures high and diverts the attention of policy makers from identification and making decisions on strategic choices.

Additional factors that limit the Government's ability to ensure more predictable and more strategic budget outcomes include:

- Priorities given to various agencies in the process of budget execution differ from the agreed budget allocations. For instance, social ministries were the most affected by de facto budget sequestration.
- The quality of budget reporting is affected by the introduction of new spending programs in the course of budget execution; many such programs have been placed under the rubric "other expenditure"/Reserve Fund and never fully disclosed according to the functional/administrative classification.
- Weaknesses in expenditure control that allow sectoral ministries in some cases to exceed their budget appropriations.
- High dependence on donor financing, which creates additional uncertainty due to constant delays with disbursement of foreign credits and grants.

Strengthening basic capacity for fiscal management is a critical element of the next stage of fiscal adjustment. The Government needs further strengthening of budget planning and forecasting and the introduction of stricter expenditure discipline in order to raise budget credibility. Introducing an efficient system of commitment control and accounting is clearly a priority. It is also critical to make a drastic cut in the existing budget liabilities to bring them in line with both the real size of the budget envelope and Government priorities. This would require a significant reduction in a number of budget dependent entities and closure of some parts of social and basic public infrastructure.

Expenditure Rationalization

The PER analysis suggests the existence of the main structural imbalances in the allocation of public expenditure in Armenia. These include:

- Excessive number of budget dependent organizations which leads to inefficient segmentation of budget allocations;
- Overcapacity in social sectors and an inherited relatively over-developed network in basic infrastructure, which became unaffordable at the current income level, while respective sectoral budgets are heavily biased towards wage bill spending;
- Imbalance between relatively high infrastructure investments that are mostly donor funded and insufficient budget allocations on current maintenance of these facilities;
- Excessive government employment at very low public sector wages;
- The public pension system that is fiscally sustainable but which can afford old age pensions that are too low to be socially acceptable;
- Large proportion of public expenditures absorbed by defense and security expenditures.[3]

The PER suggests that while the structure of budget spending has been evolving since the middle of the 90s, the accumulated inter-sectoral expenditure restructuring was insufficient, which was in part due to the government capacity limitations. Specifically, the Government failed to attain targets it set up back in 1999 in the first MTEF (2000–02), which envisioned a significant resource reallocation towards core social services. As a result, the Government is facing several urgent needs to increase expenditures, primarily in social sectors. These priority incremental expenditures have been conservatively estimated in this Report as the following:

- Primary health: increase of 0.5 percent of GDP to reach at least 2 percent of GDP target;
- Education (mostly general education): increase of 0.5 percent of GDP to reach 3 percent of GDP target;
- Labor Pensions: increase of 0.8 percent of GDP to reach 3 percent of GDP target;
- Infrastructure: increase of about 0.5 percent to reach the level that is sufficient to ensure both critical maintenance and accumulation of no new debts;
- Public sector wages: increase of 60 percent in real average wage to reach a target of 80 percent of per capita GDP.

Additional financing of these areas would come from three sources_better revenue performance, cross-sectoral expenditure reallocation, increased spending efficiency within the sectors. As mentioned above, the Government should follow a balanced strategy of simultaneous improvements in all three areas.

The Government should pursue its current policies in the energy and utility sectors to ensure a phase out of remaining subsidies in the medium term. That is, while an immediate priority for these sectors relates to an increase in explicit budget support to ensure adequate maintenance and termination of quasi-fiscal financing, the medium-term objective is to phase out budget subsidies through adequate tariff policy, strengthened payment discipline and increased efficiency of utility operators. The Government should also reduce the amount of budget credits disbursed from the Reserve Fund. It should advance its civil service reform program to ensure higher efficiency in public administration based on a streamlined structure of the Government, reduced staff levels, and increased salaries.

Health and Education Spending

Although both health status indicators and the general level of education in Armenia compare favorably to other CIS economies as well as to many other economies at the same level of income,

---

3. The Government suggested an undertaking of an additional review of defense spending.

there is evidence that years of under-financing of basic public health and education, if not addressed, could create longer term problems for the Armenia's growth and competitiveness. There is evidence of a significant decrease of health care utilization (particularly polyclinics), increased vulnerability to infectious diseases, and a growing drop-out rate from schools. The inequality of access to basic health is a major concern. Budget expenditures in these two sectors are very low by international standards, including lower than in other CIS economies. Budgetary allocations do not reflect properly the announced Government policies, while actual financing has been traditionally below budget allocations (especially in health). While inequality in general education is not so acute, children from the poorest consumption quintile enroll at lower rates at each level of education. If not addressed, these trends would become a major constraint for growth in the longer term.

At the same time, the existing expenditure patterns in these two sectors are grossly inefficient due to overcapacity and overstaffing. Introduction of per capita financing in a number of schools has been a positive strategic innovation but so far it failed to establish incentives for staff reductions at the school level. For instance, Armenia's student/teacher ratios in general education are half what is considered to be optimal in terms of learning outcomes. If not addressed, these inefficiencies will only get worse as the numbers of Armenia's 7–16 year olds will decline significantly between 2000 and 2015. In health, as follows from the recent population census, Armenia has about 4 doctors per 1,000 inhabitants, and this number did not decline in the 1990s despite a recent drastic reduction in health care utilization, one of the highest in the region.

The Government strategy in health and education should combine an increase in budget financing with the rationalization of spending at the sectoral level. Increased efficiency of sectoral expenditure programs would provide additional support for their claims for an increased share in the total budget envelop.

Other priorities in education and health financing:

- Advance implementation of Government plans for restructuring of school and health facilities to ensure reduction of excessive capacity;
- Reduce segmentation of public expenditures in health and education by incorporating off-budget grant expenditures into the budget and better accounting for private out-of-pocket spending;
- Based on an additional analysis of tertiary education, initiate a comprehensive reform of university education to include issues of financing, governance, efficiency and quality assurance, and also promote the consolidation of the system;
- Reform the system of secondary vocational education and training to increase its market relevance and reduce costs;
- Build the capacity to monitor availability of basic education and health for the poor.

Social Protection and Insurance

The introduction of the poverty family benefit program in 1999 should be considered among the major successful reforms in Armenia. Thus, this program should remain a core of the social assistance system in the country. In the medium term, the Government should refrain from introducing any additional regular monthly programs, such as for instance, a housing allowance. At the same time, efforts to improve benefit targeting as well as to improve its administration should be continued. The Government, with donors' support, should ensure that household income/expenditure surveys are conducted regularly to have adequate information for poverty monitoring. It is estimated that the budget for the family poverty benefit should not be reduced below its 2001 level of 1.4 percent of GDP to preserve a significant impact of the program on extreme poverty for the next several years. At the same time, in order to ensure a proper balance between different income sources, annual budget allocations for poverty benefits should be determined in connection with the dynamics of both average wage and average pension benefit.

With respect to social insurance, the PER recommends the following set of directions for policy and administrative reforms:

- As a medium-term objective, provide for an increase in the old age pension at a rate that would allow attaining 35–40 percent ratio between the average nominal pension and the average nominal wage;
- Improve the collection of payroll taxes by establishing stronger incentives to comply (based on the system of individual accounts) and by strengthening the payroll tax administration;
- Introduce much stricter eligibility conditions for the social pensions;
- Strictly separate financing of the social insurance benefits from other benefits, including transferring both financing and administration of social pensions out of the Pension Fund;
- Maintain tight eligibility controls: the Government should refrain from introducing any early retirement provisions or any special retirement benefits for particular employment categories, while currently existing early retirement provisions should be gradually phased out;
- Abolish unemployment insurance and introduce a flat unemployment benefit with a much stricter eligibility criteria and a much shorter eligibility period;
- Restructure the existing systems of employment support and vocational training;
- Improve the administration of the Pension Fund.

Successful implementation of the above measures in the short to medium run would allow Armenia to increase pensions and decrease the rates of payroll taxation, as well as establish an environment supportive for introduction of a new pension system based on much stronger links between individual benefits and contributions paid.

World Bank Strategy

The World Bank is committed to support, in cooperation with other donors, Government efforts to upgrade its fiscal management system and restructure its expenditure envelop. The forthcoming IDA Public Sector Modernization Project may help the Government to advance capacity building in the Treasury as well as help with broader civil service reforms, including those in the area of audit. This project would be implemented in close coordination with technical assistance projects funded by the IMF, DFID, and the US Treasury. In addition, in 2002–03, the World Bank will complete both procurement and financial accountability assessments for Armenia, which would provide additional recommendations on institutional strengthening in these two areas.

Future IDA budget support, starting from the proposed SAC5, would have a stronger focus on fiscal management issues, as well as on tax policies and tax performance. This part of the policy dialogue will be backed by technical assistance, funded from bilateral and multilateral grants. Specifically, Government efforts to strengthen capabilities for MTEF development will be backed by the PRSP grants and advisory services provided by DFID and USAID.

The World Bank will continue to assist public expenditure rationalization at the sectoral level within the framework of specific sectoral investment operations, including those in health, education, transport, irrigation, and energy. In addition, there are commitments from several bilateral donors to back up Government reforms in poverty monitoring, social protection, and pensions.

Other Assistance by the Donor Community

In addition to the above mentioned support aimed at capacity building and advancement of policy reforms, international donors could also help in the following areas:

- While Armenia's debt profile seems to become increasingly sustainable, in the medium term the country will still remain dependent on concessional external borrowing and grants.

International donors could make a major contribution to improvements in expenditure management in Armenia by making an inflow of external financing more predictable.

- Donors could also help to reduce budget seasonality by shifting a larger portion of disbursements to the first part of the calendar year.
- Donors would help to make Armenia's budget more transparent and sectoral policies more efficient if they insist on consolidation of their main non-cash grants into the budget. And donors' should become more cooperative by providing the Government (including the MOFE) with regular reports on actual grant disbursements and insisting that the Government should consolidate such reports and make them public.

INTRODUCTION

This is the first full scale World Bank Public Expenditure Review (PER) for Armenia. The only previous PER for Armenia was produced in 1997 but it was limited in scope and was based on earlier field work (1995 was the last full year of data reviewed), and as such covered the period that was characterized by high inflation and low tax collection.

The primary objective of the Report was to review the main fiscal trends in Armenia for the period of 1997–2001 and develop recommendations with respect to further fiscal adjustment, expenditure prioritization, and budget consolidation. More specifically, the following themes represent the core issues analyzed in the Report:

- Quality of fiscal adjustment: How sustainable have been the recent Government achievements to reduce fiscal deficits and budget arrears?
- Other sustainability concerns: How much potential risk for the fiscal system is associated with off-budget Government activities, including operations of the Pension Fund, quasi-fiscal subsidies provided by the energy sector, and Government guarantees.
- Fiscal transparency: How reliable are the fiscal data in Armenia? What are the main directions for improvements in reporting on fiscal operations of the public sector?
- Expenditure priorities: What are the priorities for strategic re-allocation of public spending, both at the inter-sectoral and intra-sectoral level, to maximize growth and welfare effects within fiscally sustainable limits?
- Expenditure management: What should be the short-term priorities for upgrading standards of fiscal management, given the existing economy-wide institutional constraints?

The report has the following structure. The analysis starts in Chapter 1, which reviews the main features of the Government's fiscal adjustment effort, initiated in the mid-1990s. It is focused on the analysis of aggregated indicators of fiscal performance such as deficit, public debt, budget arrears, and tax revenues. Chapter 2 looks at the main expenditure trends in the Armenia consolidated budget for 1997–2001 and makes an assessment of the quality and depth of expenditure restructuring undertaken in this period. Chapter 3 looks at the public sector's activities that remain non-reflected in the regular Government budget, which includes extra-budgetary funds, in-kind external grants, subsidies provided by the state-owned companies in the energy and utility sectors, and operations of the Social Insurance Fund.

Chapter 4 presents in-depth analysis of progress made to date in the area of expenditure management and suggests a draft medium-term action plan to address identified weaknesses in budget preparation, presentation, execution, and reporting. Annexes 1 and 2 reflect more specific recommendations with respect to upgrading budget management procedures and the regulatory framework.

Chapters 5–7 review expenditure policies in the main social sectors (health, education, social protection and insurance) and provide recommendations on: (i) how current expenditures could be made more efficient; (ii) what should be the main direction for intra-sectoral expenditure reallocation; and (iii) what should be medium-term targets for an increase in public expenditures in these sectors. Chapter 8 estimates a minimum level of budget support in core public infrastructure, which would stop deterioration of existing core assets in respective sectors and prevent the further accumulation of arrears. Sectoral Chapters 5–8 also provide recommendations for policy changes that would facilitate a return of these sectors to fiscal sustainability.

Chapter 9 presents an analysis of Armenia's public investment program.

CHAPTER I

MACROECONOMIC AND FISCAL ENVIRONMENT

Recent Economic Trends

Over the last several years, Armenia's economic performance has been rather strong. After an estimated 60 percent decline between 1991 and 1993, real GDP grew 5.4 percent in 1994. Since then, annual growth has averaged about 6 percent—a remarkably resilient performance in the face of the Russian financial crisis of 1998 and political assassinations in October 1999. Since the second half of 2000, the economy has shown an additional improvement in performance, supported by export expansion.

Overall, since the mid-1990s, Armenia has made substantial progress in both directions_macroeconomic stabilization and structural reforms. After 1997, the macroeconomic situation has remained mostly in balance, with low inflation, a stable exchange rate, and a sufficient level of international reserves (Table 1.1). The Government was also successful in advancing various sectoral reforms, including those in the energy sector, social protection, general education, as well as strengthening fiscal controls and development of basic legislation supportive of market reforms. However, these and other reform benchmarks have not been achieved easily. The reform process in 1997–2001 went through its ups and downs, was affected by political changes, government capacity constraints, and external shocks.

The country's economic expansion in 1994–2001 was fueled by a recovery from the severe contraction of the early 1990s. Factors that also contributed to growth included recovery in electricity supply, expansion of external private transfers that pushed domestic demand, and a major program of international assistance that made Armenia a leading regional recipient of donor funding in per capita terms.

However, despite a relatively strong recent performance, economic growth in Armenia has not been supported yet by strong enterprise restructuring or by massive entry of new private businesses (World Bank, 2001c). The winners from economic growth in Armenia, especially in the period before 2000, have been excessively concentrated. Growth has not yet made up for jobs lost to downsizing, and the sector and enterprise bases of growth have been narrow—a fact that explains the "mystery of growth without much poverty reduction." As a result, the country faces a noticeable

TABLE 1-1: SELECTED MACROECONOMIC INDICTORS

	1996	1997	1998	1999	2000	2001
Real Sector						
Real GDP growth (percent)	5.9%	3.3%	7.3%	3.3%	6.0%	9.6%
GDP level (1990=100)	55.9	57.8	62.0	64.1	67.9	74.4
Nominal GDP (AMD billion)	661.2	804.3	955.4	987.4	1,031.3	1,175.5
GDP (US million)	1,599.3	1,638.9	1,892.3	1,845.4	1,911.5	2,117.8
Population (thousands)	3,077.8	3,059.2	3,033.2	3,012.0	2,996.8	3,002.7
Per capita GDP ($)	519.6	535.7	623.9	612.7	637.9	705.3
Official unemployment rate (percent)	10.1%	10.8%	9.2%	11.2%	11.7%	10.4%
Monetary Sector						
Annual inflation, CPI	18.7	14.0	8.7	0.7	−0.8	3.1
Real effective exchange rate, (1995=100)	120.0	105.0	112.0	116.0	109.0	99.0
Exchange rate (AMD/$, period average)	413.4	490.8	504.9	535.1	539.5	555.1
Average Wage, AMD	9,428	11,689	15,547	18,526	21,094	23,943
Average Wage, US$	22.8	23.8	30.8	34.6	39.1	43.1
Treasury Bills: av. real yields, percent	18.6%	38.5%	33.9%	54.5%	27.7%	20.1%
Credit to economy, million AMD	37,181	48,486	81,601	90,127	109,319	103,182
−As percent of GDP	5.6%	6.0%	8.5%	9.1%	10.6%	8.8%
−Annual growth (percent)	−2.0%	30.4%	68.3%	10.5%	21.3%	−5.6%
Credits to energy sector, million AMD	n.a.	n.a.	31,121	23,814	22,605	23,938
Broad Money (M2X)	54,371	70,247	95,512	108,545	150,599	171,047
−As percent of GDP	8.3%	8.7%	10.0%	11.0%	14.6%	14.6%
−Annual growth (percent)	35.6	28.7	36.0	13.6	38.7%	13.6%
Reserves (months of imports) (a)	3.0	3.5	3.9	3.8	3.6	3.8
External Sector						
Current account balance (percent of GDP)	−18.2%	−18.7%	−21.3%	−16.6%	−14.6%	−9.5%
Exports, goods and services (US$ million)	368.0	331.0	360.0	383.0	446.8	539.6
−Annual growth (percent)	22.7%	−10.1%	8.8%	6.4%	16.7%	20.8%
−As percent of GDP	23.0%	20.2%	19.0%	20.8%	23.4%	25.5%
Imports (US$ million)	889.0	952.0	1,000.0	919.0	966.2	977.6
−Annual growth (percent)	17.4%	7.1%	5.0%	−8.1%	5.1%	1.2%
−As percent of GDP	55.6%	58.1%	52.8%	49.8%	50.5%	46.2%
Foreign Direct Investment, (net US$ million)	18.0	52.0	221.0	122.0	104.0	69.9
−As percent of GDP	1.1%	3.2%	11.7%	6.6%	5.4%	3.3%
External Debt (US$ million)	613.2	806.3	827.8	855.0	862.0	1001.0
−As percent of GDP	38.3%	49.2%	43.7%	46.3%	45.1%	47.3%
Total External Debt as percent to Exports of GS	141.4%	192.9%	223.4%	235.5%	216.9%	185.5%
Fiscal indicators, accrual basis						
As percent of GDP						
Consolidated budget revenue and grants	18.0%	20.1%	21.2%	23.7%	20.6%	20.3%
Consolidated budget revenue	16.6%	18.3%	19.5%	22.1%	19.7%	19.3%
Consolidated budget expenditure	22.8%	24.9%	25.6%	30.7%	27.3%	24.3%
Fiscal balance, accrual basis	−4.7%	−4.9%	−4.4%	−7.0%	−6.8%	−4.1%

(a) Next year import

Sources: NSS, IMF, CBA, World Bank.

imbalance between its relatively strong macroeconomic fundamentals (and substantial structural reforms), and a much weaker supply and investment response. Unless this issue is addressed, the growth rates of the last 5–6 years are likely to be unsustainable. That is, while Armenia needs and has a potential to generate a high growth episode over the next decade, without additional reforms the economy will inevitably slow down.

Generally, despite quite a comfortable macro picture and considerable fiscal adjustment since the mid-1990s, the sustainability of fiscal performance remains a major concern. It is primarily due to revenue collection, which, although improved since 1995–96, is still low and unstable and reflects persistent weaknesses in tax and customs administration as well as the sizable share of the informal economy. There are also major problems related to expenditure management that manifest themselves in both arrears accumulation and inefficiency of expenditure structure.

Overall, unfinished fiscal adjustment and associated macroeconomic uncertainties have become a serious threat to the sustainability of economic recovery. They depress expectations of the private sector and thus further delay new investments and entry of strategic foreign investors, including those from the Diaspora. Persisting fiscal problems prevent the reduction of quasi-fiscal deficits in public utilities and infrastructure as well as from improvements in financing core social services. Deterioration in infrastructure and in social services undermines longer-term growth prospects of the country and also raises a risk of social tensions.

Major Features of Fiscal Adjustment

The real level of public expenditures in Armenia decreased by about 3 times between 1990 and the mid-1990s. This resulted from a simultaneous decline in both real output (by more than 50 percent) and in the relative size of the Government (total expenditures declined from 35 percent to about 25 percent of GDP). Armenia experienced high levels of consolidated (accrual) budget deficit (48 percent of GDP in 1993) in the period of hyperinflation, which was gradually brought down to 9 percent in 1995, 7.3 in 1999, 6.7 in 2000 and 5.0 in 2001[4] (Table 1.2).

TABLE 1.2: CONSOLIDATED GOVERNMENT BUDGET, PERCENT OF GDP. ACTUAL, INCLUDING SIF							
	1995	1996	1997	1998	1999	2000	2001
							Prelim.
Total revenue (including grants)	18.2	17.8	20.1	21.4	23.6	20.5	20.0
Tax revenue	13.5	13.9	16.9	17.2	20.5	18.6	18.1
Non-tax revenue	2.5	2.7	1.4	2.5	1.6	1.1	1.3
Grants	2.2	1.2	1.8	1.7	1.5	0.8	0.8
Total cash expenditures and net lending	27.1	26.1	24.8	25.1	28.8	25.3	24.4
Current expenditures			19.4	18.8	21.3	19.8	19.1
Capital expenditures and net lending			5.4	6.4	7.4	5.6	5.3
o/w: Foreign financed			3.1	2.0	3.9	1.7	2.3
Overall cash balance	−8.9	−8.3	−4.7	−3.7	−5.2	−4.8	−4.2
Accumulation of arrears, net			0.2	0.5	2.1	1.9	−0.4
Overall accrual balance			−4.9	−4.2	-7.3	-6.7	−3.8
Financing	11.1	9.3	4.7	3.7	5.2	4.8	4.0
External (net)	10.5	6.5	5.1	1.6	4.7	2.2	2.7
Domestic (net)	0.6	2.8	−0.4	2.1	0.5	2.6	1.3
o/w: Privatization proceeds	0	0	0	2.2	1.1	2.1	0.6

Note: Excludes a write-off of budget arrears in the health sector in 2001.

Source: MOFE, Staff estimates.

---

4. Accrual basis for all years but 1995.

The reduction in deficit was achieved through both dramatic cuts in spending and improved tax collection. Total expenditures declined from 44 percent of GDP in 1994 to 30 percent in 1995 and 26 percent in 1996. Budget revenues (without grants) increased from the extremely low level of less than 13.5 percent of GDP in 1995 to 16.9 in 1997, 20.5 in 1999, 18.6 in 2000, and 17.8 in 2001.[5] Although tax collection remains quite unstable and under performed, especially in 2000, some improvement in tax performance was reported in 2001.

Donors' assistance also played a major role in sustaining fiscal stabilization. Since the mid-90s, Armenia became a leading recipient of donor assistance in the region. On average in 1995–99, donors provided about 7 percent of Armenia's GDP in annual budget support mostly through a combination of grants and low-interest credits. In 2001, however, the budget support declined to about 5 percent of GDP.[6] Figure 1.1 illustrates the overall dependence of the consolidated budget on external financing (credits and grants, combined).[7] It shows that despite declining trends, almost 20 percent of the total Government spending was financed externally.

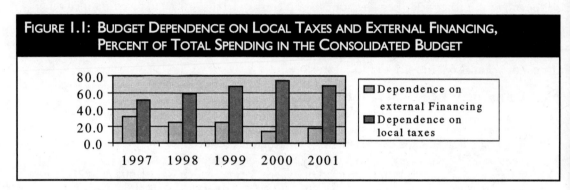

FIGURE 1.1: BUDGET DEPENDENCE ON LOCAL TAXES AND EXTERNAL FINANCING, PERCENT OF TOTAL SPENDING IN THE CONSOLIDATED BUDGET

Armenia's path of fiscal adjustment in the 90s was quite typical for lower-income countries in the CIS (see Alam and Sundberg, 2002, for a review of regional fiscal trends) and resulted in a rather typical set of problems.[8] The adjustment necessary to sustain macroeconomic stabilization was rather dramatic[9] and was undertaken in an institutional environment that could not provide for efficient comparative cost-benefit analysis of various budget cuts. These typical CIS features and outcomes of the adjustment process include:

- Restructuring and re-prioritization of budget spending in general was undertaken at a slower pace than budget compression. The institutional framework for resource allocation remained weak and non-transparent.
- The quality of achieved fiscal adjustment has been problematic: the structure of budget spending that emerged still shows too much legacy of pre-transition patterns, and as such it has considerable room for rationalization in both directions_reducing social costs of transition and facilitating economic recovery.
- Investments in public goods—public infrastructure, health and education services, social transfers—fell in both absolute and relative terms to the levels that cannot support existing

---

5. Includes payroll taxes, collected by the Pension Fund (SIF), which were rather stable at the level of 3 percent of GDP a year.

6. Still, the total inflow of official assistance in 2001, including off-budget items, amounted to US$175 million (9% of GDP) or almost US$60 per capita.

7. Estimated as a sum of grants and gross disbursement of new foreign credits divided by the total of expenditures and amortization payment on foreign credits.

8. Horvath et al. (1998) examine peculiarities of initial (1994–96) stabilization efforts in Armenia.

9. Cheasty and Davis (1996) recorded the then uneven progress on fiscal adjustment in the FSU. They recognized that the sharp reduction in deficits had contributed to stabilization but had also resulted in sharp misalignment of expenditure priorities and the expansion of unorthodox and disorderly budget procedures. See also Tanzi and Tsibouris (1999).

infrastructure assets. Moreover, poor budgetary and expenditure management practices exacerbated the impact from sharp contractions in these expenditures.

▓ Reduced spending on government transfers and public services disproportionately hurt the poor and thus contributed to the sharp deterioration in income inequality.

▓ Budget consolidation remained incomplete, with a considerable part of public expenditures being uncovered by the official budget and by the formal budget process.

▓ Fiscal risks remain high, while fiscal performance is quite sensitive to various external and internal shocks.

When measured against such a background, Armenia's fiscal performance was influenced by somewhat stronger macroeconomic discipline, primarily in the quasi-fiscal area, and had the following distinguishing features:

▓ modest successes in advancing reforms in the energy sector, reducing the volume of energy-related subsidies and incorporating a relatively large part of what remains into the regular budget;

▓ consistency in enforcing a tight monetary policy and avoiding quasi-fiscal financing of the real sector through directed credit programs;

▓ avoiding any systematic usage of non-cash payment schemes and thus escaping a trap of money substitutes;[10]

▓ lower than the regional average, tax expenditures (both tax arrears and tax exemptions).

All this actually indicates a stronger fiscal adjustment and more advanced budget consolidation. This helped to achieve relatively robust macroeconomic outcomes, such as inflation and exchange rate trends, and the level of external debt burden. In contrast to several of its neighbors, Armenia's macro performance was much less affected by the Russia crisis of 1998. Yet, given the delays in expenditure restructuring, more radical fiscal adjustment in the short term produced a larger compression in both household subsidies and social spending, and thus additional social pressures.

Table 1.3 describes Armenia's fiscal adjustment effort since 1995. It suggests a major improvement in the fiscal performance of the Government that occurred in 1997. The consolidated government deficit in 1997, as shown in the lower part of Table 1.3, declined to about 10 percent of GDP from the average of about 12.5 percent in the previous two years. The indicator for consolidated government deficit in this case includes conventional budget deficit (accrual), accumulation of pension arrears, and the deficit of the energy sector. The deficit of the energy sector is considered a good proxy for the total losses of state enterprises.

However, this achievement of 1997 was not sustained and the fiscal performance deteriorated in 1998, the year of the Russia crisis. The consolidated deficit in 1999–2000 amounted to about 7.5 percent of GDP a year, which was further improved relative to the 1997 level. While the outcomes for 2001 appear as an additional improvement, the 2001 consolidated deficit of the public sector still remained above its sustainable medium-term level, which was estimated by this Report to be about 3.5 percent of GDP.[11] As shown in Chapter 3, the level of quasi-fiscal deficit, primarily in the energy sector (power, gas, heating), while reduced, is still significant (about 2 percent of GDP in 2000–01).

It is worth noting that the fiscal adjustment since 1997 was driven by both an improvement in revenue performance and some expenditure compression. It was expected that the Government

---

10. The Government issued Treasury notes (veksels) only once in 1994–1995 in the amount of about AMD 1 billion. The Government also conducted several operations to clear mutual debts, primarily between the budget and energy and utility companies. These were eventually stopped by 1997.

11. It is believed that Armenia could afford a relatively high deficit level for the next several years because its good access to highly concessional financing, including IDA, bilateral donors, and Diaspora's sources, in a combination with high growth rates keeps its debt profile sustainable. It is worth noting that the current PRGF program contains a more ambitious deficit target of 2.5 percent of GDP.

TABLE 1.3: ARMENIA'S INDICATORS OF FISCAL ADJUSTMENT, 1995–2001
(US$ million and percent of GDP)

	1994	1995	1996	1997	1998	1999	2000	2001
Part A								
Gov. external debt, dollar, incl. IMF	200	382	547	653	748	821	840	877
Gov. domestic debt, dollar	0	0.5	24.7	47.2	40.1	43.3	55.2	57.7
Energy Sector payables, dollar	31	62	137	93	182	166	152	176
Budget arrears (including SIF), dollar		0	0	2.8	13	51	89.6	86.7
Reserve Money	37	73	95	102	103	103	131	143
Total stock of liabilities	267.5	517.1	803.5	898.6	1086.6	1183.7	1268.2	1340.3
Percent of GDP	36.3	40.2	50.3	55.4	57.2	64.2	66.2	63.0
Increase in liabilities, flow		249.6	286.4	95.1	188.0	97.1	84.4	72.1
Percent of GDP		19.4	17.9	5.9	9.9	5.3	4.4	3.4
Use of privatization proceeds, dollar		0	0	0.1	82.9	53	66.3	36.3
Loss of foreign reserves of CBA		−29.5	−58.9	−74.3	−98	9.9	0.6	−3.4
Total Loss of Assets, flow		−30.9	−58.9	−74.2	−15.1	62.9	66.9	32.9
Percent of GDP		−2.4	−3.7	−4.6	−0.8	3.4	3.5	1.5
Actuarial Deficit		−218.7	−227.5	−106.5	−172.9	−160.0	−151.3	−105.0
Percent of GDP		−17.0	−14.2	−6.6	−9.1	−8.7	−7.9	−4.9
Official Budget Deficit (accrual), percent of GDP		−8.9	−8.3	−4.9	−4.2	−7.3	−6.7	−3.8
Hidden Deficit, percent of GDP		−8.1	−5.9	−1.7	−4.9	−1.4	−1.2	−1.1
Part B								
Fiscal Deficit, gen. state budget, cash (including SIF), percent of GDP		−8.9	−8.3	−4.7	−3.6	−5.2	−4.8	−4.2
"Off-budget" Government deficit, percent of GDP		−2.4	−4.7	−5.4	−6.9	−2.6	−2.5	−1.0
Consolidated deficit, accrual (budgeted and off-budget), percent of GDP		−11.3	−13.0	−10.1	−10.5	−7.8	−7.3	−5.2
Memo: GDP, million USD		1285.7	1597.1	1,623.10	1,899.00	1,844.60	1,917.10	2,128.90

Notes:
a. External and domestic debt estimates exclude publicly guaranteed debts, but include debt write-offs.
b. Energy sector payables are considered to be a good proxy for the total liabilities accumulated by public utilities and large SOEs.
c. Non-budgeted portion of Government deficit is estimated as a proxy, based on the changes in government arrears and arrears of the energy sector, including write-offs.
Source: Staff estimates based on the data from the MOFE, Ministry of Energy, and the IMF.

would ensure that the growth in spending commitments would be slower than revenue expansion. However, actual progress on both sides was smaller than planned and needed.

In addition, Table 1.3 provides an alternative view on the quality of fiscal adjustment in Armenia by using a concept of the actuarial deficit of the public sector. These alternative estimates are based on the approach suggested by Kharas and Mishra (2001), which emphasizes limitations of the conventional budget deficit for measuring intensity of fiscal adjustment in developing countries. In the institutional environment, where a considerable portion of government fiscal activities remains off-budget, direct analysis of changes in the stock of main public assets and liabilities could provide a more accurate set of aggregate estimates for Government fiscal performance. As suggested by Kharas and Mishra, in the medium term, the actuarial deficit is a better predictor of possible macroeconomic crises at the country level than standard deficit indicators because it more explicitly reflects accumulation of net Government liabilities. Such an approach seems to be quite relevant for a fiscal analysis in transition economies, where in many cases regular budgets have insufficient coverage of public fiscal operations.

The analysis in Table 1.3 is based on consolidation of changes in five components of public liabilities (external and domestic debts, reserve money, budget arrears, and payables of public energy companies) and two types of public assets (value of state holdings in the real sector and foreign exchange reserves of the Central Bank). Dynamics of payables in the energy sector is considered to be a good proxy for the financial performance of the entire sector of large SOEs.[12] Annual changes in the value of public holdings were measured by amounts of privatization proceeds spent by the Government in the same year.[13]

The comparison between actuarial deficit of the government sector and conventional budget deficit (Figure 1.2) shows that in Armenia these two types of estimates have been comfortably close in the period 1999–2001. The similarity in trends of these two aggregate fiscal measures for 1999–2001 confirms that at least in a macroeconomic sense fiscal adjustment in Armenia in the late 1990s was quite genuine, that is, it was not accompanied by excessive growth of hidden off-budget liabilities. Unknown leakages in the system were small.

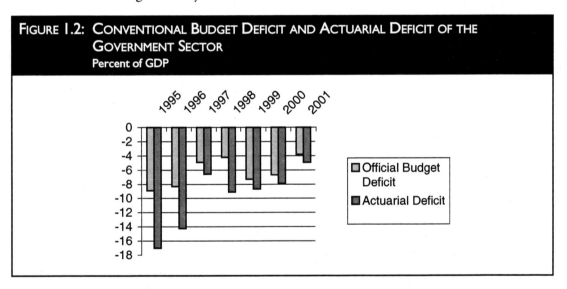

FIGURE 1.2: CONVENTIONAL BUDGET DEFICIT AND ACTUARIAL DEFICIT OF THE GOVERNMENT SECTOR
Percent of GDP

Such a trend in fiscal adjustment in Armenia could be compared with broader regional patterns. Figure 1.3 presents a case of Moldova, which is selected as rather a typical CIS economy that showed unsustainable fiscal performance in most of the 1990s. As the diagram suggests, in 1995–96, Moldova's fiscal outcomes were very similar to those of Armenia, with the actuarial deficit of about 15 percent of GDP a year. However, the next two years showed a dramatic difference. Moldova did not go through a considerable adjustment effort in 1997, and its performance in 1998 ended up in the fiscal and macroeconomic crisis with the actuarial deficit reaching almost 20 percent of GDP. It is also indicative that the 1998 actuarial deficit was two times larger than the official accrual budget

---

12. This is because the energy sector in most transition economies has been used as a main source of quasi-fiscal subsidies to state enterprises (See also Chapter 3).

13. The total for used privatization proceeds includes gas-for-equity swap in the energy sector, which has not been reflected in the budget. In 1997–2001, Armenia received more than US$120 million from this deal through free delivery of energy inputs and energy debt reductions.

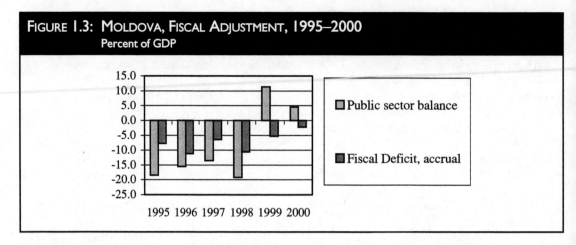

FIGURE 1.3: MOLDOVA, FISCAL ADJUSTMENT, 1995–2000
Percent of GDP

deficit. A large portion of government liabilities was accumulated outside of the budget. The average actuarial deficit in Moldova in 1995–1998 was above 16 percent of GDP, while the average reported budget deficit was 9 percent. Such a financial performance was clearly unsustainable. The major macroeconomic crisis of 1998 (triggered by the Russia crisis) was followed by a radical fiscal adjustment in 1999–2000, supported by external debt relief, debt-for-equity swap with Russia, and erosion of domestic debts due to inflation and devaluation.

Overall, there is sufficient evidence to conclude that during 1997–2000 the Government of Armenia has shown gradual consolidation of fiscal stabilization, and compared to the previous period, significant improvements in fiscal performance in several important dimensions:

- Improvements in revenue collection.
- Reduction in the overall public sector deficit, including both budgeted and quasi-fiscal portions.
- Improvement in budget coverage and transparency through more adequate budgeting of energy and utility subsidies.
- Increase in the level of social spending, primarily in general education and social protection.
- Achieving a positive level of public sector savings, and thus expanding financing of public investments from its own resources.

However, these positive shifts were not sufficient. Moreover, some backsliding occurred in 1998, which was triggered by the Russia crisis and fueled by the deteriorating revenue performance. The results of 2001 look promising but, as was seen from the earlier adjustment episode, a lot of effort would be needed to sustain them.

Sources of Deficit Financing

Table 1.4 presents the structure of deficit financing for 1997–2001. It shows that Armenia is excessively dependent upon external sources for financing its deficit. External financing covered about 72 percent of the entire deficit of this period. Moreover, in the last five years, more than 90 percent of the net total domestic financing was provided from privatization proceeds. This source is basically exhausted by now because the Government has completed privatization of all the most valuable state firms. Traditional sources of domestic financing remained insignificant.[14]

---

14. An increase in domestic financing from other sources in 2000–01 seems to be a result of a problem with the budget classification. The discussions with the authorities suggest that most inflows reflected under this line derived from external grants that did not go to the budget directly but had been originally deposited with the Central Bank. This is likely to suggest that the real level of budget deficit was about a quarter percentage point lower than is officially reported.

TABLE 1.4: SOURCES OF DEFICIT FINANCING. STATE BUDGET, 1997–2001
Percent of GDP, Cash Basis

	1997	1998	1999	2000	2001
Total	4.70	3.65	5.20	4.80	4.18
A. Domestic sources, total	−0.42	2.08	0.51	2.62	1.45
1. CBA loans	−1.48	0.47	−0.76	–	–
2. Public securities	1.14	−0.21	0.10	0.17	0.51
3. Proceeds from privatization	0.01	2.16	1.11	2.08	0.64
4. Repayment of loans from the Haiastan Fund	−0.01	−0.05	−0.06	−0.01	–
5. Other domestic sources	−0.07	−0.28	0.13	0.37	0.30
B. Foreign sources, total	5.12	1.57	4.69	2.18	2.73
1. International organizations	6.20	0.96	4.80	1.71	2.60
2. Foreign states	−1.09	0.61	−0.43	0.08	−0.20
3. Lincy and Huntsman Foundations	–	–	0.33	0.39	0.33

Note: Excludes SIF.
Source: MOFE, staff estimates.

The immediate problem with external deficit financing primarily relates to slow predictability and general delays of external disbursements, which made a significant contribution to low efficiency of budget planning. Annual inflows of external assistance fluctuate too much. In 2000, which was the most difficult year in this respect, the gross disbursement level amounted to only 40 percent of the average level for 1997–99_instead of $50 million a year, only $20 million become available.[15] As a result, in 2000, the share of external sources of deficit financing amounted to only 45 percent, while the annual budget law provided for 75 percent.

At the same time, a slower than planned pace of external disbursements became another factor that pushed down cash-based annual deficits. For all years, the actual cash deficit of the state budget was smaller that the one envisioned by the respective budget laws (Figure 1.4) primarily because availability of foreign financing was lower than budgeted.[16]

In addition, the dominance of external credits and privatization proceeds in deficit financing largely reduced flexibility of Government's expenditure policy. Privatization proceeds and a large

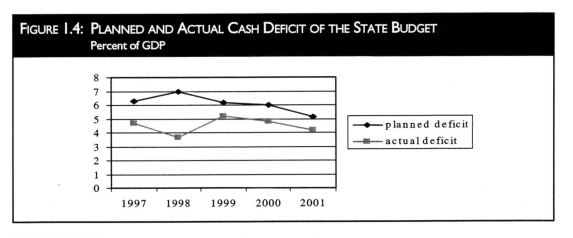

FIGURE 1.4: PLANNED AND ACTUAL CASH DEFICIT OF THE STATE BUDGET
Percent of GDP

---

15. This was primarily caused by the delays in implementation of the Government structural reform program, supported by World Bank adjustment credits.

16. The accrual deficit was much larger, given the increase in budget arrears during this period. See section 1.5 below.

part of external concessional credits have been linked to the implementation of specific investment programs and could not be reallocated in the course of budget execution in response to external shocks. On average for 1997–2001, two-thirds of the total funds used to finance Government deficit represented tied financing.

In the medium term, availability of concessional external financing for Armenia will decline, driven by reduced ADA allocations. This calls for a need for additional adjustment efforts to ensure further deficit reduction.

Table 1.5 provides additional characteristics of the state budget deficit and their dynamics for the last five years. It shows that external grants were an important channel of dependence of Armenia's budget system on external financing. Almost 50 percent reduction in budget grants in 2000–01 was another significant source for budget pressures in these years.

It is also worth mentioning that in 2000–01, as shown in the *Current Deficit* line, Government's own revenues were just sufficient to cover all of its current expenditures. It suggests a noticeable deterioration in fiscal performance relative to 1998–99, when the Government was able to contribute to the financing of public investment program 0.6 and 1.0 percent of GDP respectively.[17]

TABLE 1.5: VARIOUS INDICATORS OF THE STATE BUDGET DEFICIT IN 1997–2001
Percent of GDP, Cash Basis

	1997	1998	1999	2000	2001
1. Budget Deficit (excluding grants)	−6.45%	−5.33%	−6.73%	−5.62%	−4.98%
2. Conventional Budget Deficit (including grants)	−4.70%	−3.65%	−5.20%	−4.80%	−4.18%
3. Primary Deficit: Total revenues (excluding grants) minus Total expenses (excluding interest)	−3.98%	−3.45%	−4.80%	−4.27%	−3.89%
4. Current Deficit w/o Grants: Total revenues (excluding grants) minus Total current expenses	−1.01%	0.97%	0.59%	−0.03%	0.16%
5. Current Deficit: Total revenues (including grants) minus Total current expenses	0.74%	2.65%	2.12%	0.79%	0.96%
Memo: Budgeted Grants	1.75%	1.68%	1.53%	0.82%	0.79%

Source: MOFE and staff estimates.

Revenue Performance: The Challenge Remains Unmet

Poor tax performance represents the weakest element of the Armenian macroeconomic and fiscal framework. At the moment, the level of tax collection in Armenia is among the lowest among transition economies (Table 1.6). The relative position of Armenia deteriorated after 1999, when several CIS countries, including Kazakhstan, Azerbaijan, and Moldova, made considerable progress in their revenue effort, while in Armenia tax revenue yield has declined.

The depth of Armenia's tax under-performance has often been underestimated because external grants and non-tax sources of revenues (such as a transfer of CBA profit to the budget) contributed more to the total Government revenues in Armenia than in other countries.

---

17. Table 1.5 somewhat overestimates the level of Government savings due to problems in the budget classification. Government lending in Armenia, which largely represents hidden subsidies, is traditionally excluded from the *Current Expenditure* part of the budget. See Chapter 2.

TABLE 1.6: TOTAL GOVERNMENT TAX REVENUES IN TRANSITION ECONOMIES, PERCENT OF GDP
(excluding budget grants and non-tax revenues)

	1996	1997	1998	1999	2000	2001 Preliminary
Armenia, excluding SIF	10.8	13.3	14.4	17.3	15.5	14.83
Armenia, including SIF [a]	13.9	16.9	17.2	20.5	18.6	17.8
Georgia	10.7	12.7	12.8	13.8	14.2	18.0
Kyrgyz Republic	17.3	16.7	18.4	15.9	15.3	15.4
Kazakhstan	11.4	12.2	16.2	16.0	20.0	19.7
Azerbaijan	17.6	19.1	19.5	18.2	20.8	20.5
Moldova	27.4	29.9	28.3	21.8	22.3	23.0
Albania	18.3	16.6	20.3	21.3	22.4	22.5
Lithuania	29.6	32.6	32.6	32.1	30.2	28.5
Russia	22.5	33.0	28.6	28.8	31.3	30.9
Macedonia	35.7	34.7	33.2	34.2	35.2	38.5
Ukraine	36.7	38.0	36.0	33.4	35.6	32.8
Estonia	37.7	39.2	36.9	35.5	35.6	38.3
Latvia	37.4	39.9	43.9	40.8	37.0	38.7
Slovak Republic	45.3	42.8	40.5	41.6	39.2	34.4
Bulgaria	35.9	35.1	37.7	40.3	41.3	N/A
Croatia	48.9	47.6	50.8	47.7	45.2	38.2

Note: a. Excluding budget transfers to the SIF.
Source: IMF, MOFE.

During the last five years both the Government's overall levy ratio[18] and tax ratio[19] in Armenia rose substantially to the levels of 17.8 and 14.8 percent of GDP in 2001 compared to 13.9 and 10.8 in 1996 (Figure 1.5). The revenues increased through improved tax and customs administration, simplification of the tax structure and broadening the tax base. The general improvement in tax performance derived almost entirely from better collection of indirect taxes.

The main achievements of tax policy/administration in the second part of the 1990s included:

- change to the destination principle in VAT collection;
- shifting collection of VAT on most imports to the border;
- introduction of excise stamps for cigarettes and alcohol and increase in the levels of excises;
- introduction of presumptive taxes for SMEs;
- initiation of cash machine requirements for retail trade and services;
- reduction in profit tax and income tax rates.

At the moment, the structure of the tax system and prevailing tax rates are consistent with the best international practice (with the exception of the country's income level payroll rates being high). By now Armenia has rather modern legislation on all main type of taxes, including VAT, excises, corporate and personal income taxes. The Government also made significant investments in creation of modern tax and custom administration, which were supported by the donor community.

---

18. Tax revenue and social security contributions as a percentage of the nominal gross domestic product.
19. Tax revenue (include all taxes and duties collected by national and local governments) as a percentage of the nominal gross domestic product.

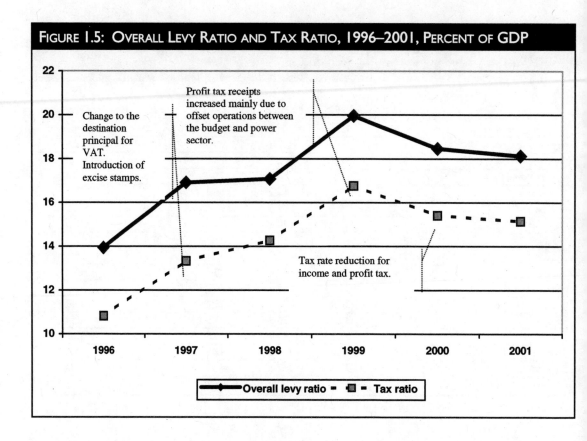

FIGURE 1.5: OVERALL LEVY RATIO AND TAX RATIO, 1996–2001, PERCENT OF GDP

These policy and administrative measures provided for a fundamental change in composition of tax revenues. In 2001, indirect taxes accounted for 79.8 percent of the total tax revenue (excluding social security contributions), which is 26 percentage points more than in 1996. A VAT share in GDP more than doubled—from 3.25 percent in 1996 to 6.75 in 2001. At the same time, the share of personal and corporate income taxes fell by more than 18 percentage points—from over 35.6 percent in 1996 to only 17.3 in 2001. This happened due to the substantial cuts of income tax rates, coupled with an increase in the nontaxable threshold for personal income tax, introduction of a more business friendly profit tax law and a significant decline in profitability of the enterprise sector. The share of social security contributions in GDP remained unchanged throughout the period (about 3 percent of GDP), albeit their rates have been substantially reduced.

The 2000 decision to reduce income tax rates was intended to:

- act as a mechanism to improve the investment climate;
- increase competitiveness of the country for FDI;
- decrease incentives for tax evasion.

While it is too early to make a conclusive assessment of the performance of the new income tax system after less than two years of its operation, it is still worth mentioning that the performance of the profit tax receipts has been well below expectations in 2001 (22 percent below the target).

Overall, as mentioned above, the improvements in tax performance are clearly insufficient. Moreover, progress in tax administration was accompanied by frequent changes in tax legislation that raised compliance costs for the private sector. The improvement in the tax performance in 1999 (the best annual outcome so far) has been based not on serious efficiency gains in administration but to a large extent on massive offsetting operations between the budget and the power sector. In addition, the Government has been regularly using a practice of tax prepayment to achieve its tax targets, which became a major concern for the private sector.

Political uncertainties of the first half of 2000 that followed the political crisis of November 1999 resulted in a significant deterioration in tax performance. Political stabilization that followed helped to recover some of this revenue loss during the second part of 2000 and in 2001. However, when measured as a percent of GDP, the 2001 tax collection remained much below the 1999 level.

Table 1.7 describes the situation with tax arrears, which have been growing in the late 1990s and by early 2000 amounted to 6 percent of GDP. The analysis shows that tax arrears are heavily concentrated: about 30 largest debtors accumulated half of the total outstanding tax debts. Many of these largest debtors are SOEs or former SOEs that are clearly non-viable and should be liquidated. Another major portion of the tax arrears has been accumulated by energy companies and to a large extent reflects the fact that these companies in the past were not properly paid by the budget and state-owned firms.

TABLE 1.7: TAX ARREARS, STOCKS BY THE YEAR END
Million Dram

	1996	1997	1998	1999	2000	2001
Total tax arrears	19,986	27,181	46,474	55,566	64,503	64,612
as percent of GDP	3.02%	3.38%	4.86%	5.63%	6.25%	5.50%
o/w: arrears to the SIF	6,779	6,548	7,225	7,353	8,989	9,683
as percent of GDP	1.03%	0.81%	0.76%	0.74%	0.87%	0.82%

Note: Excluding penalties and fines.

Source: Ministry of State Revenues.

The results of 2001 were successful in a sense that the further growth in tax arrears was practically stopped. It is worth noting, however, that tax arrears have been growing for most of 2001 at their average trend rate, but the Government managed to reduce the stock of outstanding arrears by 7 billion drams over the last two months of the year. It remains to be seen how sustainable this decline will be.

Overall, while the level of tax arrears and tax discipline is of concern, it is clear that the deterioration in revenue performance in 2000–01 cannot be explained by the recent growth in tax debts. The real source of the problem is tax evasion, including smuggling, but not non-payment.[20] The existing system of tax administration has been failing to register a large portion of tax liabilities in the economy.

The Government has been addressing this problem by accelerating capacity building in tax and customs administration with the assistance from the IMF and bilateral donors (Corfmat et al., 2001). However, the return on these efforts was disappointing so far. Moreover, the developments in the last three years suggest that a radical improvement in revenue performance requires, in addition to the reforms in administration, a much stronger Government's ownership of the reform process is needed that would allow address the problem of powerful vested interests. Also, surprisingly little was done to strengthen compliance with personal income tax legislation by the wealthiest quintile of the population, especially by business managers and business owners.

This report argues that immediate improvements in revenue performance should be among the top fiscal priorities for the Government. It sounds realistic, based on experience of other CIS states, to establish an increase of 2 percentage points of GDP as a medium-term (three-year) target, which would provide for attaining a 20 percent of GDP mark.[21] At the same time, tax collection is the

---

20. Analysis by Ebrill et al. (2001) suggests, based on cross-country comparisons, that Armenia's tax administration has been missing a large chunk of potential revenues from the VAT tax.

21. In the earlier analysis, Barbone and Polachkova (1996, pp. 22–25), based on the cross-country regression models, determined Armenia's tax capacity as 21 percent of GDP.

most informative indicator of Government's commitment to fight vested interests and address broader problems of governance and unfair competition (See Box 1.1).

It is critical to ensure proper balance and sequencing between future improvements in tax administration, expenditure rationalization and quality of public sector accounts. Government accountability for budget outcomes as well as rational spending of available resources are the main pre-conditions for expanding the budget envelope, including the one in social sectors. The Government has to demonstrate its real commitment to higher standards of expenditure policy before making an additional tax collection effort.

The initial steps to boost collections should be concentrated in the areas that are known as the worst offenders. They include:

- Improved revenue flow from taxation of main excisable goods (such as petrol and tobacco) by reducing their under-reporting and smuggling;
- Improved car registration and budget revenues from car importation;
- Increased revenue yield from a limited number of largest retail markets in Yerevan to ensure level playing field in the sector;
- Improving administration of the personal income tax by introducing Personal Identification Numbers/Tax Identification Numbers (PINs/TINs) and expanding coverage of mandatory tax declarations to include entrepreneurs and business owners;
- Making progress in the administration of VAT refund for exporters.

The Government should ensure that future steps to improve efficiency of tax and customs administration are specific and well targeted at closing particular tax loopholes in the existing system, some of which are listed above; others could be identified based on additional analysis of tax incidence. It is worth mentioning that the experience of the last several years, especially of 2000–01, suggests that non-specific administrative efforts in this area are unproductive. When the Government simply asks for a specific amount of taxes collected by a specific date at any cost, it does more harm than good. This practice leads to additional economic distortions (such as advance tax payments)

BOX 1.1: AID DEPENDENCY, ACCOUNTABILITY AND CAPACITY BUILDING

The capacity to raise taxes is increasingly used by political scientists as a key indicator of state capacity. Governments that are financially dependent on their own taxpayers tend to be more democratic, effective, and accountable than those that rely rather heavily on rents, "unearned incomes."

Where government income sources are few and concentrated, there are especially strong incentives for collusion between the state and those who control those main income sources. This collusion is usually aimed at preserving the political status quo. Adversely, the existence of a broad and diversified tax base makes the state more dependent on society, that is, more sensitive to interests of large social groups.

High aid inflows undermine Government's dependence on domestic taxation. For ruling elites in developing countries, high levels of foreign aid could become a type of rent that exacerbates existing problems of Government's accountability and incentive structure.

As the history of European states suggests, the strategic interaction between a state and various social groups in relation to taxation mechanisms was, together with inter-state competition, a powerful tool of state building and modernization. Interdependence between state and society is a key to enhancing both state capacity and accountability.

The revenue itself may not be the most valuable product of increased efficiency in tax administration. Improved tax collection may require a stronger trust between the state and general public, but when achieved, it would further support an erosion of the current "disconnect" between the state and society.

Source: Based on Moore (1998).

and creates more problems for the business environment_smaller and the most disciplined taxpayers face an additional tax burden, while those with political connections remain practically unaffected.

Low Credibility of the Budget

The only previous PER for Armenia was produced in 1997 (World Bank, 1997) but it was based on the earlier field work (1995 was the last full year of data reviewed), and as such covered the period that was characterized by high inflation and low tax collection. It charted the dramatic effects on public expenditure of Armenia's exceptionally difficult economic circumstances in the early 1990s, but was able to present only rather limited analytical data. The PER's main messages included:

- the need to establish overall levels of public expenditure consistent with economic stability and growth;
- the need to review the functions of the state and concentrate activities, and hence public expenditures, on appropriate core functions only_this would require disengagement from commercial activities, a greater relative emphasis on basic health and education services, and better targeting of social welfare expenditure on the needy;
- the need to complement improvements in short-term cash management (restricting expenditure to match revenues) by strengthening medium-term planning of public expenditure in line with appropriate sector strategies.

Since the last PER was prepared, there has been substantial improvement in the macroeconomic and fiscal situation. The Government succeeded in the building capacity of the Treasury, reducing explicit and implicit subsidies, advancing privatization, improving efficiency of social assistance spending, and providing for some recovery of public expenditure in education and health.

However, some of the strategic issues that the previous PER highlighted are still relevant. This includes issues of budget planning and expenditure prioritization.[22] Despite the years of macroeconomic stability and some recovery in the overall spending level, budget execution is still undertaken in a "crisis management" mode, while the uncertainty and seasonality of expenditure releases remains high.

Figure 1.6 illustrates typical seasonality patterns in the execution of the annual budget. On average, within the year inter-quarter differences in budget spending on core social services such as education and health used to exceed 350 percent. This seasonality partially reflects structural features of the economy, such as its dependence on agriculture and remittances. Donor support also has been traditionally concentrated in the second part of the year, thus it further reinforced inter-quarter variation in budget spending that became both a socially and politically sensitive issue.

This report emphasizes the importance of making the budget credible in order to ensure that planned Government policies can be achieved. Budget credibility requires actual budgetary releases to be similar to budget plans and calls for appropriate fiscal discipline to be in place. Also frequent changes in authorized budget amounts should be avoided.

In Armenia, actual budget outcomes do not correlate much with the adopted budget laws, especially at the disaggregated level, which severely under-mines credibility of both the budget process and agreed budgetary allocations (Tables 1.8 and 1.9). While the Government did push for an increase in the size of the budget as a share of GDP, this trend continued only up to 1999. The results for 2000–01 were disappointing. The budget outcome for 2001 was very close to the level of 1997—just above 20 percent of GDP.

The use of the budget deviation index is a simple methodology for measuring overall budget predictability_whether the Budget Law gives an accurate estimate of final expenditures. The index expresses the sum of the absolute value of budget deviations by sector as a percentage of

---

22. As noted by the Armenia IGR (World Bank, 2000a), ". . . reforms seem to have been driven mostly by short-term fiscal constraints and little emphasis has been put on institutional development or the given institutional constraints."

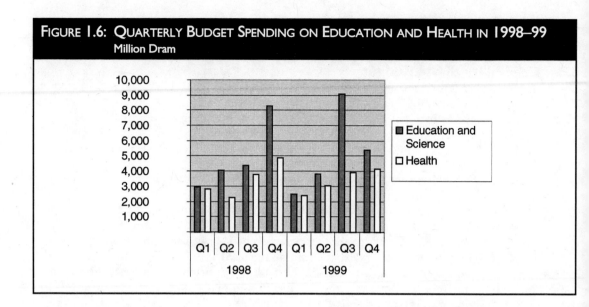

FIGURE 1.6: QUARTERLY BUDGET SPENDING ON EDUCATION AND HEALTH IN 1998–99
Million Dram

TABLE 1.8: THE LEVEL OF STATE BUDGET EXECUTION: BUDGET EXPENDITURES

	1997	1998	1999	2000	2001
Budget Law, percent of GDP	21.00	23.60	26.33	25.80	21.67
Actual, percent of GDP	20.45	21.42	24.57	21.57	20.59
–as percent of the approved budget	97.4	92.1	93.3	83.3	96.2

Note: Excludes use of privatization proceeds.

TABLE 1.9: BUDGET EXECUTION ACROSS VARIOUS SECTORS, PERCENT OF THE APPROVED STATE BUDGET ALLOCATIONS, 1998–2001

	1998	1999	2000	2001
Total Expenditures	96.6	89.2	83.0	98.2
General State Services	100.3	87.4	96.5	116.3
Defense	101.1	86.9	97.1	99.9
Public Security	96.1	92.8	96.8	100.6
Education and Science	92.1	77.6	87.6	88.5
Health Care	77.5	65.6	48.5	86.3
Social Security	93.8	87.6	75.2	92.9
Culture, Sport and Religion	96.2	75.9	72.7	91.6
Non-classified expenditures	113.2	109.3	94.3	116.0
o/w: Debt service	124.1	123.8	80.9	84.0
Transfers to local governments	99.2	48.3	58.5	89.0
Other Programs	104.2	112.7	111.4	153.6
Memo:				
–Budget deviation index, non- weighted	4	7	17	13
–Budget deviation index, weighted	11	20	17	11

Note: Excludes use of privatization proceeds.

Source: MOFE, Staff estimates

the originally approved budget expenditures. The analysis indicates that the deviations between the approved and executed budgets were significant, and the deviations increased in 1999–2000 compared to 1998: deviations increased from approximately 4 percent of the original budget in 1998 to 7 percent in 1999 and 17 percent in 2000. When the index is calculated using weighted averages, which gives proportionally greater weight to the deviations of the largest spending sectors, the measure of budget predictability is considerably lower for the earlier years but the 1998 budget is still rated as more credible than for later years. One more time, the preliminary data for 2001 suggests a significant improvement in 2001 relative to 1999–2000.

This budget uncertainty and associated loss of credibility derives from several factors. Its primary source, however, reflects failure to resolve the underlying imbalance between expenditure commitments and resources available. The Armenian budget is overcommitted: the Government was not able to concentrate spending in a fewer number of functions/institutions, it struggles to support too many pieces of the traditional expenditure structure but in many cases provides funding at unsustainable low levels. Chronic underfunding across the board keeps the fiscal pressures high and diverts the attention of policymakers from identifying and pushing through strategic choices.

Additional factors that limit the Government's ability to ensure more predictable and more strategic budget outcomes include:

- Priorities given to various agencies in the process of budget execution differ from the agreed budget allocations. For instance, social ministries were the most affected by de facto budget sequestration, with public health being hit the most severely in 1999–2000.
- Introduction of new spending programs in the course of budget execution; many such programs have been placed under the rubric "other expenditure"/ Reserve Fund and never fully disclosed according to the functional/administrative classification.
- Weaknesses in the expenditure management area that allows some line ministries to exceed their budgetary appropriations and accumulate arrears.
- High dependence on donor financing, which creates additional uncertainty due to constant delays with disbursement of foreign credits (Table 1.10).[23]

In the late 1990s, there have been several initiatives to help the Government with developing a more strategic approach to budget management to address the above mentioned problems.[24] Many of these recommendations are still relevant. Chapter 4 uses them as a starting point and provides a detailed action plan on strengthening expenditure management processes.

TABLE 1.10: CONTRIBUTION OF DELAYS IN EXTERNAL DISBURSEMENTS TO THE OVERALL EXPENDITURE CUTS. 2000 STATE BUDGET
Million Dram

	Planned	Actual	Difference	Actual as a Share of Planned
Total budget funds	252,780	222,887	−29,894	0.88
Domestic	186,416	191,863	5,447	1.03
—revenues	184,524	163,630	−20,894	0.89
—domestic deficit financing	1,893	28,233	21,304	14.92
Foreign	66,364	31,023	−35,341	0.47
—grants	17,574	8,503	−9,071	0.48
—external deficit financing	48,790	22,520	−26,270	0.46
Share of foreign financing, percent	26.3	13.9		

---

23. As suggested by Table 1.10, total external disbursements in 2000 were less than a half of their planned level. It caused a decline of about 14 percent of the originally planned expenditures.

24. See e.g., De Maria (2000), World Bank (2000a).

Budget Arrears

Budget arrears in Armenia have been generated by the combined effect of feeble revenue performance and weak budget discipline. It is worth noting that budget arrears are a relatively new phenomena in Armenia: during 1997–98, the initial years of fiscal adjustment, the Government managed to avoid any significant accumulation of arrears. By early 1999, the stock of budget arrears was less than 1 percent of GDP. Budget arrears, including those of the Pension Fund, have been growing by 2 percent of GDP a year in 1999–2000.[25]

In 2001, the Government provided for a significant decline in the stock of budget arrears—from 4.7 to 3.7 percent of GDP (Table 1.11). The Government cleared a large share of pension arrears. Moreover, the overall improvement in dynamics of arrears came primarily from a one-time large write-off of Government arrears to public health providers in the amount of 10 billion Drams (1 percent of GDP). The Government unilaterally decided that these liabilities were not envisioned by the earlier budgets and should not be paid with public funds. This improved the overall picture of outstanding debts but did not prevent from accumulation of new budget arrears in 2001, including those on wages and social benefits.

It is worth mentioning that at least part of the increase in arrears in 1999–2000 could be linked to strengthening performance in the energy sector. The GOA has succeeded in reducing quasi-fiscal deficits in energy through, *inter alia*, more accurate consolidation of both energy subsidies to utilities and energy consumption of budget organizations in the regular budget (see Chapter 3). Total arrears of the energy sector declined by more than 50 percent between 1997 and 2000 (or by about 3 percent of 2001 GDP). This definitely improved transparency of the entire public sector. However, while progressing with consolidation, the government was much less successful in reducing its other, non-energy budget commitments in line with its overall financing capacity, which accelerated

TABLE 1.11: BUDGET ARREARS, INCLUDING THE PENSION FUND
Million Dram

	Arrears as of 1.1.98	Arrears as of 1.1.99	Arrears as of 1.1.2000	Arrears as of 1.1.01	Arrears as of 1.1.02
Total arrears, consolidated	1,367	6,568	27,308	48,331	43,632
budget as percent of GDP	0.2	0.7	2.8	4.7	3.7
Budget	1,042.8	5,070	24,490	44,535	42,214
Current Expenditures		4,235	20,475	34,813	31,415
Wages		14	335	493	388
Subsidies		0	64	901	844
Interest payments		0	0	3,392	3,119
Current Transfers		0	5,684	9,044	7,888
Goods and services		4,222	14,393	20,984	19,176
Health		3,978	6,378	12,666	11,446
Education		0	541	1,733	2,191
Other		244	7,474	6,585	5,539
Capital exp.		835	4,015	2,690	4,383
Amortization of external debt		0	0	7,033	6,414
Pension Fund	324.5	1,498	2,818	3,795	1,418

Note: 2001-preliminary data.

---

25. Reliability of statistics on budget arrears is low because the system of commitment control remained under-developed (See also Chapter 4). As a result, the Treasury does not produce reports on budget arrears itself. Instead, the available data are based on reports from sectoral ministries, which have quite outdated accounting procedures.

accumulation of budget arrears. In a sense, arrears to foreign energy suppliers were partially substituted by debts to local doctors, teachers, and pensioners.

Public Debt

As is the case in most of the other CIS countries, Armenia has assumed no external debt after the collapse of the former Soviet Union. Basically, all its public debt has emerged after independence. The public debt has been growing at a very high rate between 1993 and 1997, which was unsustainable. By the end of 1995, the total official public debt amounted to 29 percent of GDP while by the end of 1997 to 45 percent of GDP (to its current level), with the external debt making 92 percent of the total. The accumulation of public debt in the more recent period has been much more effectively controlled.

Armenia's public external debt, including guarantees, stood at US$905 million or 45 percent of GDP by the end of 2001. The debt's relatively large grant element (about 40 percent) reflects the large share of highly concessional IDA credits and the small share of non-concessional commercial debt. Less than one-fourth of total nominal debts carry variable interest rates. This composition of debt protects Armenia reasonably well against higher international interest rates or significant shifts in value of the major international currencies. There is a moratorium on non-concessional borrowing. Armenia has a good record of servicing its external debt.

Overall debt service (interest only) amounted to almost 10 percent of consolidated budget spending in 1997 but it declined to 7 percent in 1999 and to on average less than 5 percent in 2000–01. As a percent of GDP, debt service costs declined from 2.5 percent in 1997 to 1.1 in 2001. Both domestic and external debt became on average much less expensive, however, during 1997–2000 total actual costs of servicing domestic debt were twice higher than those for external debt. In 2001, these two became almost equal – it means that in per unit terms the domestic debt is on average at least 15 times more expensive than foreign borrowing.

With respect to the external public debt, starting from 2000, the Armenian Government has provided for a major improvement in its debt profile. This improvement came through three main channels: (i) repayment of some of the most expensive debts with privatization proceeds; (ii) slower than expected disbursement of new credits; and (iii) major expansion in Armenian exports (by more than 40 percent in two years, 2000–01), which helped to change assessment of Armenia's longer-term capacity for debt servicing.

At the end of 1999, in terms of net present value (NPV), Armenia's external debt was estimated at 153 percent of export of goods and services, meaning that while the debt burden was modest in terms of the size of the economy, it was high relative to expected export earnings (World Bank, 2001b). This debt ratio improved to 116 percent of exports by the end of 2001, which is comfortably below the conventional risk threshold of 150 percent.[26] Simultaneously, other main debt ratios have also improved, though less significantly.

The current medium-term forecast suggests further gradual improvements in Armenia's debt profile over the next several years. The authorities have been negotiating a concessional repayment of its largest non-concessional debts with CIS creditors (Russia, Turkmenistan), including through debt-for-equity swap and repayment with domestic consumer goods. If completed, it would result in both significant fiscal benefits as well as in BOP improvements. It is estimated that after full repayment of these credits, NPV of external debt will decline from 29 to 27 percent of GDP.

Overall, Armenia's debt should remain manageable as export performance continues to improve. However, the World Bank does not envisage that Armenia will become creditworthy for IBRD lending during the next three years. It is important that external support in the next several years still be provided as grants or on a highly concessional basis.

---

26. Respectively, the ratio of total public debt service (including amortization) to export declined from 41 percent in 1997 and 49 in 1999 to 26 in 2001.

The Government should look to further strengthening a legal and regulatory framework for accounting/reporting on public debt developments either through amendments to the Budgetary Systems Law or through an adoption of separate Law on Public Debt Management. The issues that require a special attention in the process of legal drafting include both definition and classification of the public debt, coverage and level of details in Government's debt reports to Parliament (for example, to ensure an inclusion of debt guarantees), introduction of the public debt register, introduction of the internationally recognized indicators of the debt burden, etc.

Domestic Debt

The Government initiated a formation of the modern TB market in 1996. Respectively, 1998 was the last year when the Central Bank provided direct financing of the budget deficit. However, despite significant improvements in the last three years, domestic borrowing remained very expensive, and its contribution to deficit financing remains rather insignificant. The stock of outstanding TBs has never exceeded 4 percent of GDP. By the end of 2001, it amounted to 2.9 percent of GDP, of which 18 percent was held by the Central Bank.

Table 1.12 provides a comparison between contribution of TBs to deficit financing and related debt service costs. In 1998–2000, the financing role of TBs has been negligible but it used to be a major effective budget subsidy to the local banking sector (a main domestic holder of TBs).

Since 1999, the authorities have been rather consistent in rationalizing the TB market structure, making rules more transparent, and strengthening market infrastructure. Some improvement has been observed in coordination of monetary and fiscal policies on the part of the CBA and the MOFE. This strategy helped to ensure a gradual decline in yields and extension in average maturities of TBs (Table 1.13). While the average yield on Treasury Bills exceeded 50 percent in 1999, it declined to 20 percent in 2001.[27]

The main reasons for a slow expansion of the TB market relate to low level of savings as well as to the underdeveloped financial sector, which is incapable of successful mobilization of even the existing savings. The existing TB market remains primarily an instrument of monetary policy, not a real source for additional financing of government spending.

TABLE 1.12: TREASURY BILLS: CONTRIBUTION TO DEFICIT FINANCING AND SERVICE COSTS, PERCENT OF GDP

	1997	1998	1999	2000	2001
Net deficit financing	1.14	−0.21	0.10	0.17	0.51
Debt service costs	0.58	0.98	1.09	0.91	0.56

Source: MOFE, Staff estimates.

TABLE 1.13: TREASURY BILLS: AVERAGE MATURITY AND YIELDS

	1997	1998	1999	2000	2001
Average maturity, days	141	87	107	152	210
Yield, percent	53.8	46.6	52.5	23.5	20.1

Source: CBA.

Conclusions and Recommendations

The main conclusions from this chapter could be summarized as follows.

▨ While Armenia's fiscal adjustment effort has been significant, especially in 1997, it is still incomplete. Remaining fiscal problems and related macroeconomic uncertainties are serious enough to affect investment decisions by the private sector, and thus are detrimental for economic growth.

---

27. In the first half of 2002, the yield has been fluctuated in the 12–17 percent interval. The sustainability of this interest level remains to be seen and will largely depend upon the soundness of the banking system.

- The important policy priority is to improve revenue performance by at least two percentage points of GDP. This additional tax effort should be properly balanced with the steps to improve both efficiency and transparency of current spending. While some additional reduction in budget deficit is desirable, most incremental resources should go to increase expenditures, including arrears clearance.
- The Government needs to strengthen budget planning and forecasting and introduce stricter expenditure discipline in order to raise budget credibility.
- International donors could make a major contribution to improvements in expenditure management by making an inflow of external financing more predictable. Donors could also help to reduce budget seasonality by shifting a larger portion of disbursements to the first part of the calendar year.
- While Armenia's debt situation seems to become increasingly sustainable, in the medium term the country will remain dependent on concessional external borrowing and grants. If the current growth trends continue and the Government resolves its revenue problems, Armenia may become eligible for mixed IDA/IBRD lending in about 2006–7.

CHAPTER 2

MAIN EXPENDITURE TRENDS

Expenditure Trends in Functional Classification

Table 2.1 presents a basic expenditure structure of the Armenian state budget as it is usually reported by the Government. Main spending proportions in the late 90s could be summarized as follows: 30 percent of total spending goes for core social spending (social protection, education, and health), almost 20 percent to defense and internal security; 10 percent basic infrastructure in agriculture (primarily irrigation) and transport (road network), 10 percent government administration, 6–10 percent to debt service, and 1–2 percent for transfers to local budgets; about 10 percent of total expenditures remain non-classified.

This chapter goes beyond this standard presentation to look into main expenditure trends for the last five years. The analysis is based on the data for the consolidated (not just state) budget. With the assistance of Treasury staff, a special database on budget expenditure was prepared to ensure consistency in budget presentation and classification between different years, to consolidate information on original and amended annual budget laws together with actual expenditures, disbursements, and financing, as well as provide access to more detailed data on economic classification of actual spending. The concluding section of the chapter identifies main weaknesses of the existing budget classification that limit expenditure analysis and make the entire budget picture quite non-transparent.

Table 2.2 presents an institutional structure of Armenia's consolidated budget for 1997–2001, which combines expenditure of the regular budget and the Social Insurance Fund (SIF – Pension Fund). Table 2.2 also provides a breakdown between two levels of the Armenian Government: National/Republican and Local/Municipal. Armenia remains among the most fiscally centralized economies: the consolidated local budget is quite small (less than 1.5 percent of GDP) and municipalities remain very dependent on transfers from the republican budget.

Table 2.3 presents the levels of budget expenditures for six aggregated budget categories. Table 2.3, as well as Table 2.4, both suggest that the expenditure structure has been evolving, especially in 2000–01. The data show an increase in expenditure shares of social sectors and

TABLE 2.1: STATE BUDGET IN FUNCTIONAL CLASSIFICATION, 1997–2001
Percent of total (cash based)

	1997	1998	1999	2000	2001
Total Expenditures	100	100	100	100	100
General State Services	9.45	10.71	8.37	8.66	9.66
Defense	21.41	16.46	15.05	16.44	15.05
Public Order Protection and State Security	7.44	6.4	5.99	6.75	6.25
Education and Science	10.53	9.64	9.1	12.93	11.87
Health Care	6.5	6.68	5.61	4.5	6.44
Social Security and Social Protection	8.59	9.75	10.76	9.9	10.68
Culture, Sport and Religion	2.17	1.99	1.53	1.67	2.27
Public Housing and Utilities	1.84	4.53	5.51	6.18	2.90
Fuel and Energy	0.98	3.96	1.96	1.37	2.84
Agriculture, Forestry, Fishery and Water Management	1.73	5.94	11.06	7.52	6.96
Mining, Manufacturing and Construction	0.77	0.69	2.3	0.21	0.24
Transport and Communications	2.21	4.89	3.95	2.74	2.85
Other economic services	0.75	1.4	1.55	0.16	0.23
Non-classified expenditures	25.65	16.96	17.29	20.94	21.75
o/w: Debt service	12.71	8.47	8.18	6.23	6.06
Transfers to local governments	n.a.	n.a.	0.93	1.62	2.78
Other non-classified	12.94	8.49	8.18	13.09	12.90

Note: excludes the SIF.

Source: MOFE, Treasury, staff estimates.

TABLE 2.2: CONSOLIDATED BUDGET EXPENDITURES
Percent of GDP

	1997	1998	1999	2000	2001
Consolidated budget expenditures	24.78	25.08	28.75	25.34	24.41
Expenditures of the state budget (including inter-budgetary transfers)	20.45	21.42	24.57	21.57	20.75
Expenditures of the State Social Insurance Fund (including inter-budgetary transfers)	3.67	3.23	3.78	3.62	3.51
Expenditures of local community budgets (including inter-budgetary transfers)	1.19	1.20	1.17	1.23	1.34

TABLE 2.3: MAIN EXPENDITURE CATEGORIES OF THE CONSOLIDATED BUDGET
Percent of GDP

	1997	1998	1999	2000	2001
Total Expenditures	24.78%	25.08%	28.75%	25.34%	24.41%
1. Social	9.14%	9.32%	10.46%	9.63%	9.77%
2. Defense and Public Order	5.18%	4.90%	5.15%	4.88%	4.28%
3. Real Sector	3.94%	4.96%	6.70%	4.07%	3.61%
4. State Administration	2.11%	2.62%	2.47%	2.44%	2.27%
5. Debt Service	2.47%	1.93%	2.01%	1.35%	1.24%
6. Other Sectors	1.94%	1.36%	1.96%	2.98%	3.23%

TABLE 2.4: STRUCTURE OF THE CONSOLIDATED BUDGET: MAIN EXPENDITURE CATEGORIES					
	1997	1998	1999	2000	2001
1. Social	36.90%	37.15%	36.39%	37.99%	40.01%
2. Defense and Public Order	20.89%	19.53%	17.90%	19.26%	17.56%
3. Real Sector	15.90%	19.79%	23.32%	16.06%	14.78%
4. State Administration	8.51%	10.43%	8.58%	9.61%	9.30%
5. Debt Service	9.98%	7.68%	6.99%	5.32%	5.11%
6. Other Sectors	7.81%	5.42%	6.78%	11.76%	13.24%

public administration, and a much larger expansion on non-classified spending ("other sectors"). At the same time, shares of spending on defense, public security, and real economy declined. And, as was mentioned in Chapter 1, starting from 2000, the Government has been spending much less than before on debt service, due to sharply falling interest rates at the T-Bill market.[28]

While the total Government spending did not expand in the last five years as a share of GDP, it is worth noting that the Armenia budget system did expand considerably in that period due to relatively high GDP growth rates. In real terms (using GDP deflator), the level of Government spending in 2001 was 27 percent higher than in 1997. Figure 2.1 illustrates variation in rates of real growth between six expenditure categories.

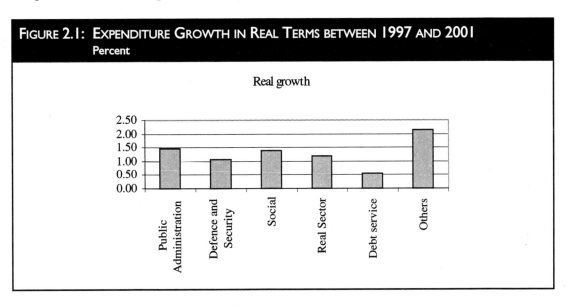

FIGURE 2.1: EXPENDITURE GROWTH IN REAL TERMS BETWEEN 1997 AND 2001
Percent

Figure 2.2 shows how the overall increase in the budget spending between 1997 and 2001 was shared between the main sectors. Social sectors were indeed a big winner: almost half of the total expenditure increase of 77 billion Dram (in 1997 prices) was channeled to social sectors. Another quarter of the increase went to financing of "other sectors."

Such a shift of budget resources towards social spending has been very appropriate, given an extreme under-financing of main social services. It is worth noting that a large part of this increase took place in 2000–01 but this restructuring of budget spending is still insufficient. Total social spending is still below 10 percent of GDP. Overall Armenia considerably under-spends on education

---

28. See discussion of debt service costs in Chapter 1 (section on public debt).

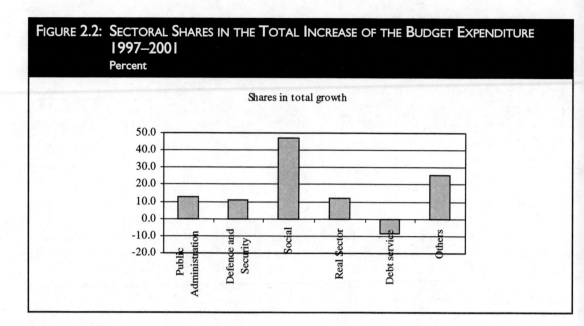

FIGURE 2.2: SECTORAL SHARES IN THE TOTAL INCREASE OF THE BUDGET EXPENDITURE 1997–2001
Percent

and especially on public health (see also Table 2.5), while the Government spends more than usual at this income level on defense and internal security. The Government suggested an undertaking of an additional review of defense spending.

TABLE 2.5: PUBLIC SPENDING ON EDUCATION AND HEALTH
Percent of GDP

	Education	Health
Armenia, 2001	2.55	1.34
Central Europe & Baltics	4.6	5.1
CIS	4.6	3.6
Europe & Central Asia	4.1	4.0
East Asia & Pacific	1.7	1.7
South Asia	3.1	0.9
Sub-Saharan Africa	4.7	1.7
Low Income	2.9	1.2
Middle Income	3.5	2.5
High Income	4.8	6.1

Note: Simple averages have been used for the regional averages.

Source: Alam and Sundberg (2001). Data are for the most recent year available.

Table 2.6 presents several expenditure ratios for basic economic sectors. It confirms that Armenia under-spends on social sectors relative to other economies in transition. Armenia also spends relatively little on government administration (primarily due to low wages) but too much on support of the real sector. The table also reflects a significant improvement in financing of the education sector in 2000–01 (but not of health and social protection).

In fact, the actual pace of expenditure restructuring has been much slower than the Government's own medium-term plans. Figure 2.3 compares main benchmarks for 2002, which were set up in the original MTEF for 2000–02, with the latest 2002 annual budget law. This comparison suggests that back in 1999 the Government planned for quite a radical shift of resources towards social sectors but these plans were adjusted later towards status quo. While both the MTEF and 2002 Budget Law planned for a similar level of state government spending in 2002 (about 20.5 percent of GDP), the initial plan was to spend much more on education, health, social protection and government administration.

Overall, the restructuring of public expenditure in the second part of the 1990s has been slow and so far insufficient, which was in part due to the government capacity limitations. Modification

TABLE 2.6: EXPENDITURE RATIOS IN SELECTED ECONOMIES

	Armenia, average for 1997–2000	Armenia, average for 2000–2001	6 CEE countries, average for 1997–2000	5 CIS countries, average for 1997–2000	5 LAC countries, average for 1997–2000
Health/Education	0.56	0.43	1.51	0.70	0.33
Social/Education	2.37	1.92	4.80	3.23	1.75
Defense/Education	1.63	1.24	0.71	0.82	0.50
State Administration/Education	1.07	0.87	1.35	2.00	1.02
Real Sector/Education	1.63	1.24	0.71	1.46	1.28

Note: 6 CEE countries: Bulgaria, Czech Republic, Hungary, Poland, Romania, Slovak Republic.[29]
5 CIS Countries: Georgia, Kazakhstan, Kyrgyz Republic, Moldova, Tajikistan.
5 LAC Countries: Argentina, Bolivia, Brazil, Columbia, Chile.

Source: IMF, Staff estimates.

of budget priorities and, therefore, changes in expenditure proportions has been slower and less radical than the pace of budget cuts in the mid-1990s. There is excessive inertia in the system, with the budget support segmented among too many institutions, as for instance, is the case of budget spending on research and development (Box 2.1). Too much budgeting is done on an incremental basis, determined primarily by the last year's actual expenditures but not by longer-term priorities,

FIGURE 2.3: THE GOVERNMENT'S ADJUSTED BUDGET PLANS. COMPARISONS OF BUDGET TARGETS FOR THE STATE BUDGET, ADOPTED IN 1999 (MTEF) AND IN 2001 (2002 BUDGET LAW)

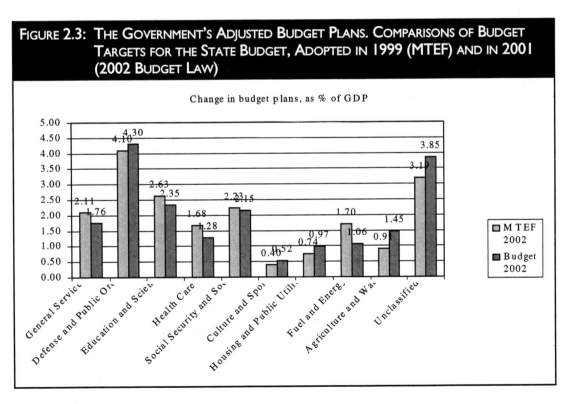

29. Fakin and Crombrugghe (1997) suggest that CEE countries had the excessive average level of public expenditures on social insurance in the mid 90s.

BOX 2.1: BUDGET SUPPORT OF BASIC RESEARCH

Armenia inherited from the Soviet era quite a developed network of R&D facilities. In 1991, the country had 124 research organizations, which employed about 25,300 employees. Given the dramatic decline in the country's incomes in the course of the 90s, it is rather clear that Armenia cannot afford any more of its pre-reform research capacity. There is an urgent need to reorganize both administration and financing of basic and applied research, downsize the sector and reduce the number of independent institutes. So far, insufficient progress was made in this direction. While total employment in the R&D sector (without universities) declined fivefold to about 5,000, in early 2002, Armenia still had 120 independent R&D organizations. The sector became excessively segmented, with many very small units and a highly decentralized management system. In 2002, only 13 research organizations reported directly to the Ministry of Education and Science, 41 to the National Academy of Science, while the rest were attached to various sectoral ministries.

Given that in 2001 the official country budget on science was just above US$2.5 million, the average research institute was getting about US$21,000 a year in budget funds (or US$530 per employee per year). This is an inefficient, very segmented way of financing basic research, which would not in most cases allow the development of products and ideas that meet international standards. In fact, in 2001, Armenian scientists received more funding from international foundations and charities (about US$3.5 million) than from the Armenian budget. The reforms in the sector should be accelerated and linked to the future reforms in university education, while most of the existing R&D facilities should be privatized.

Source: NSS, Ministry of Education and Science.

which are strategically selected in the course of public discussions. Further fiscal adjustment has to focus more on the qualitative side of the process to ensure improvements in the expenditure structure at both national and sectoral levels. This could be attained through radically different future growth rates of specific expenditure categories.

Table 2.7 presents the detailed structure of budget spending on *social services* for 1997–2001. It covers expenditures on social security and insurance, health, education and science, as well as culture, sports and mass media. Overall for the period, the largest expansion occurred in the educa-

TABLE 2.7: SOCIAL SPENDING IN THE CONSOLIDATED BUDGET, 1997–2001
Percent

	1997	1998	1999	2000	2001
As Percent of GDP					
Social and Cultural Sectors, total	9.14%	9.32%	10.46%	9.63%	9.77%
Including:					
1. Education	1.97%	2.07%	2.30%	2.86%	2.55%
2. Social Insurance and Social Protection	5.18%	4.94%	6.05%	5.20%	5.14%
3. Health	1.19%	1.43%	1.38%	0.94%	1.34%
4. Culture, Mass Media, Sports and Religion	0.59%	0.61%	0.55%	0.49%	0.59%
5. Science	0.23%	0.27%	0.19%	0.14%	0.15%
As Percent of total budget expenditures					
Social and Cultural Sectors, total	36.90%	37.15%	36.39%	37.99%	40.01%
Including:					
1. Education	7.95%	8.25%	7.99%	11.28%	10.43%
2. Social Insurance and Social Protection	20.89%	19.71%	21.05%	20.53%	21.07%
3. Health	4.79%	5.71%	4.79%	3.69%	5.48%
4. Culture, Mass Media, Sports and Religion	2.36%	2.42%	1.90%	1.95%	2.43%
5. Science	0.91%	1.06%	0.66%	0.54%	0.60%

tion and health sectors.[30] In education, the 1998 Government program, supported by SACIII Credit, called for the sectoral share to reach at least 11 percent of total state budget expenditures. This was achieved starting from 2000.

However, there is a worrisome instability in budget financing of social services. Health spending was cut by almost 50 percent in 2000 compared to the previous year (measured as percent of GDP) before recovering basically to the original level in 2001. In 1999, spending on social protection and insurance was increased by 25 percent in real terms, triggered by the introduction of new family poverty benefits. Such an expansion proved to be fiscally unsustainable and was scaled back in 2000–01. Still, in terms of social spending, for the country's income level, social protection (poverty benefits) receives disproportionably more funding than is spent on social insurance (pensions).[31]

Table 2.8 provides a breakdown of expenditures on *the real sector* between main recipients of Government support. This budget category combines public investments and budget subsidies in various economic sectors, and, as shown below, considerably underestimates the degree of Government involvement in the economy due to under-reporting of subsidies. As reported, main Government spending is made in irrigation, road rehabilitation and maintenance, housing and urban utilities (including those in the Earthquake Zone), and the power sector. The main driver of public spending in this category is various donor-funded investment projects in infrastructure. For instance, road projects of the IDA accounted for 42 percent of the entire budget spending in 1997–2001 on transport. Irrigation projects of the IDA and IFAD provided for almost a half of budget spending on agriculture and irrigation.

TABLE 2.8: BUDGET EXPENDITURES ON THE REAL SECTOR
Percent of Total

	1997	1998	1999	2000	2001
Real Sector, total	15.90%	19.79%	23.32%	16.06%	14.78%
Agriculture, Forestry and Irrigation	2.46%	5.07%	9.45%	6.41%	5.92%
Residential Housing and Communal Services	4.51%	5.36%	5.51%	5.92%	3.54%
Transport, Roads and Communication	4.43%	4.18%	3.40%	2.35%	2.46%
Energy and Fuel	3.39%	3.39%	1.67%	1.19%	2.41%
Industry, Mining (except Fuel), Construction and Environment	0.50%	0.51%	1.90%	0.15%	0.21%
Other Economic Services	0.61%	1.27%	1.39%	0.03%	0.23%

Another important determinant of budget spending on these items is subsidization in utility sectors as well as a degree of reflection of these subsidies in the budget. This explains a sudden expansion of total spending on the real sector in 1999: it was a year when the Government tried its best to reflect the full amount of quasi-fiscal subsidies in the budget. This spending level declined by more than 50 percent in 2000 due to some improvements in cost recovery but also because off-budget subsidization of utilities increased again.[32]

Armenia's *defense and internal security* budget amounted to 4.8 percent of GDP in 2001 (o/w defense_3.1 percent of GDP[33]) and 17.6 percent of the total budget spending. This is lower

---

30. However, it should be noted that an expansion in education spending in 2000 and 2001 was seriously helped by largely increased funding from irregular budget sources?disbursements under the IDA Education Credit and extensive use of privatization proceeds for school rehabilitation. Longer-term sustainability of such expansion is of concern.

31. See Chapter 7 on social spending for a more detailed analysis.

32. Chapter 3 provides analysis of a quasi-fiscal component in the budget system.

33. In fact, defense spending was reduced considerably in 2001, from the average level of about 3.5 percent of GDP in the previous years.

than the recent level: in 1997–2000, the share of such spending was pretty stable and amounted to 5 percent of GDP and about 19 percent of the total budget spending. Still, the current level of the year 2001 is high for the country at Armenia's income level. There are also concerns about possible additional quasi-fiscal and misclassified budget sources of defense spending (for example, reported as loans to Nagorny Karabagh). The excessive military spending heavily tax both Armenia's growth prospects and poverty reduction. This also demonstrates the size of a future "piece dividend", associated with potential trimming of defense spending to a more "normal" level and utilization of released funds on top priority development needs. Cross-country comparisons above suggest that under the conditions of peace settlement, the share of defense/security spending in the budget could be gradually reduced by as much as 50 percent.

Expenditure Trends in Economic Classification and Quality of Budgetary Information

Table 2.9 describes the structure of consolidated budgets in economic classification. It suggests rather stable proportions between current and investment expenditures[34] in the budget: current spending made between 75 and 78 percent of the total.

The detailed analysis of the current expenditures is difficult due to several major distortions in the way, how the existing budget classification is applied. Those include: (a) under-reporting of both subsidies and budget wages; (b) biased upwards estimates for purchase of goods and services; and (c) one-third of the budget that remains under "other" expenditures. The remaining part of this chapter reviews these distortions and related implications for fiscal policy.

TABLE 2.9: CONSOLIDATED BUDGET EXPENDITURES IN ECONOMIC CLASSIFICATION, PERCENT OF TOTAL

	1997	1998	1999	2000	2001
Current expenditures	78.07%	74.70%	74.23%	77.96%	78.25%
o/w: –Interest and payments	9.98%	7.68%	6.99%	5.32%	5.15%
–Subsidies	1.50%	0.68%	5.12%	2.83%	2.35%
–Current transfers	24.11%	22.92%	22.17%	23.45%	24.02%
–Wages	11.44%	11.95%	7.51%	8.94%	8.71%
–Purchase of goods and services	31.03%	31.47%	32.43%	37.42%	38.02%
O/w: Other expenditures	14.88%	14.65%	29.01%	32.80%	33.54%
Capital expenditures including net lending	21.93%	25.30%	25.77%	22.04%	21.75%

Subsidies

The budget data suggest that budget financing of subsidies was highly volatile. It changed from 0.7 percent of GDP in 1998 to 5.1 percent in 1999. Such fluctuations were a result of two main factors. First, the Government policy on incorporation of quasi-fiscal deficits in the budget was inconsistent: in 1997–1999, it showed a trend towards better consolidation of quasi-fiscal elements but this process backslided partially in 2000–01. Second, in fact, the Government had another major channel of *de facto* budget subsidies_under the rubric "budget loans"_that was rather intensively used in 1997–98 and 2001.[35] This considerably distorted the whole picture of budgetary subsidy incidence in Armenia.[36]

Table 2.10 presents more realistic estimates for the current level of subsidies in the budget system. Indeed, the level of subsidization is excessive. In 1999, more than 9 percent of total bud-

---

34. Chapter 9 analyzed the public investment program.
35. In 2001, by its Decree 440, the Government wrote off 11.7 billion drams (more than 1 percent of 2001 GDP) of budget credits granted in 1998 to irrigation, admitting de facto that those were subsidies to the sector.
36. It also causes a serious distortion for national accounts, especially for those done on a quarterly basis.

TABLE 2.10: BUDGET SUBSIDIES AND DIRECT BUDGET CREDITS TO LARGE SOES

	1997	1998	1999	2000	2001
Total subsidies and direct credits	4,986.2	6,579.3	26,314.1	10,266.0	11,865.4
As percent of GDP	0.62	0.69	2.66	0.99	1.01
As percent of total budget expenditures	2.50	2.75	9.27	3.92	4.13
Budget subsidies	2,986.2	1,629.4	14,546.3	7,404.3	6,749.4
As percent of GDP	0.37	0.17	1.47	0.72	0.57
Total budget credit to non-financial institutions	2,000.0	5,099.4	11,767.8	2,861.7	5,116.0
As percent of GDP	0.25	0.52	1.19	0.28	0.43
Irrigation		1,795.0	2,443.4		
Airline and airport		507.9	1,824.6	3,531.2	1,844.6
Drinking water companies	2,000.0	2,000.0	1,200.0		
Energy companies			1,899.8		3,200.0
Nairit			4,400.0		
Residential housing		647.0		421.9	71.4

get spending was spent on subsidies,[37] while in 2000–01, it was about 4 percent of the total. Main recipients of budgetary support in Armenia are state-owned companies in energy and infrastructure. The subsidies reflect both performance problems (especially, low collection levels) as well as insufficient cost recovery in tariffs (primarily in irrigation).

In the second half of the 1990s, the Government basically stopped direct subsidization of commercial companies outside of the infrastructure. The main exemption was the chemical company, Nairit, which remained a recipient of considerable direct Government support in the late 1990s. Nairit is considered by the authorities to be too large to fail. It was estimated that total average annual subsidies (explicit and implicit) received by Nairit in 1996–99 amounted to 0.6 percent of GDP (World Bank, 2000c). In dollar equivalent, every one of the 4000 employees was a recipient of an annual subsidy that amounted to about US$2,500. This should be compared to an average industrial wage of about US$600 a year, and the average salary of a teacher of US$350 a year. In 2002, a UK company signed with the GOA a private management contract for Nairit. It is expected to close a major drain on the country budget.

Net Budget Lending

Another confusing budget line in the Armenian budget is "Net budget lending," which combines three qualitatively rather different items:

- direct credits to loss-making public SOEs that nobody expects to be repaid, i.e. subsidies as discussed above;
- credits to Nagorno-Karabakh, which should be classified as inter-governmental grants;
- genuine lending operations to the economy, which in most cases represent Government participation in the donor-funded credit lines (on-lending).

Table 2.11 describes levels of three main types of budget lending. It shows that budget credits have expanded considerably since 1999, and in 1999–2001, on average exceeded 7.5 percent of total budget expenditures. This increase occurred mostly due to the expansion of the various on-lending schemes, including credit lines of the World Bank, German Government, Lincy and Huntsman Foundations.

---

37. A portion of 1999 subsidies was spent on clearing enterprises' arrears accumulated earlier, i.e. it cashed out unpaid subsidies of the previous years.

TABLE 2.11: BUDGET LENDING					
	1997	1998	1999	2000	2001
Total Net Lending	**8,511.7**	**13,864.2**	**26,148.3**	**18,052.6**	**20,080.3**
As percent of total budget expenditures	4.3	5.8	9.2	6.9	7.4
Quasi-Subsidies: Credit to utilities,	2,000.0	5,099.4	11,767.8	2,861.7	5,116.0
On-lending: Credits to commercial borrowers through local banks	895.3	1,598.6	7,080.7	6,054.0	7,410.0
Credits to NKR	6,464.2	7,689.0	8,207.0	9,508.8	9,000.0
Memo: Total repayment of budget credits	–847.8	–522.8	–907.2	–371.9	–445.7

In contrast to budget credits to utilities, which are used primarily for covering operational losses, on-lending schemes actually expand availability of credit to the private sector and as such may have a significant potential development impact. The problem in Armenia is that expansion in credit lines was too rapid and as such was not accompanied by appropriate institutional strengthening of the banking sector. By the end of 2001, Government-backed credit lines amounted to almost 20 percent of total outstanding private credit in the economy. More importantly, starting from 1999, almost the entire expansion in banking credit to the private sector was funded by credit lines, while domestic intermediation has stagnated. This suggests that the incentive structure of local banks is seriously distorted.

Wage Bill

Another major weakness of the Government budget statistics derives from the absence of any comprehensive reporting on the consolidated salary fund in the budgetary sector. The official budget data show that after 1999 the share of wages in the total budget expenditures declined drastically, from about 15 percent to 10–11 percent in 2000–01. This decline reflects a change in budgetary presentation and reporting and it does not relate to any serious reductions in Government staffing or wage policy in 1999–2001. Instead, the primary reason derives from the introduction of new financing mechanisms in several sectors, primarily education and health. Most public hospitals and about 20 percent of country schools were transferred to the new system, under which they receive their global budget without item-by-item breakdown and could allocate it among various categories of spending independently. In economic classification of the budget, such budget financing is reflected as "acquisition of goods and services." Somewhat surprisingly, the entities covered by the new financing system do not report back to the Government (neither to the MOFE nor to a sectoral Ministry) at a sufficient level of details on how they ultimately spend their allocations.

As a result, the Ministry of Finance and Economy does not have the capability of monitoring the dynamics of total salary fund in the budget sector, which is rather an important indicator of overall fiscal management.[38] Due to the weaknesses in the reporting system, the Ministry (and the Government in general) does not have up-to-date estimates of how many positions are in budget-funded entities and how many people are in reality on the Government payroll. This affects budgetary planning, hampers control over staffing and overall wage costs, and it also would hamper forthcoming reforms of public sector employment.[39] Lack of proper salary reporting also creates problems for current budgetary management because it reduces opportunities for both the MOFE

---

38. The 2002 annual Budget Law provides explicit financing for only 12,000 employees of the central Government administration with a total salary fund of Dram 6.2 billion (0.6 percent of GDP).

39. The Government has initiated a major reform of civil service in 2001. However, so far this effort has been narrowly focused on the core employment in central administration (i.e., only on those who would become civil servants), and it does not yet cover more general problems of managing the entire budget sector employment. Most of the employees in public health and education will remain outside of the civil servant corp.

and budget managers in sectoral ministries to monitor timely wage payments by budget organizations. Funds intended for wage payments could be disbursed by the Treasury but used by organizations' managers for other non-salary purposes. This creates additional accumulation of wage arrears and tensions in the system, in particular in the health sector.

In the absence of official Government statistics on public employment, everyone is using indirect estimates. The available data suggest that the Armenian Government is overextended. Armenia's budgetary sector employment in 1998–99 comprised at least 300,000 or 10 percent of the Armenia population, while in the OECD states the similar share on average amounts to 7.7 percent and in the FSU states_about 8 percent (World Bank, 1999a). About a half of Armenia budgetary employment is concentrated in health and education. At the same time, Armenian Government officials are underpaid, which generates problems for attracting highly qualified people to the administration. The official average wage in the Government administration in the late 1990s was estimated as 50 percent of Armenia's GDP per capita, which is an extremely low level by international standards (Fig. 2.4). A combination of overstaffing and over-regulation with low salaries creates an environment supportive of corruption. While the core wages are very low (Fig. 2.5), as it is shown in the next chapters, in core public sectors the public wage bill has a very high share of total spending, which is not sustainable in the long term.

Indirect estimates suggest that the total public sector wage bill (without defense and security forces, and without employees of public enterprises) amounted to about 5 percent of GDP in 1999–2000, or 18–20 percent of the total budget expenditures of respective years.

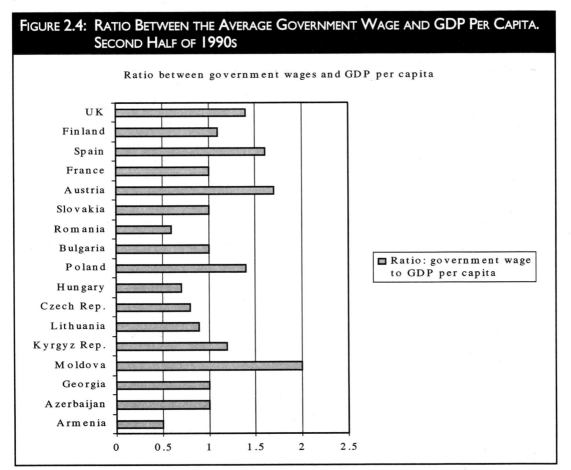

FIGURE 2.4: RATIO BETWEEN THE AVERAGE GOVERNMENT WAGE AND GDP PER CAPITA.
SECOND HALF OF 1990s

Source: IBRD.

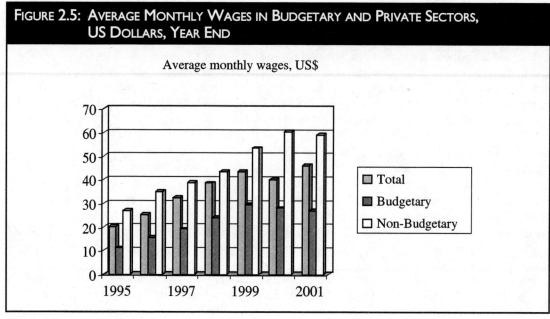

FIGURE 2.5: AVERAGE MONTHLY WAGES IN BUDGETARY AND PRIVATE SECTORS, US DOLLARS, YEAR END

Source: IMF.

This analysis highlights once again an importance of civil service reform for Armenia: the Government should accelerate implementation of its civil service reform program to ensure higher efficiency in public administration based on a streamlined structure of the Government, reduced staff levels, and increased salaries.

Additional Problems with the Quality of Budget Data

The previous section identified specific problems with budget data on main expenditure aggregates in economic classification (subsidies, wages, net lending). The resulting distortions as well as the fact that one-third of total expenditure is not classified greatly limits productivity of economic analysis of Government spending. While functional classification of the budget is of much higher quality, it also has serious deficiencies that derive from incomplete compliance with the principles of GFS budget classification. This section discusses the main source of these problems in functional classification, which derives from an inflated use of budget category "expenditure on other sectors."

Table 2.12 presents the basic structure of this category. It shows that it expanded largely in the last two years, from 6.8 percent in 1999 of total expenditures to 13.2 percent in 2001. Because the budget does not provide any explanation which sectors/entities were recipients of these funds, this represents a serious deterioration in the level of budget transparency and government accountability.

Table 2.12 shows that "expenditure on other sectors" includes three main components for which the budget documents do not provide a functional/sectoral breakdown. Each component remains quite a heterogeneous aggregate and ultimately unclear. More than 50 percent of total spending under this budget line is simply identified as either "other expenditures" or "other services."

The discussions with the MOFE officials helped to clarify the qualitative features of these three aggregates and suggest main implications of such excessive use of this expenditure item.

■ "Repayment of budget arrears" contains a considerable amount of Government cash spending on social sectors. This is just a reflection of the fact that budget arrears are heavily con-

TABLE 2.12: BUDGET EXPENDITURES ON OTHER SECTORS

	1997	1998	1999	2000	2001
Other sectors, total	15,576.2	13,000.1	19,355.6	30,799.0	38,061.2
–share in GDP	1.94%	1.36%	1.96%	2.98%	3.23%
–share in total	7.81%	5.42%	6.78%	11.76%	13.24%
1. Repayment of budget arrears	6,854.9	1,042.8	–	9,444.1	8,792.1
–share in GDP	0.85%	0.11%	–	0.91%	0.75%
–share in total	3.44%	0.44%	–	0.61%	3.06%
2. Government reserve fund	1,738.8	2,534.5	8,534.5	9,381.2	10,891.7
–share in GDP	0.22%	0.27%	0.86%	0.91%	0.93%
–share in total	0.87%	1.06%	3.01%	3.58%	3.79%
o/w: 2.1. Net lending to the non-financial sector		111.0		2,439.8	5,044.6
2.2. Other services	1,621.8	1,000.9	875.4	6,131.9	5,076.2
3. Other expenditures	6,982.5	9,422.8	10,821.1	11,973.7	18,377.4
–share in GDP	0.87%	0.99%	1.10%	1.16%	1.56%
–share in total	3.50%	3.93%	3.81%	4.57%	6.39%

centrated in these sectors. Thus, actual budget spending, e.g. on health and education in Armenia have been somewhat higher recently compared to the levels reported in the standard budget documents (Table 2.13). These deviations could be quite significant. For instance, total 2001 cash spending on public health (including repayment of arrears on 2000 commitments) were 7.7 percent above the officially reported level. Respectively, total 2001 accrual expenditures on health were 10.5 percent higher.

▓ Budget credits under "Net lending" (0.5 percent of GDP in 2001) from the Reserve Fund, which similar in their nature to budget subsidies; the experience from other economies in transition suggests that budget credits to large state enterprises are rarely repaid by the borrowers.

▓ "Other services" from the Reserve Fund include rather standard Government expenditures such as subsidies and social transfers which could and should be easily classified under respective sectoral rubrics.

▓ The third sub-group "Other expenditures" reflects spending in various sectors which are funded under different donor-funded projects that do not have a specific sectoral focus,

TABLE 2.13: BUDGET ARREARS AND TOTAL SPENDING IN SOCIAL SECTORS IN 2001, MILLION DRAM

	Budget Report (without repayment and accumulation of arrears)	Re-payment of arrears	Accumulation of Arrears	Cash Expenditures (include repayment of arrears)	Accrual Expenditures (include accumulated arrears)	Ratio: Cash/Budget Report	Ratio: Accrual/ Budget Report
Total Expenditures	276,605.4	8,792.3	11,764.0	285,397.7	288,369.4		
Education and Science	31,697.5	776.8	1,379.2	32,474.3	33,076.7	1.025	1.044
Health	15,746.7	1,219.9	1,650.7	16,966.5	17,397.4	1.077	1.105
Social Security and Social Insurance	60,564.8	1,467.7	300.4	62,032.5	60,865.2	1.024	1.005

including World Bank's SIF, credit lines, projects of Lincy and Huntsman Foundations. Most of these expenditures should and could be classified under specific sectoral rubrics. As it is now, some public investments (e.g. under the SIF) and budget transfers to commercial enterprises (through credit lines) are not accounted for properly.

Overall, most of the "Other sectors" category could be easily reported elsewhere within the existing functional classification (see Annex 4). But for this to happen, the budget should be prepared and approved in a different structure, with a much smaller share of other spending. The MOFE has also to prepare a new internal budget classification instruction, which would aim at the reduction of the "other sectors" category and provide definitions for all expenditure items that fully reflect internationally accepted classification principles.

As it follows from the above discussion, the existing budget statistics in Armenia have numerous problems. While the Government adopted the budget classification consistent with the GFS requirements, in practice implementation of the GFS is still incomplete. As a result, the available budget reporting does not have a necessary degree of either adequacy or transparency. Strengthening the quality of fiscal data is a necessary step to improve expenditure analysis as well as design an efficient expenditure rationalization strategy.

Aside from the problems with specific budget classification entries such as investments, subsidies, wages, etc., there are additional weaknesses in expenditure data that are usually available for analysis:

- the lack of expenditure time series by organization (ministries, central agencies): it is organizations, not functions, who hold the budgets, and organization-wise data are therefore essential to understanding budget formulation and implementation;
- annual changes in budget classification that make very difficult analysis of budget time series;
- insufficient reflection in the budget of donors' assistance in social sectors.[40]

Overall, the general public doesn't have access to a sufficiently accurate picture of public expenditures. The data that are readily available for Armenia, such as the standard summary tables published in Armenia Economic Trends (AET) and the IMF's Recent Economic Developments (RED), are rather limited. They usually reproduce the standard budget publication as in Table 2.1, which is based on unreliable budget classification, has incomplete coverage, and is excessively aggregated.

It is problematic to conduct public expenditure analysis at too high a level of aggregation such as national summaries of functional and economic classification. Further disaggregation is necessary for at least two reasons: (a) highly aggregated data do not explain enough about the distribution of resources or the efficiency and effectiveness of resource use; (b) the aggregates abstract from the organizations that hold the budgets; analysis at the organizational level is essential to an understanding of the dynamics of public expenditure management.

For the first time, the Government published the detailed report on 2001 actual budget execution in the same format and with the same level of details as the Annual Budget Laws (which have been published since 1996). This practice should be continued.

Recommendations

The analysis in the chapter suggests the existence of the main structural imbalances in the allocation of public expenditure in Armenia. Current imbalances derive from fundamental institutional weaknesses, which are relatively well understood (though there is scope to raise the level of public understanding and debate). Given the existing political economy of Armenia's reform process (strong populist sentiments and internal divisions within the political elite), it is difficult to expect

---

40. Chapter 3 discusses the budget coverage.

that a major change in budget performance could emerge quickly and easily. Fundamental institutional reforms would take time, during which one may expect only gradual progress in strengthening the process for inter-sectoral budget allocations, including shifts in such ratios as recurrent vs. capital expenditure and wages vs. other recurrent spending. While it may be technically correct to argue that these shifts are badly needed, recommendations at such an aggregated level are not really operational under prevailing institutional constraints.

In addition, given the expenditure cuts that have already taken place, the scope for further aggregate expenditure compression in most sectors is quite limited, which further limits room for improvements in expenditure efficiency through inter-sectoral re-allocation.

At the same time, there is an urgent need to increase the existing funding of social sectors, which seems to be socially unacceptable and would become a major constraint for growth in the longer term. While the improved financing of health, primary education, and pensions should come from three sources_better revenue performance, expenditure reallocation, increased efficiency within the sector_in the short term, the revenue factor would prevail. In short, the top priority for the Government is to improve tax collection by about 2 percent of GDP and channel at least 75 percent of this increase to the social sectors.

Rationalization of spending at the sectoral level, especially in social sectors, should be another priority. As it is argued in Chapter 4, this could be achieved by expanding the role of line ministries in budgeting and their responsibility for outcomes. Increased efficiency of sectoral expenditure programs would provide additional support for their claims for an increased share in the total budget envelop.

At the same time, the Government has to broaden public debate on expenditure strategy and available strategic options, as a part of the PRSP process. There is a major need for updating (and in some cases, clearly formulating) expenditure priorities. It is important to raise public awareness about actual budget trends and realistic alternatives.

This would require a major improvement in the quality of budget reporting at all levels_budgetary organizations, line ministries, and the central Treasury. Strengthening the quality of fiscal data is a necessary initial step to improve expenditure analysis and design an expenditure rationalization strategy, including proper reallocation between sectors. The MOFE has to improve transparency of operations of the Reserve Fund and greatly reduce the amount of budget credits disbursed from the Reserve Fund. Further budget transparency should be achieved quickly through better reporting on operations with budget arrears and on multi-sectoral donor projects. Another priority relates to improvements in reporting on salaries in the budgetary sector as well as in statistics of public employment, including establishment of a database on all budgetary-funded staff positions. There is also a need to improve general statistics on the public sector that is important for budgetary planning. This would include items such as the number of students in public schools and universities, public housing, length of publicly funded roads, etc.

In the medium term, the Government is expected to achieve significant reductions in subsidies that go to utilities and infrastructure. This would provide room for an additional reallocation of funds to concentrate limited resources in the most critical areas, especially those related to support of primary social services and basic infrastructure.

CHAPTER 3

OFF-BUDGET ELEMENTS OF THE FISCAL SYSTEM

In order to ensure efficient use of public resources and appropriate macroeconomic management, the budget should include, in line with the GFS recommendations and internationally recognized definitions of the government sector, total revenues received and all budgeted expenditures made by Government agencies.

Since the adoption of the 1997 Budget Systems Law, the Ministry of Finance and Economy has improved the coverage of the annual budget, in particular as it relates to the coverage of external credits and budgetary support grants. However, the Government budget still excludes several major components of both government revenues and expenditures, primarily:

▓ Own revenues raised by particular ministries, such as e.g. extra-budgetary funds.
▓ External grants that are received in the form of commodities.
▓ Losses and contingent liabilities, accumulated by state-owned enterprises – quasi-fiscal deficits.

In addition, there are considerable gaps in reporting on Government guarantees for banking credits (both domestic and external) granted to local commercial firms.

Also, as was mentioned in Chapter 1, the Government has been keeping off-budget a large portion of privatization proceeds received through the gas-for-equity swap in the gas sector. About US$120 million were received in "free" gas and reductions of energy debts in 1997–2001, which has been an important source of quasi-fiscal financing in this period. Overall, the Government has to improve recording of operations with privatization proceeds. At the moment, budget documents include only the use of privatization receipts for purposes of debt reduction and capital expenditure. The budget does not describe an amount of privatization proceeds planned to be received during the year. Respectively, the Government does not report on the actual inflow of such proceeds.

This Chapter reviews the magnitude of off-budget activities within each of the above mentioned components. It concludes that budget consolidation in Armenia is far from being completed, while there has been some progress recently. The Chapter does not discuss issues related to the performance of the Pension Fund/SIF, which is instead reviewed in Chapter 7. While the SIF is a separate entity within the Armenian fiscal system, it does not represent an off-budget activity in a sense of other items discussed in this Chapter. In 2001, the Government adopted amendments to the Pension Fund Charter and introduced new requirements for transparency and accountability of the SIF, which are basically comparable with those for a regular Government budget.

Extra-Budgetary Funds

At least ten central ministries/agencies in Armenia hold extra-budgetary funds (EBFs), including the Ministry of State Revenues, State Customs Committee, Ministry of Transport and Communication, and the Ministry of Interior. A total of 16 billion Drams (representing 1.5 percent of GDP and around 8 percent of revenues of the consolidated budget) were collected by these ministries/agencies in 2001 (Table 3.1). This does not include dozens (potentially hundreds) of very small EBFs, which are created by individual budgetary entities, such as schools and hospitals.

TABLE 3.1: CONSOLIDATED BALANCE OF ARMENIA'S EXTRA-BUDGETARY FUNDS IN 2000–01
Million Dram

	2000	2001
Opening balance	—	1,107
Receipts	5,607	16,045
Expenditures	4,500	15,424
Closing balance	1,107	1,728

Source: MOFE.

The own-source receipts and expenditures of most ministries/agencies are not included in the budget. Only the receipts and expenditures by the EBFs that are held by the MOFE and the Ministry of State Revenue (MOSR), including the Customs Committee, are required to be included in the budget, according to the Budget Systems Law. The Fund which is held by the MoSR is also unique (Table 3.2) in a sense that it was established based on the Law. All other funds are set up by individual Government decisions, which identify revenue sources for these funds on a case-by-case basis. In the case of the MOSR, the Ministry is allowed to keep 10 percent of additional tax revenues it managed to raise as a result of its auditing activities.

Before 1999, there was no common framework to regulate activities of EBFs. The Government adopted two decisions in 1999–2000, which introduced the reporting requirements for line ministries on their respective EBFs spending. However, there is no a requirement in legislation to report to Parliament on EBFs' expenditures, and no detailed information is available to general public on their actual spending. At the same time, accounts of the largest EBFs are kept with the Treasury, so the Ministry of Finance and Economy has a potential possibility for both monitoring and reporting on this part of extra-budgetary flows.

As Table 3.2 suggests, the size of the EBFs may be rather significant relative to the regular budget of respective ministries. In the case of the MOSR, it amounts to 60 percent of its regular budget.

As these EBF resources represent government revenues and are used to purchase goods and services in support of delivery of regular Government services, the EBFs should be included explicitly

TABLE 3.2: EXTRA-BUDGETARY FUND OF THE MINISTRY OF STATE REVENUES, INCLUDING THE CUSTOMS COMMITTEE
Million Dram

	1998	1999	2000	2001
Expenditures from the Extra-budgetary Fund	344.4	433.2	709.4	800.0
Memo: MoSR regular budget (State budget provision)	577.2	717.5	1,113.4	
EBF/Regular budget, percent	59.7%	60.4%	63.7%	

Source: MOSR.

in the budget and voted on by Parliament. The first best solution is full consolidation of these funds with the regular budget to avoid budget segmentation. If this is not politically feasible in some cases, as a minimum, each ministry/agency should provide in its budget submission a forecast for expected extra-budgetary receipts, and the use of these receipts should be shown by program. Requests for this information should be included in the annual Budget Instructions approved by the MOFE. Respectively, the ministries should report on utilization of actual EBF receipts in the same format.

The MOFE should fully enforce the existing legislation that requires maintaining of all extra-budgetary accounts with the Treasury, while the Treasury has to be able to produce regular consolidated reports on operations of the EBFs.

Grants

Since the mid-1990s the Government has significantly improved reflection of cash-based external grants in the regular budget. However, the budget excludes most externally-financed grants that are received in the form of commodities, and this leads to a major under-estimation of the actual volume of available public resources, especially in the social sectors.

By a number of reasons, the level of incoming commodity grants to Armenia has been quite high if compared to some of her neighbors. In 2000, total import of humanitarian aid amounted to US$75.6 million or 8.5 percent of total imports. The factors that explain such a higher than average inflow include: (i) existence of massive and clearly identifiable humanitarian needs (refugees, Earthquake zone); (ii) Armenia's established track record of being "poor but reform minded"_an advanced reformer in the region; and (iii) intensive Diaspora support. As a result, Armenia has numerous providers of humanitarian assistance.[41] However, as reported by the Government Commission on Humanitarian Assistance (GCHA), in the recent years, 20 largest donors provided more than 85 percent of total registered assistance.

At the moment, the Government has rather limited capacity for monitoring and coordination of this massive inflow and its adequate integration into its regular (funded from its regular budget) activities. The existing Government coordination system is highly segmented.[42] Several government units focused primarily at monitoring of incoming "decentralized assistance," that is, aid arriving through non-Governmental channels. At the same time, assistance provided by official donors according to inter-Governmental agreements remain mostly outside of centralized Government monitoring. However, as estimated, official donors contribute about 75 percent of the total aid. The computerized system for donor coordination, sponsored by the UNDP in the late 1990s, has not been fully utilized recently.

At the sectoral level, the situation varies considerably from ministry to ministry. Some ministries, for example, the Ministry of Social Security, seems to have established rather a reliable system of regular reporting and controls over received aid but this best practice has not been disseminated efficiently.[43]

This lack of coordination and monitoring affects policy decisions. Where grants in kind are used to finance public expenditure or substitute conventional budget spending (such as in social protection and other social sectors), it is important for budget comprehensiveness that these figures are included in the budget. Otherwise, it reduces accountability of recipients to the Government, to Parliament, and to donors. In several sectors, off-budget grant-funded assistance represents a major share of the sector expenditures. Their exclusion from the budgetary framework undermines efficiency of decisions on the resource allocation between and within sectors. The more adequate inclusion of external finance into the budget will also assist the Government in programming future donor resources.

---

41. In 2001, the GCHA received regular reports from 145 non-governmental donor organizations.

42. The Government reorganized its donor coordination system in February 2001. Under the previous arrangements, the GCHA was responsible for monitoring and reporting on the entire aid flow (official and non-official).

43. In particular, in the past the Government did not reflect in the budget major grant-based programs of public investments funded by the Lincy Foundations. In early 2003, the Government made a commitment to start reporting to Parliament on this grant program on a quarterly basis.

As part of the preparation for this report, the team undertook a pilot survey of off-budget quasi-public health spending that is funded by international donors, NGOs and Diaspora organizations (Table 3.3). Detailed interviews were held with representatives of 37 major providers and recipients (main hospitals) of aid. The results suggest that incoming assistance to the sector amounted to about a half of the regular Government health budget. When technical assistance is excluded, the volume of aid amounts to about 35 percent of the regular sectoral budget.

TABLE 3.3: OFF-BUDGET DONOR ASSISTANCE IN THE HEALTH SECTOR
US$ thousands

	1997	1998	1999	2000	2001	Total
Technical Assistance	1,148	1,365	932	1,228	1,824	6,498
Equipment	603	1,424	5,718	2,157	981	10,883
Training	288	446	654	598	4,878	6,864
Medicine	1,226	1,139	2,096	1,929	8,291	14,681
Construction	450	451	469	1,510	566	3,445
Medical Services	387	526	867	433	319	2,532
Maintenance	96	57	270	300	192	914
Transport and fuel	163	64	293	195	122	837
Other	301	289	248	618	781	2,236
Total grants	**4,661**	**5,760**	**11,548**	**8,968**	**17,953**	**48,890**
Memo: Official health budget, US$ million			25.4	18.6	28.5	
—Grants as percent of the official health budget			45.4	48.2	62.9	

Source: Survey results.

Table 3.4 provides some rough conservative estimates for the total inflow of humanitarian assistance (commodity grants) to Armenia that remains outside of the budget. It suggests that the total average volume amounted recently to US$40 million or 2 percent of GDP. This is much more than budgeted (cash) grants.

TABLE 3.4: OFF-BUDGET GRANT ASSISTANCE
US$ million

	1999	2000	2001
TOTAL	**34.4**	**41.4**	**46.1**
o/w: Health	9.7	6.6	10.4
—Education	6.1	9.7	9.8
—Social Protection	11	20.6	20.8
—Construction in the EQZ	7.6	4.5	5.1
Memo: Budgeted grants	28.2	15.8	16.9

Note: Excludes funding of technical assistance.

Source: Staff estimates based on interviews with donors and Government officials.

Because policy makers in Armenia do not take off-budget resources explicitly into account, this creates additional problems with planning and policy design. The main concern is that off-budget mechanisms for implementation of aid projects undermine equity in resource allocation. For instance, they create pockets of better funded public institutions in health. They also sponsor formation of parallel systems of allocation of poverty benefits that inflate overall administrative costs (See Box 3.1).[44]

---

44. In some cases, donors should review the existing practice of administering their own systems of poverty benefits, especially when they do distribution of food and other in-kind benefits. It could be more efficient to switch to regular cash grants that would be earmarked for additional funding of the main Government social assistance program, family poverty benefits. See also Chapter 7.

Box 3.1: UMCOR: NGO's Participation in Delivery of Social Assistance

UMCOR (United Methodist Committee on Relief) is the main NGO contractor for the humanitarian part of USAID's Social Transition Program, which provides in-kind poverty alleviation in 5 out of 11 marzes (regions) of the country. UMCOR coordinates activities of other NGOs, including Mission Armenia, Save the Children, Catholic Relief Services, and others, which actually distribute this assistance. As estimated by the Ministry of Social Security (MSS), the total number of staff engaged in the program amounts to 280. Main elements of the program include:

- Food assistance. In 2000/01 fiscal year, 84,000 families from these 5 marzes received food baskets. In the year 2001/02 the number of beneficiaries is expected to be 40,000. The selection of recipients is based on the database of eligible households, which is managed by the MSS.
- Free lunches in 20 schools as selected by the Ministry of Education and Science.
- Free basic medicines to individual communities as selected by the Ministry of Health.
- Agricultural inputs, provided to vulnerable households as identified by communities.

The comprehensiveness of external finance in the Budget needs to be improved, specifically to capture grants from bilateral agencies, and flows from major NGOs and foundations. This could be accomplished through requiring the relevant information on grants from bilaterals and multilaterals to be systematically collected by the Ministry of Finance and Economy. The Budget Department could be responsible for liaising with the Government Commission on Humanitarian Assistance, which at the moment has access to the most systematic data. Where such grants are provided to support public expenditure (including public investment), these flows should be captured in the budgetary documents. This relates to all stages of the budget process: the MOFE should capture the majority of incoming grants during budget preparation (as estimates of future disbursements) as well as during preparation of the annual budget execution report (as reported amounts of disbursed assistance). In cases when large additional grants become available in the course of the year (for example, in case of emergency relief assistance), the Government may need to do an official amendment to its annual budget law.

Better reporting would also require an additional effort from the donors.[45] First, the donors, especially official donors, should insist on proper reflection of incoming aid in the budget and request respective Government's commitments in their grant agreements. The largest donors should be prepared to provide quarterly disbursement information to the GCHA and copy it to the MOFE and a responsible sectoral Ministry. These reports would include: (i) the value of disbursements during the quarter and year-to-date (cumulative); (ii) the type of disbursements (such as type of supplies) and receiving institutions; and (iii) planned disbursement for the next reporting period. Although separate reports would potentially require extra work from donors, on balance, the benefits to Government planning are likely to outweigh the additional inconvenience. In the longer term, this reporting system should be supported by the strengthening of appropriate aid management units in the sector ministries.

Quasi-fiscal Deficits and Losses Generated by State Enterprises

The problem of quasi-fiscal deficits, which usually emerge as a result of quasi-fiscal (hidden off-budget) subsidies to enterprises and households, has two inter-related and equally important dimensions that relate respectively to macroeconomic and enterprise sector performance. Accumulated experience with transition since 1990 suggests that dramatic reduction in total subsidies

---

45. The World Bank Report (2001f, Chapter IV) provides a detailed set of suggestions that would increase efficiency of aid flows to the IDA countries. Specifically, the report argues for a larger shift from project aid to budget support, for multi-year donor commitments linked to the recipient's budget calendar, and for avoiding off-budget support.

(budgeted and non-budgeted) is a critical prerequisite for macroeconomic stabilization, enterprise restructuring, and the credibility of the entire reform process (Pinto et al., 2000). Overall, and especially when compared to several largest CIS economies, it seems that the budget constraints in Armenia were modestly tight for most of the enterprise sector in the late 1990s. While the level of quasi-fiscal subsides (especially utility arrears) remained high, those were heavily concentrated in the household sector as well as in a limited number of largest companies (SOEs and recently privatized). As was concluded in the earlier study (World Bank, 2001c), arrears and quasi-fiscal subsidies in Armenia are much more fiscal than a restructuring problem. There is no evidence so far that softness of budget constraint for a few largest companies was among the major factors that had slowed down the overall enterprise restructuring process. The Government should accelerate liquidation and/or forced restructuring of these largest loss-making firms, which would have a beneficial impact on both the fiscal system and the entire enterprise sector.

The purpose of this section, which is based on the earlier analysis by the World Bank (2001c), is to review the structure and the level of quasi-fiscal deficits and subsidies remaining in the Armenian economy and to identify main beneficiaries of the current subsidies.

Table 3.5 provides a summary of main estimates for annual subsidies that were entering the economy through three main channels: (a) explicit budget support;(b) accumulation of tax arrears; and (c) quasi-fiscal subsidies received by economic agents through accumulation of arrears to public and publicly-controlled companies in the utility/energy sector.[46] It reveals that the incidence of subsidies remains high and until recently most subsidization has been kept outside of the regular budget. In 1996–98, quasi-fiscal financing of subsidies amounted to 4.2–5.4 percent of GDP, which was 4–7 times higher that the volume of budgeted subsidies. This level of quasi-fiscal financing was comparable with the size of official cash-based deficit of the Government budget. Subsidization through tax arrears was rather modest (on average amounted to about 1 percent of GDP).

TABLE 3.5: BUDGETED SUBSIDIES, QUASI-FISCAL SUBSIDIES AND TAX ARREARS
Percent of GDP

	1996	1997	1998	1999	2000	2001
1. Budgeted subsidies and direct credits	1.3	0.6	0.7	2.7	1.2	1.4
2. Increase in tax arrears	0.3	0.9	2.0	0.9	0.9	0.0
3. Total fiscal (1+2)	1.6	1.5	2.7	3.6	2.1	1.4
4. Quasi-fiscal financing of subsidies	5.4	4.2	4.5	2.9	2.3	1.6
5. Total financing of subsidies (3+4)	7.0	5.7	7.2	6.5	4.4	3.0
Net Recipients of subsidies (on the consolidated basis)						
Population	2.6	2.2	3.0	2.2	1.4	1.0
Energy	−1.5	0.4	0.7	1.0	−0.2	0.1
Utilities	0.0	0.3	1.2	2.3	1.5	0.9
Industry	0.9	1.6	1.1	1.6	0.3	0.3
Others	0.7	0.8	0.8	0.5	0.8	0.4
Memo: implicit tariff subsidies			2.0	1.5	—	—

Source: Staff estimates based on data from the MOFE, NSS, and public utilities.

---

46. Table 3.5, however, only partially covers another source of subsidization—subsidization through tariffs—that derives from a combination of low tariffs for utility services and insufficient budget compensation of utilities with explicit subsidies. This causes some underestimation of subsidies received by final consumers of energy and utility services (population and the enterprise sector). However, because main energy inputs were imported to Armenia at non-subsidized prices, it does not create distortion in the level of the overall subsidies in the system.

Starting from 1999, the Government managed to shift a larger portion of subsidy financing from the energy sector to the fiscal system. While the budget itself still contains only a small fraction of overall subsidies, in 1998–2001, total fiscal subsidies (including tax arrears) became comparable in size with the quasi-fiscal subsidies financed by public utilities. This is clearly a sign of the system becoming more transparent. Better budgeting of quasi-fiscal subsidies since 1999 has been accompanied by the Government's efforts to increase cost recovery in tariffs and improve payment discipline. As a result, tariff subsidies have been mostly eliminated in 1999.

Still, the level of quasi-fiscal subsidies, which showed a clear sign of declining since 1999, remained high (about 1.5 percent of GDP in 2001).[47]

Non-payments by consumers for energy and utility consumption were a single main form of quasi-fiscal subsidization. The culture of non-payment is well rooted in Armenia and it supports long-chains of overdue payables within the economy. The overall annual flow of non-payments in main utilities amounted to 8.7 percent of GDP in 1996, 7.0 percent of GDP in 1998, but it was reduced considerably since 1999 (to about 2.4 percent of GDP in 2001) due to a stronger Government reform effort.

Thus, the funding of quasi-fiscal subsidies was coming primarily from the operational cash flow of (mostly publicly-owned) energy companies first of all in the gas and power sectors. Heating and water companies provided smaller amounts of subsidies in particular years. In turn, gas and power companies incurred significant losses and financed their operational deficits by building debts to their suppliers and commercial banks as well as through under-maintenance of companies' assets. Annex 3 presents a flow-of-funds type of description for subsidy financing in Armenia in 1999.

The gas sector has been a major source of net quasi-fiscal subsidies in the economy. From the gas industry, subsidies have been diverted to power and heating companies, while the power sector channeled most of them further to irrigation, water, and industry. Finally, all major sectors such as power, water, irrigation, and heating were involved in subsidization of households.

Therefore, various sectors of Armenia's economy may be grouped as the following:

- Main donors in the energy sector.
- Intermediaries: sectors (heating, water, irrigation) that receive budget and quasi-budget subsidies but transfer most of them to the final recipients.
- Final recipients (households and the enterprise sector) of quasi-fiscal/fiscal subsidies.
- Minor recipients of budget subsidies (transport, publishing).

The household sector is a major final recipient of quasi-fiscal subsidies. In all years before 2000 it exceeded 2 percent of GDP, while it declined to about 1 percent of GDP in 2001. These include household payables to the energy, water, heat, and gas sectors as well as an increase in land tax arrears. In addition, in 1997–98, households received tariff subsidies which could be roughly estimated as 1 percent of GDP.

The amount of quasi-fiscal subsidies to population has been quite high in comparison with the volume of public cash expenditures on social assistance and social insurance (pension, poverty benefits and similar programs). Quasi-fiscal subsidies to the population fluctuated between a third and half of total social public expenditures in 1996–2000. As the international experience suggests, subsidization of households through non-transparent quasi-fiscal channels is very inefficient because it is non-transparent and regressive.

The losses, accumulated by public companies in utilities and infrastructure because of excessive subsidization of the rest of economy, represent the single largest component of quasi-fiscal deficits in Armenia. This is quite typical for economies in transition. What makes Armenia a little different is that: (a) such deficits were somewhat smaller;[48] and (b) a relatively larger part of these deficits

---

47. The data for 2001 are preliminary and need an additional check.

48. For instance, in Kyrgyz Republic, total quasi-fiscal deficit in the energy sector amounted to 9 percent of GDP in the mid 1990s.

was admitted to be a direct liability of the state, and therefore was made rather explicit. To reduce the outstanding debts in the sector, the budget provided energy companies with subsidies and transfers through various channels, some of which were quite non-transparent (Box 3.2). Those included directed budget credits, tax offsets and write-offs, investment grants (funded from external credits), and using a gas-for-equity swap with the Russian gas suppliers.

BOX 3.2: A FORGOTTEN BUDGETARY CREDIT TO THE IRRIGATION SECTOR

The irrigation sector remains among major debtors of the power companies. In the second part of the 1990s, the Government funded several rounds of arrears clearance in irrigation. In particular, in 1998, the decision was made to provide irrigation with Dram 9.2 billion (1 percent of 1998 GDP) in budget credits to clear the sector's energy arrears. This budget support had two components. First, in the amount of Dram 1.8 billion was a regular cash credit, which was transferred directly to power companies by the Treasury. The second, much larger at Dram 7.2 billion, has never been monetized. Instead, the Government undertook an offset operation to write off both irrigation's debts for energy and tax arrears of the power sector. The interesting part of this offset is that it was reflected neither in the 1998 budget nor in any consequent Government budgets. While Dram 7.2 billion remained on the books of the irrigation sector as its debt to the budget, it was lost in the budgetary accounts. This credit was re-discovered in 2001, when the Government finally decided to write-off most of its budget credits to irrigation (i.e. admitting that these were budgetary subsidies).

This experience suggests once again that the existing most basic procedures on expenditure registration and commitment control require significant improvements.

Table 3.6 suggests that because of better budgeting and advanced energy sector reforms, the power sector companies managed to stop accumulation of new commercial bank credits after 1998. In fact, the total level of commercial debts declined from 7.5 percent to 5.1 percent of GDP. Still, this is a significant amount and should be taken into account when one estimates the total stock of public sector's liabilities in Armenia.

Overall, direct budgetary financing of quasi-fiscal deficits in the energy sector made a significant contribution to the build-up of Armenia's external debt in the 1990s. Yet, at the same time, it reduced a quasi-fiscal part of public sector liabilities, and by providing policy makers with more accurate costs of bad policies, it helped to advance the reform process and made an overall debt situation more transparent and thus manageable.

TABLE 3.6: COMMERCIAL DEBTS ACCUMULATED BY SOES IN THE POWER SECTOR
Million Dram, at the Year End

	1998	1999	2000	2001
External suppliers	0	8,465	13,443	14,247
Domestic suppliers	40,768	21,417	16,754	21,475
Commercial banks	31,121	21,754	22,605	23,941
Total	71,889	51,636	52,802	59,663
as percent of GDP	7.5	5.2	5.1	5.1

Source: Ministry of Energy.

Financial Performance of the SOE Sector
Table 3.7 describes the consolidated financial results of the SOE sector for 1998–2000. In 2000, the Government retained control over almost 300 large and medium state enterprises.[49] This represents about 25 percent of all major commercial enterprises in Armenia. The number of SOEs has been declining at the rate of about 5 percent a year as a result of the ongoing privatization program.

---

49. More than 90 percent of all SOEs are fully owned by the state, and of the remaining, the state owns more than 50 percent of all shares.

TABLE 3.7: FINANCIAL PERFORMANCE OF THE CONSOLIDATED SECTOR OF STATE ENTERPRISES
Million Dram

	1998	1999			2000		
			o/w:			o/w:	
	Total	Total	power sector	MTED	Total	power sector	MTED
1. Number of companies	317	292		187	287	34	187
Total revenues/losses	2,768	−120,837		2,030	−163,989	−153,904	−5,259
−as percent of GDP	0.3	−12.2		0.2	−15.9		−0.5
2. Number of loss-makers	122	132		73	138	26	74
Total losses	−21,545	−121,784	−111,600	−4,525	−182,276	−172,171	−5,320
−as percent of GDP	−2.2	−12.3	−11.3	−0.5	−17.6	−16.7	−0.5

Source: NSS, Ministry of Trade and Economic Development (MTED), Ministry of Energy, Staff estimates.

The number of remaining SOEs is somewhat surprising, given the scale of the Government's recent privatization efforts.[50] In fact, it confirms that privatization has slowed down considerably in the late 1990s relative to the earlier period. At the same time, it is worth noting that many of the remaining SOEs have not been operational for several years and probably do not have any privatization potential. These should be liquidated.

As Table 3.7 suggests, about 50 percent of all SOEs are loss-making and this share has been gradually increasing. The total losses of the consolidated SOE sector were astounding in 1999–2000 and on average amount to 15 percent of GDP.[51] Practically all losses were concentrated in the power sector, which reflects the central role of this sector in the financing of quasi-fiscal subsidies as discussed in the previous section. So far, the total annual losses of all SOEs outside of the energy and utility sector have been modest (less than 1 percent of GDP) but these losses could be disastrous rather quickly if they remain unchecked.

How are the current losses in the power sector financed? The funding has been coming from the three primary sources: (i) budget support, mostly in the form of hidden subsidies, including donor credits and grants; on average this support exceeded 4 percent of GDP a year in 1998–2000; (ii) amortization funds, i.e. at the cost of depletion of sector assets; this estimated to amount about 0.5 percent of GDP a year; and (iii) writing-off old bad debts of customers.[52]

At the moment, the monitoring of financial performance of SOEs is weak and segmented. SOEs in commercial sectors report to their sectoral ministries but neither to the Ministry of Finance and Economy nor to the Ministry of State Property. In other sectors, such as education and health, even sectoral ministries do not receive regular adequate financial information from large state-owned entities (universities, hospitals). As a result, the Government does not have a full picture for consolidated losses in this sector and therefore cannot manage properly risks related to such public sector liabilities. Overall, the combination of poor financial performance with a weak centralized government oversight poses a serious risk for the fiscal system.

---

50. The Ministry of Trade and Economic Development has responsibility for exercising Government's oversight functions over the largest number of SOEs – almost 200 in 1999–2001, which are mostly companies in manufacturing and mining. Only two-thirds of these SOEs provided the Ministry with the information on results of their financial performance.

51. The preliminary estimates for 2001 suggest only a modest improvement in SOEs' performance, with the total losses close to 10 percent of GDP.

52. It also suggests that a considerable part of the reported losses in the power sector are not real operational losses but a purely accounting phenomena. The real financial losses from current operations are much smaller.

The Government should establish an efficient system for monitoring the financial performance of state-owned enterprises to ensure that they have restricted access to new financing and thus expansion of their debts is under control. The Government should also initiate regular reporting to Parliament on the financial performance of SOEs, including their debts and major contingent liabilities.

Government Guarantees on Commercial Credits

Over the last several years the GOA has been experiencing an accumulation of contingent liabilities by granting state guarantees to loans obtained by commercial companies, primarily companies in the infrastructure and energy sectors. While the Law on Budgetary System introduced the ceiling for annual amounts of newly-issued state guaranties at the level of 10 percent of the tax receipts for the previous fiscal year, in practice this requirement has been several times violated. For instance, guarantees granted in 1998 were double the legally established ceiling.

So far, the known volumes of government guarantees were not high (never exceeded 2 percent of GDP a year), and their overall stock does not yet constitute a serious increment to the existing stock of the conventional public debt (Table 3.8). Thus, the current fiscal risks associated with these guarantees are modest.

TABLE 3.8:	GOVERNMENT GUARANTEES ISSUED FOR BANKING CREDITS GRANTED TO COMMERCIAL ENTITIES. ANNUAL FLOW US$ million						
	1995	1996	1997	1998	1999	2000	2001
State guaranteed commercial credits	0.3	17.3	18.2	42.3	0	18.1	10.0

Source: MOFE.

However, the existing budget accounting and reporting mechanisms do not provide for sufficient coverage and transparency of recording for state guarantees, and this constitutes a potential risk for integrity of the fiscal system. First, budget documents reflect only the amounts of guarantees granted for external credits, while state-backed domestic credits are not reported. As proposed in the existing draft Law on Public Debt Management, the Government should ensure comprehensive accounting and reporting on all budget guarantees. Second, the reports on annual budget execution do not provide an explicit account for total actual budget costs of guarantees, that is, how much the Government did pay for borrowers who failed to repay their credits. In several recent cases, the Government managed to avoid a direct repayment of guaranteed credits with budget funds by issuing new direct budget credits to borrowers that enabled them to pay back the original credits. Such practices further distort the budget accounting framework and do not allow for proper estimates of budget risks and full fiscal costs associated with guarantees.

Overall, government guarantees on commercial credits lead to various inefficiencies in resource allocation and should be avoided. State guarantees are a source of a non-transparent budget subsidy to beneficiaries in the commercial sector. Usually they provide a disincentive for beneficiaries to utilize credits effectively. They involve commercial banks in quasi-fiscal operations, while the state budget becomes engaged in quasi-banking. In addition, guarantees create fiscal risks and uncertainties with respect to future Government liabilities.

Recommendations

From the macroeconomic perspective, the process of fiscal consolidation in Armenia is still far from completed. The scope of off-budget operation is still excessive, while the level of quasi-fiscal deficit, especially in the energy sector (power, gas, heating), while reduced, is still significant and could be a potential threat to both macroeconomic stability and the imposition of the hard budget constraint in the enterprise sector.

Main elements of the fiscal system, which should be moved to the regular budget include non-cash external grants, sectoral extra-budgetary funds, and quasi-fiscal subsidies that are funded by state-owned companies in the energy sector.

Table 3.9 presents a consolidated picture of fiscal operation of the public sector. It suggests that total expenditures of the public sector, when fully consolidated, amounted to more than 30 percent of GDP in 2000.

While almost 50 percent of the total medium and large SOEs reported losses in 2000, the Government system of monitoring the financial performance of state enterprises remains weak and segmented. The Government should establish a modern consolidated system of financial reporting by state enterprises on their performance, including accumulated liabilities, and introduce stronger control over their borrowing. This should cover public sector entities in education and health. It should also advance liquidation and/or forced restructuring of the largest loss-making firms, which would have a beneficial impact on both the fiscal system and the entire enterprise sector. It should also revitalize its privatization program, which slowed down considerably in 2000–01.

TABLE 3.9: ILLUSTRATIVE ENLARGED BUDGET FOR THE PUBLIC SECTOR THAT REFLECTS MAIN OFF-BUDGET ACTIVITIES, 2000
Percent of GDP

Revenues, Total	22.9
1. Consolidated budget	20.5
O/w: Pension Fund	3.6
2. Extra-budgetary funds	0.4
3. External grants	2.0
Expenditures, Total	32.0
1. Consolidated budget, cash	25.3
O/w: Pension Fund	3.6
2. Extra-budgetary funds	0.4
3. External grants	2.0
4. Quasi-fiscal subsidies	2.4
5. Accumulation of budget arrears	1.9
Deficit	9.1
1. Consolidated budget	6.7
O/w: cash deficit	4.8
Increase in budget arrears	1.9
2. Quasi-fiscal (public enterprises in the energy sector)	2.3

Source: Staff estimates.

CHAPTER 4

STRENGTHENING PUBLIC EXPENDITURE MANAGEMENT

The strengthening of the institutional arrangements for sound expenditure management is a key component of the fiscal reform effort by the Armenian Government. In particular, an effective system for public expenditure management will play a central role in the realization of the full PRSP. The PRSP, in turn, is dependent for its success on effective public expenditure planning and management, as good public expenditure management should provide the resource framework to guide the preparation and implementation of the PRSP.

The Government of Armenia began reforming its public sector resource management system in 1994, with the preparation of its first Public Investment Program (PIP), as a way to improve its aid management and prioritize its post-independence investment plans to fit within its much-reduced resource constraints. Since then, the Ministry of Finance and Economy has introduced changes to its budget legislation, the presentation and coverage of its budget, the budget formulation process, the Treasury system and overall budget execution, procurement arrangements and internal and external audit systems. This chapter provides an assessment of these public expenditure management (PEM) reforms as the basis for identifying future steps to strengthen PEM.

The assessment of the PEM in this chapter covers:

- Contextual background to this chapter of the PER, including a review of the previous Institutional and Governance Review (IGR) evaluation, and a description of the criteria used for the PER's assessment;
- Structure of the budget system, including budget legislation and budget presentation;
- Budget preparation process, including strategic budgeting, the link between Government policies and budgets, and the role of sector ministries in the process; and;
- Budget execution and budgetary control.

Two annexes summarize the recommendations made in the chapter: Annex 1 provides a summary of the measures recommended for the budget system as a whole, based on the assessment of

Armenia's PEM system, whilst Annex 2 sets out an action plan for strengthening the MTEF. This chapter will not address issues concerning the audit system or inter-governmental finance, as these are being addressed in other fora.

Existing Situation Analysis

Recommendations from the Institutional and Governance Review

The assessment in this PER on public expenditure management follows on from the World Bank's Institutional and Governance Review (IGR), completed in 2000.[53] That study focused primarily on the issue of budget accountability, specifically, the role of the budget as a tool for implementing policy. It analyzed: (i) how well budget outcomes reflected budget plans; (ii) the ability of the budget formulation process to link budget plans with Government policies; (iii) whether or not the budget execution system was able to provide Government with accurate information on the utilization of the budget and how this compared with budget plans; and (iv) whether public procurement and audit procedures provided an appropriate level of discipline and oversight to public expenditures.

The main conclusions from the IGR's analysis were:

- Even when taking into account external shocks, budget deviations between the approved budget and the actual outturns were significant, although the extent of deviations varied by sector, with defense, state security and public order categories faring relatively better than other sectors.
- Accountability of the budget process was found to be hampered by the absence of a strategic medium-term budget framework, which should be based on a realistic estimate of overall resource availability and which should contain appropriately costed budget proposals from sector ministries, and a transparent process of resource allocations across sectors.
- Despite significant progress in establishing the Treasury system, budget execution was undermined by the fact that spending agencies do not adhere to cash limits and sometimes over-commit their budgets, resulting in informal budget reallocations and evasion of aggregate budget constraints.
- There was found to be a need to address institutional issues in the nascent public procurement system, including the establishment of an oversight committee.
- The independence of the Chamber of Control was hampered by a lack of clarity in its role and inadequate Parliamentary oversight.
- Poor co-ordination was found between internal and external audit activities and duplication in responsibilities between the MOFE, the President's Supervisory Service, the Government Control Department and sector ministries' internal audit departments.
- Weak accountability and transparency measures at local government level hampered the Government's ability to decentralize budget decisions to lower levels.

As indicated in the current chapter of the PER, the extent of progress since the IGR was completed is mixed: most significant progress has been made on procurement and external audit and relatively less on budget formulation. Box 4.1 sets out the current status of each of the IGR recommendations.

PER Assessment Criteria

The criteria against which Armenia's budget management system is appraised in this chapter are those required for a modern budget management system, which: (i) can support the implementation of Government policy through appropriate targeting of resources; (ii) is formulated within a realistic resource framework; and (iii) uses budgetary resources efficiently. In contrast to previous

---

53. Chapter 4, Armenia: Institutional and Governance Review, World Bank (2000).

Box 4.1: IGR Recommendations on Budget Management and Control

IGR Recommendations	Progress/Current Status	Remarks
Short term measures		
Enact modern public procurement legislation.	Legislation promulgated. Central Procurement Agency operating as sole public procurement organization.	PER makes recommendations on changes to the centralized procurement model.
Promulgate implementing regulations and country-specific bidding documents.	Completed.	
Establish independent oversight for public procurement through the setting up of an oversight committee.	Parliamentary oversight established for public procurement process.	
Clarify external audit role of Chamber of Control (COC).	Under preparation.	
Revised Law on Chamber of Control to enhance its independence.	Under preparation.	Amendments to the law were drafted.
Require COC to prepare an annual statement of conformity of government budgetary operations and an annual audit report on government's financial statement to Parliament.	Completed.	
Develop an independent work program for the COC.	Still outstanding.	
Eliminate overlap between MOFE Main Financial Control Department, President's Supervisory Service, Government Control Department and line ministries' internal audit bodies.	Still outstanding.	
Prepare a plan for creating internal audit capacity.	Still outstanding.	
Review intergovernmental finance system.	In process, with assistance from USAID.	
Medium-term measures		
Adopt strategic and resource-bound medium-term expenditure framework (MTEF).	Non-strategic MTEF has been prepared during each of the last three years (1999–2001), and recently updated for 2003–2005. Its role has been largely one of ex-post (or cotemporaneous in 2002) analysis following the budget's adoption by Government.	PER makes recommendations and provides a draft action plan for strengthening the MTEF.
Strengthen implementation of Treasury controls.	Treasury currently working on a commitment control system.	Recommendations have been made for strengthening Treasury and introducing second generation reforms.
Move towards comprehensive budget coverage.	Budget coverage continues to require significant improvements.	PER makes recommendations on improving budget coverage.
Strengthen capacity of oversight bodies and central procuring entities.	In process.	
Adopt and implement generally accepted audit principles, standards and codes of conduct for government auditors.	Still outstanding.	
Strengthen technical and institutional capacity of the COC.	Still outstanding.	

(continued)

BOX 4.1: IGR RECOMMENDATIONS ON BUDGET MANAGEMENT AND CONTROL (*CONTINUED*)

IGR Recommendations	Progress/Current Status	Remarks
Improve transparency of procedures for auditors' appointment and dismissal.	Still outstanding.	
Establish co-operation and co-ordination between external and internal audit.	Still outstanding.	
Modernize internal audit principles.	Still outstanding.	
Implement streamlined internal audit structure.	Still outstanding.	
Enhance capacity by strengthening professional skills of auditors.	In process.	
Develop longer-term program for decentralization and capacity building.	In process, with assistance from USAID.	
Adapt international accounting standards.	Still outstanding.	The Government aims to prepare a plan in 2003 on gradual implementation of IAS in the budget sector.
Develop private sector accounting association.	Established.	
Longer-term measures		
Extend procurement to regional and local levels.	Process not yet begun.	
Procurement database to improve transparency.	Process not yet begun.	

donor attempts to encourage the Government to reform its budget management system, this assessment stresses the current imbalance in reforms undertaken to date and emphasizes practical recommendations which take current practice as their starting point.

The following budget criteria underpin the chapter's assessment of Armenia's public expenditure management system:

- Transparent – the budget documents should show a clear trail from summary of revenues and expenditures through detailed estimates of expenditures and revenues by accountable budget heads (i.e. ministries or agencies), and they should clearly indicate which agency is being voted funds and for what purpose;
- Accountable – a single budget manager should be identified as being responsible for monitoring and achieving results from each particular budget appropriation item;
- Legitimate – spending units believe that the approved budget is implemented to a large degree and decision-makers (i.e. politicians) who can change policies during implementation must take part in and agree to the original policy decision;
- Credible – budgets should be achievable and relatively close to eventual actual figures;
- Predictable – it is important for efficient and effective planning and implementation of policies and programs;
- Comprehensive – the budget must encompass all fiscal operations of the government, including all public expenditures;
- Clear link with Government policies – budgetary allocations should be linked to performance or the achievement of Government objectives;
- Robust and flexible – budgets should be capable of responding to changed circumstances (e.g. external shocks) and providing budget managers with some discretion over the use of funds in delivering services, provided expenditure do not exceed authorized amounts;
- Appropriately strategic – budgets should have a medium-term view; and
- Controlled – budgets should ensure an appropriate degree of control over public expenditure by the legislature, and facilitate effective and comprehensive control by the executive.

PEM Reform Measures

While the IGR concentrated on how effectively the budget could be used as a tool of Government policy, this PER chapter is focused more broadly on the PEM system as a whole, including how well the different parts of the PEM system work together. Unsurprisingly, the assessment in this chapter concentrates relatively more heavily on those areas in which less progress has been made in order to identify key directions for future reforms.

Armenia's budgetary reforms have followed a pattern similar to other CIS countries. Much of the early reform efforts focused on the more technical aspects of budgetary reform, such as introducing a Budget Systems Law, revising the budget classification, improving budget presentation, updating the budget calendar, and introducing a Treasury system. Once the basic foundations for a modern budget system were largely in place, the Government turned to the much more difficult phase of undertaking strategic reforms, such as introducing a strategic phase to budget formulation. Further reforms will need the support of wider public sector improvements, through, for example, restructuring government institutions, their incentive structures, and their institutional/analytical capacities. Both technical and strategic reforms need to work together, and the recommendations given in this chapter serve to strengthen this balance.

Box 4.2 provides an overview of the main PEM reform measures undertaken by the Government to date. Most of the reforms have focused on: (i) establishing a solid legislative framework to underpin a modern budgeting system; (ii) reforming the classification system to ensure that it complies with international standards; and (iii) introducing a Central Treasury supported by field

BOX 4.2: OVERVIEW OF PUBLIC EXPENDITURE REFORM MEASURES UNDERTAKEN, 1991–2002

PEM Area	Reforms Undertaken	Next Steps
Legislative/regulatory framework		
Budget System Legislation.	Promulgation of Budget Systems Law, Treasury Law and Procurement Law as legal framework for the budget system.	Laws provide reasonably comprehensive basis for budget system. However, there is the need for these laws to be updated to take account of the reforms being introduced. The Budget Systems Law should be amended to stipulate: (i) what cannot be re-appropriated without the approval of Parliament; and (ii) any other restrictions on virement.[54]
Budget preparation		
Budget calendar	Lengthened to allow more time for Government/Parliamentary approval.	These changes have been largely appropriate. However, there is the need to incorporate explicitly the MTEF into the budget calendar, particularly its preparation and Government approval in the first half of the year.
Budget classification	GFS86 functional and economic classification introduced. Administrative classification introduced.	A stable classification chart is a major recent improvement in PEM. To improve accountability, the use of administrative classification of budget spending should be expanded. There is also the need to switch to the new GFS2001 budget classification.

(continued)

54. Virement is the process of transferring expenditure provision from one line-item to another during the budget year.

BOX 4.2: OVERVIEW OF PUBLIC EXPENDITURE REFORM MEASURES UNDERTAKEN, 1991–2002 (CONTINUED)

PEM Area	Reforms Undertaken	Next Steps
Budget presentation	Budget presented in detail by functional, economic and administrative classifications.	To improve transparency, the trail from one classification to other should be clearer; at present, the mapping of functional to administrative classification is incomplete. Appropriation of the Budget is very detailed, increasing budgetary control but inhibiting flexibility of input use.
MTEF	MTEF document has been prepared annually since 1999, setting out the medium-term macro objectives and broad sectoral priorities. As yet, these priorities have not been explicitly linked to budget plans.	Plans are under way to expand the strategic basis of the budget. This will involve the setting of sector resource ceilings, and in time the preparation of detailed medium-term sector expenditure plans.
Budget execution		
Treasury system	Introduction of the Central Treasury and establishment of field treasury branches. Amalgamation of government accounts into the Single Treasury Account. Development of a set of accounts to handle inter-treasury, intra-treasury and treasury-CBA transactions.	The Government plans to build on these "first-generation" reforms in the second round of Treasury reforms, including the establishment and expansion of the internal and external audit functions. The second generation treasury reform is intended to make communications between budgetary institutions and the Treasury on-line. Improved financial planning and cash management is also on the agenda.
Expenditure reporting and control	Development of budget execution reporting system, supplemented with monthly reports on arrears and quarterly reports on receivables and payables. Initial computerized commitment recording/control system being developed.	There is the need to ensure that the classification system facilitates the execution of the budget as appropriated. This will require: (i) classification codes to be included in the budget documents; (ii) consistency in application of classification between budget preparation and execution by all stakeholders; (iii) reporting on budget execution in same format as appropriated budget; and (iv) improved commitment controls and reporting on budget arrears. The Government plans to introduce accounting reform, including accrual accounting in government and strengthened consolidated reporting.
Other		
Procurement	Procurement Law passed. Central Procurement Agency established, staffed and operating.	Revenue shortfalls are causing significant delays in payment for procured goods and services. Ceiling for value of tenders before open tender procedures must be used is too low. Procurement system should be less centralized.
Internal Audit	Decree promulgated establishing internal audit in line ministries and their subordinate organizations.	Ensure that international internal audit standards are followed.
External audit	Chamber of Control (CoC) established, answering to Parliament.	CoC should be made operationally independent, with an independent work program.

treasuries and consolidating all existing government accounts into the Treasury Single Account (TSA). The work to establish an appropriate legislative framework for the budget has been essential in providing a cornerstone for more wide-ranging reforms.

The next two sections look at the budget structure and the budget preparation process. It will look in particular at the following key areas for effective and efficient budgeting:

- The budget process should be guided by an appropriate legislative basis.
- Budgets should be comprehensive. In particular, extra-budgetary resources should be minimized, aid agency funds should be included in the budget, and the budgets of lower levels of government reflected in Government budget reporting.
- Budget presentation should follow international standards, and the budget should be implemented as presented.
- Budgets should be based on a comprehensive budget classification system that follows international standards and includes administrative, economic, functional and programmatic categories.
- The budget should be appropriated by ministry/agency (the administrative classification) to facilitate accountability and improve transparency of budgetary spending, with supporting documentation presenting budget figures by economic item and by function.
- Budgets should be prepared within a medium-term programmatic context. The medium-term expenditure framework should be well integrated, taking into account overall resource constraints and clearly linked (through expenditure programs) to the achievement of Government priority policy objectives.

Each of these issues will be discussed in the sections below.

Structure of the Budget System

Budget System Legislation

Armenia's budget management system is based on three main pieces of legislation: (i) the Budget Systems Law, promulgated in 1997; (ii) the Treasury System Law, brought into force on 1 January 2002; and (iii) the Procurement Law, introduced in June 2000. The Treasury System Law has been supplemented by regulations setting out the specific roles and responsibilities for all stakeholders in Treasury operations. These laws have served to strengthen the basis for the preparation, execution, reporting and the methodological framework of the budget. In particular, they have provided a clear calendar within which the budget is to be prepared, set out clear objectives and institutional responsibilities for the preparation and execution of the budget and identified clear sanctions for breaches of these responsibilities.

Budget Systems Law. The Budget Systems Law contains the formal regulations concerning preparation, execution, reporting and the methodological framework of the budgets. These are supplemented by regulations contained in the Annual Budget Law, including virement rules, and the detailed budget classification. The Law is comprehensive and covers both State and local budgets. Formal rules and procedures for approval and changes to the budget are transparent. The timetable and responsibilities for budget stakeholders are clear, as are relations between State and local budget entities.

However, a number of weaknesses and omissions in the Budget Systems Law act to limit the effectiveness of the budget process.[55] These include:

- The current Law does not provide for the preparation and implementation of the MTEF (including the setting, approval and circulation of sector expenditure ceilings) as a necessary

---

55. See also J. Zohrab, <u>Status Report: An Assessment of the Current Status of the Treasury of the Republic of Armenia and Scope for Further Enhancement</u>, IMF (2002).

element of the annual budget cycle, and thus it weakens the strategic focus of fiscal policy. In particular, the Law does not require an explicit link between budget allocations, the MTEF and the achievement of Government policies.

▨ Regarding the budget calendar, the period allowed for budget preparation in the line ministries is too short to allow sufficient time for the planning, scrutiny and analysis that the exercise deserves.

▨ Although the annual budget is the Government's most important short-term policy document, the political leadership does not become involved until too late in the process, leading to substantial ad hoc revisions being requested to the draft budget during its presentation to the Government. This makes for a more inefficient budget approval process and can lead to ad hoc changes that are inconsistent with overall budget strategy.

▨ The existing legislation is weak on assigning responsibility for the control of expenditure and the description of sanctions for non-compliance (overspending or poor budget performance) with the Budget Law. At a fundamental level, the legislation does not provide specific restrictions and sanctions to prevent expenditure without parliamentary appropriation.

▨ Current arrangements for internal/external audit are not explicitly mentioned. There is no mention of efficiency of expenditure and seeking value-for-money.

▨ Weaknesses in the Budget Systems Law relating to the budget execution process (i.e. treatment of budgetary arrears, sequestration procedures). These include:[56]

⟶ Sequestration procedures are inflexible, which prevent MOFE from dealing with revenue shortfalls by making in-year budget reductions without resorting to sequestration, which requires Parliamentary approval. At the same time, sequestration requires proportional cuts across all budget items, which further restricts the flexibility of the MOFE to identify low-priority areas.[57]

⟶ The role of the appropriated budget in the face of revenue shortfalls is not clear. Specifically, the Budget Systems Law does not make it clear whether appropriated expenditures must be executed even in the fact of revenue shortfalls. This is due to a lack of clarity in the roles of spending ministries and budget institutions in the Law, which appears to give them the right to spend the whole of their appropriated amount on identified programs, rather than an amount made available to them (up to the appropriated amount) as a result of realized receipts, e.g. through a system of cash and commitment limits. This also appears to affect the way the virement rules are interpreted; i.e. reallocations are only permitted if they do not result in the under-fulfillment of identified expenditure programs, which restricts substantially the flexibility that virement would otherwise create.

⟶ The Budget System Law is not an organic law superior to an Annual Budget Law. The fact that provisions in the Annual Budget Law can therefore in effect override articles in the Budget Systems Law indicates that the basic legislative framework is not as robust as it should be.

⟶ There is an absence of any provision to deal with expenditure payment arrears, which is related to the inflexible sequestration process.

▨ The Budget System Law does not cover the operations (such as budget preparation, adoption, execution, and reporting) of the State Fund for Social Insurance, which is a major part of the Armenia's budget system, but basically remains outside of the basic legal framework for the budget management system.

---

56. For further discussion of each of these points, see Desai, Parry, Rao and Saunders (1998) and Zohrab (2002).

57. However, Annual Budget Laws usually introduce opportunities for the Government to make budget reallocations by its own decision. For instance, in 2001, the Government was allowed to reallocate 3% of initial allocations for each budget group.

Treasury System Law. It is too early to assess the impact of the new Treasury System Law. However, a few comments may be made on the legislation itself. While the Budget Systems Law and the Treasury System Law authorize the Government to execute the budget within the limits specified against each functional classification, the Treasury System Law also introduces a position of Chief Financial Officer for every ministry and Government agency who should be personally responsible for budget execution and reporting. This clarifies responsibilities for controlling budgets and respective lines of accountability. The Government should accelerate implementation of this requirement of the Law to strengthen fiscal discipline in the system. In addition, the Treasury legislation should be amended to introduce explicit sanction procedures for overspending or poor budget performance.[58]

Procurement Law. The Procurement Law is adequately drafted and sets out an appropriate institutional framework for international-standard procurement to take place. The main criticism of the Law is that it sets too low a ceiling above which competitive procurement should occur. Armenia's public procurement system is based around the Central Procurement Agency (CPA), which is accountable to Parliament and whose role is to carry out all state procurement, including tendering procedures. However, given staffing and other resource constraints of the Agency, this leads to an inefficient and overly cumbersome procurement process. In a less centralized model, the Central Procurement Agency would be responsible for supervising the procurement activities of contracting entities in line ministries and other public sector agencies covered by the Procurement Law. The role of the Agency would then be to develop more detailed procurement rules and regulations in line with procurement legislation, create a government-wide information and publication system, ensure that government entities carrying out procurement employed trained personnel, develop a training system and maintain general supervision of procurement systems.

Recommendations on Budget Legislation

Notwithstanding the issues identified above, the series of Budget Systems Laws, supported by supplementary regulations, has provided an adequate legislative foundation for the establishment of an initial post-independence public expenditure management system. However, as the second phase of reforms takes place, there will be the need to update the legislation to take account of existing and planned changes in the PEM system to overcome the weaknesses described above. It is important that changes to the legislation are not undertaken in a piecemeal fashion.

Specifically, the PER makes recommendations to four areas of improvement to the Budget Systems Law.[59] First, a section on the MTEF should be added to the Law, setting out the objectives, timing, roles and responsibilities for the preparation, approval and implementation of the MTEF. These should include:

- **A statement of the objectives of the MTEF** as an instrument to enable the Government to manage public sector resources in accordance with the Government's medium-term policy priorities.
- **Responsibility for co-ordination of the preparation of the MTEF**, based on submissions by sector ministries, should be given to MOFE.
- **Coverage of the MTEF**: the MTEF should cover the 3 years following the year of preparation (i.e. the next budget year plus two outer years), plus actual expenditures for the previous budget year and the revised estimates of the current budget year; fiscal indicators to be incorporated should include budget revenues with main tax and other revenue sources specified, budget expenditures by major spending groups, including the development (capital) budget, and the budget deficit and sources to cover it.

---

58. This issue is discussed further in Section 4.4 below.

59. It should be noted that the MOFE is currently preparing a number of amendments to the Law; some of these recommendations may already have been taken into account.

■ **Policy guidance for MTEF preparation**: overall Government policy statements, such as the Poverty Reduction Strategy Paper (PRSP).

■ **Timing of submission of MTEF** by MOFE to the Government (or to an Economic Policy Committee), and of review and approval of the MTEF by Government (see Box 4.3 below).

BOX 4.3: RECOMMENDATIONS FOR THE ANNUAL BUDGET CALENDAR

Date	Task
January/February	MOFE prepares initial macro/fiscal framework for MTEF period to Government, including fiscal principles, proposed short and long term fiscal indicators and advice on strategic expenditure priorities.
February	MOFE prepares MTEF methodological guidelines including key economic and demographic assumptions to be used by line ministries in preparing their MTEF submissions.
End February	Presentation of initial macro/fiscal framework for MTEF period and MTEF Guidelines to Government. Government approves a fiscal framework and MTEF Guidelines.
March	Line ministries prepare MTEF submissions, including three year expenditure projections (for existing commitments) and identifying any additional expenditure needs (for new policy initiatives, increased volumes, etc).
Early April	MOFE updates revenue and debt servicing forecasts.
April	MOFE and Government examine MTEF submissions and consider overall expenditure needs, priorities and proposals for additional funding in light of updated forecast information (early April) and agreed fiscal principles (February).
May	Indicative budget ceilings determined by Government, together with a new initiatives 'resource envelope' and preliminary agreement of the sectors and agencies that will be accorded a high priority for additional funding.
May	Finalization of MTEF: Part A (Fiscal Policy Statement by MOFE) and Part B: (Expenditure Policy Strategy by line ministries and MOFE). MTEF is presented to Government for approval.
June	Government approves MTEF - it is published and tabled in the National Assembly.
June	Issuance of budget preparation instructions and budget forms. Budget Instructions include MTEF decisions on indicative budget ceilings and priority areas for any additional funding.
June/July	Ministries prepare budget requests in line with Government's MTEF decisions on areas of spending priority and indicative budget ceiling. Submission to MOFE by 20 July.
August	MOFE to scrutinize submissions and to resolve minor discrepancies with spending ministries.
August/September	Meetings with ministries at MOFE.
Late August	MOFE updates forecasts, prepares revised economic and fiscal outlook and (if necessary) revises the MTEF resource envelope in light of revised forecasts. Collation and summarization of budget data.
15 September	Submission of draft Budget to Government.
15 October	Submission of draft Budget to Budgetary Committee of Parliament.
October	Preparation of Budget Message and update of Economic and Fiscal Outlook Report in line with the country's Economic Development Policy document.
1 November	Submission of Budget to Parliament.
1 December	Approval of Annual Budget Law by Parliament.
1 January	Issuance of authorities to spend.
1 January	Public distribution of Budget.
April, July, October, January	Quarterly reports by line ministries to MOFE on budget execution.
April/May	Annual report by GoA to Parliament on execution of previous year's State Budget.

- **Relationship between MTEF and Annual Budget**: following approval of the MTEF and approval and circulation of sector ceilings, the fact that MTEF should be the basis of Annual Budget preparation.
- **Arrangements for updating and reviewing the MTEF resource framework**, e.g. twice annually (May for initial approval and September/October, just before submission of annual budget to Parliament).

Second, the Budget calendar should be revised to include the MTEF, to give sector ministries more time to prepare their submissions following the setting of sector ceilings, and to enable MOFE to have more time for analysis of the budget submissions and negotiations with sector ministries. Recommendations for a revised Budget calendar are made in Box 4.3.

Third, the Budget Systems Law should be made an organic law superior to the annual budget laws, which may require a change in the Constitution.

Finally, articles currently referring to procurement in the Budget Systems Law should be moved to the Procurement Law.

Budget Coverage

In order to ensure the efficient use of Government resources and appropriate macroeconomic management, the budget should include total revenues and all public expenditures, including funds that are often not reflected, e.g. extra-budgetary funds.[60] Activities that are outside of the budget are not subject to Parliamentary scrutiny and the associated discipline of the resource allocation process.

Since the adoption of the 1997 Budget Systems Law the Ministry of Finance and Economy has improved the coverage of the annual budget. In particular, external credits and budgetary support grants (cash grants) have been almost fully included since 1998. However, as was shown in the previous chapter, the Budget excludes many externally-financed grants, primarily those that are received in the form of commodities and of technical assistance. Other major exclusions from the Budget documents include extra-budgetary funds and the accumulation of public liabilities by the largest state enterprises, primarily in the energy and utility sector.

The Government recognizes the need to improve the comprehensiveness of the budget. Chapter 3 suggests specific steps to capture grants from major donors and introduce a regular reporting on debts and deficits in the largest SOEs.

Budget Presentation and Classification

At present, the Government's budget documents are very detailed[61] and presented in a way which makes it relatively difficult to track expenditures across the system. As indicated above, the principle behind good budget presentation is that the Budget documents should: (i) show a clear trail from summary of revenues and expenditures through detailed estimates of expenditures and revenues by accountable budget heads (i.e. ministries or agencies); and (ii) clearly indicate which agency is being voted funds, how much they are authorized to spend, and for what purpose.

The current budget structure and style of presentation do not yet meet these criteria. Firstly, although Budget funds are shown by budget agency, function and economic item, resources are appropriated primarily by function and economic item, making it difficult to assign responsibility for these funds to an individual manager in an appropriate ministry, since more than one ministry/agency often contributes to a single function. Indeed, it is not yet possible to assign all resources categorized by function and sub-function to individual spending agencies, as some overlaps in the

---

60. Defined in the Armenian context as revenues raised by a spending agency or line ministry through charging fees for providing some specified services.

61. This issue is different from that of the appropriate level of detail of budgetary appropriations, which is addressed below.

classification remain. Secondly, Parliament votes on the detailed budget (as shown by the functional, economic and administrative classifications), subjecting each type of authorization to virement rules and thereby limiting the flexibility of budget managers to manage their resources efficiently (e.g. through altering the balance of inputs between personnel and goods and services, for example, to improve efficiency). Whilst giving greater flexibility to budget managers is being piloted in the health and education sectors, a disadvantage to MOFE is the loss of detailed control over these resources. If appropriate safeguards are in place, this need not be a problem, but the lessons from the experiments in the health and education sectors should be studied in order to improve accountability for future delegation of expenditure control authority.

Finally, even though there is significant detail shown in the budget, the picture is nonetheless not yet comprehensive (see above).

A stable classification chart is a major recent improvement in PEM.[62] The Budget is presented and approved according to the classification structure and coding (revenue, economic, function, administrative, and financing sources) recorded in the Budget Systems Law and in subsequent regulations by MOFE; these are based on the classification in the IMF's *Manual of Government Financial Statistics* (GFS86). Annual and quarterly reports by the Central Treasury showing a summary of the utilization of the budget (according to the classifications for revenue, economic item, function, and financing sources) are consistent with the breakdown shown in Articles 6-8 of the (2002) Annual Budget Law; these classifications are based on GFS86.

The main weaknesses of the use of the classification system are that: (i) classification codes are not included in the budget documents, inhibiting comparative analysis and reporting; (ii) the existing system is not widely and consistently used by sector ministries in the reporting of their expenditures; (iii) the Treasury has been regularly reporting on budget execution in a format which is different from the approved budget; and (iv) the way that the standard GFS classification has been applied leads to under-reporting of key categories of expenditures.

At present, the Central Treasury does not report on the utilization of the budget by administrative classification. In fact, it is difficult for it to do so since line ministries use a different accounting system from those used by the Treasury. Treasury uses the cash-based GFS86 accounting and reporting system, whereas sector ministries use the Soviet accounting quasi-accrual system for accounting and the Soviet system's Chart of Accounts to prepare their quarterly reports on expenditure to the Central Treasury. Reconciliation in information between the two systems is difficult to achieve. The PER recommendation made above to ensure the main budgetary appropriation is based on the administrative classification will require the consolidation of the two systems into a common accounting framework, based on the same budget classification, accounting principles and chart of accounts. In the short-run, this issue is expected to be addressed through the Treasury's planned improvements to the Financial Management Information System (FMIS), while in the longer–term, the implementation of the Second Generation Treasury Reforms, including the migration to the GFS2001 and International Accounting Standards in the public sector, will largely help to resolve the issue.

At the same time, current reports from spending ministries give no information on the implementation of sector programs. The strengthening of the MTEF and the introduction of a program structure to budgetary appropriations would need to be accompanied by reporting on budget execution by the same program structure.

Finally, as was discussed in detail in Chapter 2, the way that the standard GFS functional classification system has been applied by MOFE distorts expenditure analysis. In particular, expenditures on some sectors are regularly under-reported, including those on health and education. The new GFS classification (2001) potentially assists in improving the functional classification of expenditures (see Box 4.4). Under GFS 2001, the catch-all category, Function 14 ("other, not elsewhere

---

62. The classification chart began being applied in 2000. Prior to that, there was no stable and published budgetary classification system, making budget comparisons across years difficult.

BOX 4.4: GFS CLASSIFICATION AND THE BUDGET

The IMF's Government Financial Statistics (GFS) classification is used widely throughout the world as a tool for international comparisons of the allocation and use of budgetary resources. However, whilst the IMF recommends the breakdown of Government activities into standard functional and economic groupings, it does not necessarily follow that the paragraph numbers used for these classifications should be adopted as each country's Chart of Accounts. Whilst the budget classification system should allow expenditure allocations to be categorized according to the major GFS functions, the GFS itself is unlikely to provide an appropriate program classification to be used in the planning and setting of budgets. In particular, the IMF format is unsuitable for Parliamentary presentations and budgetary control purposes. Organizations need to assess their own budgeting, accounting and reporting needs to ensure that the most appropriate coding structure for them is adopted.

---

classified"), has been eliminated, and the number of functions reduced to ten. Many of the economic sector categories (such as agriculture, fuel and energy, mining, etc.) have been combined in a new Function 4, "Economic Affairs." Thus, most of the miscellaneous expenditures currently classified under Function 14 would under GFS2001 most likely be classified under Function 1, "General Public Services".[63]

Recommendations on Budget Presentation and Classification

Other papers have recently made recommendations on improvements to budget presentation and classification, of which the PER supports the following priority measures:[64]

- reducing the level of detail required for promulgation in the Annual Budget Law,[65] in order to provide government managers with increased flexibility with which to meet organizational goals and objectives;
- changing the Annual Budget Law to emphasize appropriations by administrative classification, in order to improve organizational accountability;
- considering the abandoning in the main budget document the matrix presentation that crosses the three classification schemes and moving to a format based on budgetary organizations in order to make budgetary and appropriation information more transparent and easier to comprehend; at same time, considering a move of the functional classification information to the appendices of the Annual Budget Law, to present it at two levels for budget preparation purposes, but to collect it at three levels for budget execution purposes; and
- removing the budget classification system specification from the Budget Systems Law and giving the MOFE the authority to maintain and update the classification for incorporation in Annual Budget Laws.

Budget Formulation

Overview of Budget Formulation Process

During the 1990s, the Ministry of Finance and Economy achieved considerable success in implementing aggregate budget and expenditure controls and in reducing the budget deficit. Nonetheless,

---

63. At the same time, if the Treasury moves to GFS2001, as currently planned, then accounting would be on an accrual basis, rather than on a cash basis as at present. This means that consumption of fixed capital would in future need to be included in the budget as an expenditure item.

64. Zohrab (2002).

65. This reduced level of detail does not necessarily apply to accounting or reporting but only to the level of detail *approved* by Parliament and thus subject to virement and sequestration rules.

the Government continued to struggle with the chronic underfunding of sector expenditure requirements, which are unsustainable within the current level of resources. In practice, salaries and payroll deductions have become treated as fixed costs, with all other items acting as a residual; however, it is not possible to sustain a system where people are employed but cannot work properly because of inadequate facilities and equipment and because they are insufficiently paid. Whilst Armenia has made a lot of progress in moving away from FSU practices, the Government has not yet been able to put in place strategic budgeting techniques in order to prioritize its much-reduced post-independence level of resources.[66] Instead, the MOFE, in line with MOFEs in other CIS countries, has tended to cut expenditures across-the-board rather than strategically.

Sector budgets continue to be allocated on the basis of norms and inputs (economic items),[67] rather than on outputs and outcomes (Box 4.5). The system has not been replaced because of a significant lack of accountability in the system, leading to fears that the loosening of spending controls will lead to greater corruption. The continued reliance on line-item budgeting[68] prevents any mechanism for linking budgets to Government policies. With the wagebill dominating the recur-

---

BOX 4.5: THE PROBLEM WITH NORMS AND AN ALTERNATIVE APPROACH

As in many CIS countries, the Armenian process of budget formulation utilizes normative budgeting techniques, which involves the use of specified input ratios to which standard unit costs are applied. These normatives are set out in subsidiary regulations. An advantage of normative budget techniques is their simplicity in approach. Budget determination becomes a simple multiplication exercise, minimizing the analytical demands on those responsible for preparing and evaluating budget requests. Their use throughout the public sector is likely to contribute to inefficiencies in public service delivery by:

- removing from program managers the responsibility for introducing innovations that allow for improvements in productivity and in the quality of public service provision;
- providing incentives to managers to increase input use as a means of maximizing their budget allocations; and
- reducing budget analysis in sector ministries to a process of checking whether norms have been applied correctly rather than challenging the assumptions on which budgets are based and considering alternatives.

There is a further risk of norms being set without adequate recognition of resource constraints or of becoming outdated and inappropriate to present circumstances.

Approaches to budgeting in other countries emphasize the analysis of budget at the program level, the consideration of alternative means of achieving program objectives, and an active dialogue with the Ministry of Finance over funding levels and performance. Within such a process legislated norms are replaced by resource allocation guidelines, which themselves are subject to regular review and updating. Such an approach to budget formulation places additional analytical demands on both the Ministry of Finance and Economy and line ministries, as well as requires much stronger standards of accountability. However, it is particularly relevant to transition economies where governments are faced with a wide-ranging agenda of reforms to improve both the sustainability and efficiency of public spending programs. This emphasizes the importance that governments should attach to the reform of budget planning systems and the strengthening of policy, programming and budgeting capacities.

---

66. This is the objective of the MTEF, which the Government plans to strengthen over the medium term.
67. A budget methodology based on calculating the costs of required inputs according to an established set of physical norms, such as the number of personnel per hospital bed. This methodology does not take into account the demand for public services (i.e., the number of people requiring treatment) nor the cost implications of alternative treatment methods. At the same time, it does not link budget requests to performance information or expected program outcomes. The MOFE monitors and controls input items, not the cost of a program or outcome. See Box 4.5 for a further discussion of the issue.
68. Preparing and showing budgets by inputs, or line items, such as salaries, business trips, etc.

rent portion of the budget, the remaining economic items, particularly non-wage operations and maintenance, tend to get squeezed when there is shortfall of funding.

Thus, in the absence of more strategic budget allocation procedures, budgets become led by inertia rather than by policy, with incremental budgeting the result.[69] Thus, sectoral expenditure planning becomes an exercise of managing budgetary inputs (staff and supplies and materials), with relatively little attention being given to the outputs and outcomes of public expenditure in terms of the efficiency and effectiveness of public services and their impact on the realization of government policies; the objective of budget formulation at the sectoral level becomes one of trying to obtain as many resources as possible, rather than ensuring that available resources are used to achieve policy objectives. Hence, guidance from the Ministry of Finance and Economy at the start of the annual budget preparation process focuses primarily on the level of increase to be applied to the main expenditure items (wage increases, increases in utility costs).

The strengthening of the MTEF, currently under way in the Ministry of Finance and Economy, is expected to address the issue of a change in the basis of budget formulation by initiating a gradual shift from an emphasis on inputs to a focus on outputs. Future MTEFs are also expected to specify overall and sectoral resource constraints in order to prevent the introduction of policy initiatives which are unaffordable and to facilitate budget preparation by sector ministries.

Other areas requiring future reform include:

- *Integrating the processes for programming, budgeting and reporting domestic and foreign aid resources.* The externally-financed part of the budget is programmed separately from the domestic portion; this can lead to a mismatch between investment and recurrent spending allocations. Instead, the focus should be on building an integrated approach to the planning of capital and recurrent and to aid and domestically-financed activities, linked to policies and programs and including the recurrent implications of capital expenditures.
- *Boosting the role of sector ministries in budget-making.* Sector ministries should produce their own contestable budgets within resource ceilings set by the Ministry of Finance and Economy. The role of sector ministries in budget formulation is expected to be enhanced through the strengthening of the MTEF process.
- *Improving the degree of strategic direction from the Government and the Ministry of Finance and Economy.* As indicated above, the prior lack of sector resource ceilings provided at the outset of budget preparation has resulted in budgetary requests exceeding, often by several times, the available resource envelope. The resulting cuts to budget requests imposed by the MOFE has had the effect of negating much of the early budget preparation work by sector ministries and of contributing to an inefficient allocation of budgetary resources since there has been little incentive for ministries to review and prioritize their expenditure plans.
- *Greater incentives to seek cost-saving alternatives.* The current normative basis of budgeting penalizes sectors which reduce their nominal physical capacity in order to deliver more effective services with the resources available because budgetary resources are provided on the basis of physical resources (see Box 4.5 above). As indicated above, the basis of budget formulation is expected to move gradually from an emphasis on inputs to a greater focus on outputs, which should facilitate changes in input-mix to improve efficient delivery of services. At the same time, the preparation of detailed sector expenditure strategies and medium-term expenditure plans, as part of MTEF strengthening, should assist highlighting areas where efficiency can be improved and cost-saving alternatives are possible.

---

69. Incremental budgeting refers to the practice by sector ministries of merely add percentages, guided by an inflation projection in the budget circular, to their previous year's budget. With this "bottom-up" approach, sector ministries are able to overstate their needs, exerting upward pressure on overall spending.

Role of Sector Ministries

Spending ministries and other independent bodies that are directly accountable to Parliament and the President should be responsible for compiling their own draft estimates within prescribed ceilings and in accordance with instructions issued by MOFE. They should prepare their drafts to reflect ministry priorities and objectives. For health and education services, the line ministries are also obliged to oversee the budget preparations of regional and local administrations to ensure that sufficient budgetary resources are included to fund minimum service levels. However, final budget preparation work is carried out primarily by MOFE staff, with relatively limited active participation by ministry and department heads.

In practice, sector ministries have a limited role in the budget formulation process due to two aspects of Armenia's budget system. Firstly, the absence of budgetary ceilings given to sector ministries by the MOFE means that sector/function budget submissions are significantly above the likely resources available (see Box 4.6); consequently, it is the MOFE who makes final decisions on individual budgetary allocations. However, because of the lack of an effective MTEF to date, the mechanism used by MOFE to allocate budgetary resources across sectors is not as transparent as it should be. This further exacerbates the separation between sector policies and budgets and prevents greater flexibility being given to budget managers. This situation is expected to improve over the next few years with the strengthening of the MTEF and the increase in the Government's policy role in identifying priorities across sectors.

Secondly, in some important sectors, such as education, the sector ministry has a minimal role in the budget submissions themselves. Once budget requirements have been determined by individual budget cost-centers (e.g. schools), using norms or pre-set input ratios, these budget needs are aggregated at the regional level before being sent on to the Ministry of Finance and Economy. Though the information is sent to the Ministry of Education and Science in this case, it is for information, rather than for their approval. The Ministry's role is mainly limited to gathering the policy-based statistical information (e.g. numbers of teachers) required to apply the norms.

BOX 4.6: THE IMPORTANCE OF SECTORAL CEILINGS

Failure to place financial ceilings on ministries' initial requests for budget funds can have a number of consequences for the budget planning process:

- it is likely to be extremely wasteful of staff time. If budget requests have to be reduced at later stages to a fraction of the initial submission, much of the preparatory work will have been of little value in determining the eventual allocation of budgetary resources;
- it provides a tactical incentive for ministries to inflate their initial requests in the hope of maximizing their eventual allocations;
- it allows ministries to avoid having to make hard decisions about the priorities for public sector resources in their sectors; and
- it gives rise to the danger that the final budget will be allocated between too many programs, resulting in the available resources being spread too thinly rather than concentrated on priority areas.

The result can be that the budgeting process becomes discredited in at least two ways. First, the Ministry of Finance and Economy may be seen as imposing arbitrary cuts on sector ministries with the "real" budget being determined in haste at the last minute by a small group of officials who may have little understanding of the programs being funded. Second, for externally financed projects, the preparation of an unrealistic program carries the danger that the external agencies end up selecting projects for financing, while other higher priority projects remain underfinanced.

It is important to note that, for the credibility of the budget process, once the sector ceilings are set, the Ministry of Finance and Economy adheres to them and rejects any ministry/sector budget submission that is above the relevant ceiling.

Thus, whilst sector ministries such as the Ministry of Education and Science are responsible for setting Government policies, they lack the role/ability to influence how resources are used to meet these policy objectives. This lack of a link between policies and budgets is further exacerbated on the budget execution side by the fact that cash releases tend to be *ad hoc*, thereby preventing sector ministries from effectively planning their expenditures during the year and encouraging *ad hoc* and non-strategic expenditure decisions.

Recommendations for Strengthening Budget Formulation

The Government recognizes the need to strengthen Armenia's budget preparation process still further. The objective of the recommendations in the next two sections is to ensure that the appropriate basic processes are put in place.

Move away from line-item budgeting. An important step in strengthening the budget system will be to change the basis of budget estimation from line-items to estimates based on activities needed to achieve broader program areas. The current system needs improving since it provides little linkage between resource allocations and the purpose of expenditure programs, thus making it difficult to evaluate budget plans in terms of sector policy objectives (see Box 4.7).

Moving away from a reliance on line-item budgeting will require longer-term, integrated and sequenced reforms, beginning with the elaboration of medium-term sector policy strategies, as part of MTEF strengthening (see Annex 2). These will identify the relevant programs and activities to

---

BOX 4.7: BUDGET PRESENTATION BY PROGRAM

The discussion above emphasizes the importance of presenting ministry/agency budgets by broad program area. The following table shows an example of a presentation which has been prepared in an Annual Budget format. This type of programmatic presentation should also be used for the MTEF. The main criteria for a programmatic presentation include (see also Box 4.8 below):

- Classification presented by <u>ministry</u> and main department/agency, then by broad program;
- Investment expenditures shown separately from recurrent expenditures;
- Expenditure figures shown for previous year's actuals, revised current year and next year's budget;
- Broad expenditure categories shown (e.g. recurrent/investment/total or further broken down into e.g. wagebill/ other recurrent/investment or further disaggregated to wagebill/ operations & maintenance/ subsidies/transfers/ investment).

Breakdown of Expenditure by Program Area

| Programs | Dram million | | | | | | | | |
| | 2000 Actual | | | 2001 Estimated | | | 2002 Budget | | |
	Rec.	Inv.	Total	Rec.	Inv.	Total	Rec.	Inv.	Total
Ministry of Health									
1. Primary health care									
2. Secondary health care									
3. Tertiary health care									
4. Medical/health education & research									
5. Public Health Services									
6. Planning, management & administration									
Total Expenditure									

achieve priority sector policies. In the medium term, the costing of these programs would be made, and alternative methodologies for carrying out activities would be compared. Under the MTEF, lower priority activities would be phased out or eliminated. These changes will need to be accompanied by appropriate legislative/regulation changes, including changes to the classification and virement rules.

Greater involvement of sector ministries in the budget process. The move to budgets based on broad program areas will need to be accompanied by strengthening of sector ministries' responsibilities and their capacities for preparing budgets so that sector ministries have the primary role in programming and implementing sector policies and budgets. This would give responsibility for budget estimations to sector ministries, which could plan their budgets by broad program areas. The introduction of a simple program area classification within the budget can help to make explicit the linkages between sector policies and budgetary allocations and to facilitate the analysis of budget requests, thereby contributing to improved targeting of the budget and monitoring of budgetary performance in relation to the achievement of Government policies.

The suggested MTEF action plan (Annex 2), building on progress to date, includes the introduction of broad programs into the budgetary system. The definition of program areas within the budget should be derived from the definition of a ministry's objectives and the means by which these objectives are to be realized. At least initially, the focus should be on defining a limited number (e.g. 5-10 for a large ministry) of major programs that are comprehensive of expenditures in the sector (see Box 4.8). Subsequently, a more detailed breakdown may be introduced. However, it should be noted that introducing programs results in greater complexity in budget preparation and presentation, placing additional demands on limited budget planning capacities. As far as possible, the definition of program areas needs to be linked to clearly defined responsibilities for program management in order to ensure appropriate responsibility and accountability for budget outputs and outcomes. The exercise of defining program areas can be useful in helping to determine requirements for the reorganization of a ministry's structure.

BOX 4.8: EXAMPLE OF PROGRAMS IN THE HEALTH SECTOR

In an effort to strengthen their MTEFs, many transition countries are moving towards planning their budgetary resources on the basis of sectoral programs. This process begins with a comprehensive review of the programs in a given sector and the implications for the MTEF of medium-term sector policies within the overall sector's resource envelope.

In the health sector, programs are being defined on the basis of the level of health care, since this facilitates the movement of resources towards priority areas, such as primary and public health care, and away from lower priority services, such as tertiary care. Programs cover both recurrent and capital expenditures. Responsibility for overseeing these programs would be undertaken by the Ministry of Health, in conjunction with local authorities.

Examples of health sector programs include:

- **Primary health care services** – covering initial, non-referral care at health centers/ambulatories, polyclinics, and at outpatient centers. Also covers some disease prevention services, such as vaccinations.
- **Secondary health care services** – covering basic referral services at inpatient hospital facilities.
- **Tertiary health care services** – covering specialized referral services in specialized facilities as well as services at health research institutes.
- **Public health care services** – covering environmental health services, health promotion campaigns and epidemiological services.
- **Medical/health education and research** – covering design, development and delivery of medical education, research and training programs.
- **Planning, management and finance** – covering policy and strategy formulation for all health services and licensing, regulation and standard setting for the provision of medical services.

As indicated above, this increase in the role of sector ministries in the budget process will need to be accompanied by giving responsibility for sector budgets to sector ministries. This means that budget appropriations should contain information, which is presented in administrative classification codes. This will give authority to sector ministers and accounting officers to program and manage their budgets to fulfill sector policies. It should be noted that building up sector ministry capacities will take significant time and substantial technical assistance inputs.

More flexibility/budget authority given to budget managers. The changes outlined above would give greater flexibility to budget managers.[70] Global budget experiments are already taking place in health and education, where budget users are responsible for lump-sum budgets. Lessons from these experiments should focus particularly on accountability and disciplinary sanctions against budget managers responsible for overspending. Training will be needed in financial management for budget managers both in budget centers and in sector ministries. This should be accompanied by a more appropriate role for the Ministry of Finance and Economy (see below).

Appropriate role for the Ministry of Finance and Economy. In addition to strengthening the roles of sector ministries in budget formulation, there is the need to alter the role of the MOFE in line with these changes. Specifically, the budget, macro/revenue and sector departments in the MOFE should primarily be involved in setting overall budget policy, determining the scope and size of the government's expenditure program overall between sectors (sector expenditure ceilings) and analyzing sectoral budgetary submissions in relation to sectoral policies. This contrasts with its current role in being the primary determinant of intra and inter-sectoral (functional) budgetary allocations.[71] At the moment, the MOFE has been dealing primarily with the traditional functions of the Finance Ministry, while the functions that are usually performed by the Ministry of Economy remained under-developed. The change in its role will necessitate greater analytical capacities and a better understanding of strategic policymaking and is likely to require the design and implementation of a comprehensive training program. In addition, in order for the sector departments in the MOFE to concentrate on its budget formulation role, the PER recommends the transfer of their current budget execution role to Treasury.

More transparent budget formulation process. The move towards ensuring primary budget appropriation by spending ministry (administrative classification) and the presentation of budgets by program area will increase the transparency of budget formulation. Greater transparency is needed for Government and Parliament to have appropriate oversight of budgets. At the same time, the greater responsibilities given to budget managers to manage their budgets will require better accountability for budgetary allocations, which in turn will require more transparency in budgets.

Improving links between policies and budgets. One of the major planks of a modern strategic budget system is ensuring a strong link between Government policies and priorities and budgetary allocations. This will be the main objective of strengthening the MTEF, which is described in more detail in the section below and in Annex 2. The PER agrees with the current approach of building up a strategic and operational MTEF gradually, including sector strategies which set out short, medium and long-term policies and provide appropriate resources to fulfill these policies. These resource allocations are to be based on MOFE-set sectoral ceilings, which would be circulated to sector ministries before the Annual Budget process begins. These ceilings would be based on a strategic analysis of inter-sectoral public expenditure priorities that is consistent with government policies for economic reform and fiscal sustainability. It is recommended that this capacity for sectoral policy analysis be built up progressively as part of MTEF strengthening, beginning perhaps initially with pilot ministries in 2003.

---

70. Defined as someone who is responsible for managing an institution's budgetary resources (e.g. a financial manager in a hospital or the Director of the Budget Department in a sector ministry).

71. Which tend to be done incrementally, rather than strategically.

Medium-term Expenditure Framework (MTEF)

The Government prepared its first MTEF in 1999, covering the period 2000-2002. The MTEF was rolled over in each of the following three years (2000 to 2002 inclusive), with each MTEF covering the subsequent three years. Although limited in scope, the initial MTEF exercises have shown the potential for a move to a more strategic approach and a willingness of the Government to continue with the exercise. Whilst the first MTEF was prepared with assistance from the World Bank and USAID, the Ministry of Finance and Economy prepared its subsequent MTEF document without significant external assistance. From the beginning, the MTEF was not included in the Budget Systems Law or incorporated into the budget calendar. The initial MTEFs have focused primarily on setting out a realistic macro/fiscal framework and articulating policies in education for example, which are well advanced.

The PER acknowledges the on-going efforts of the Government to strengthen the strategic focus of the budget preparation process; MOFE is currently working with technical assistance to build on and improve the MTEF process. The following assessment is based on the situation in mid-2002.

The MTEF is not at present used as a decision-making tool for Government. Whilst the MTEF concept has been established within the budget cycle, its use as a strategic tool to direct budgetary resources to meet Government policies has not been thus far established. Although Government may review the MTEF document, it has not approved it in order to provide guidance to ministries in preparing their annual budget submissions, nor does the document currently contain sufficient policy and budgetary analysis to enable them to make relevant decisions to guide the preparation of subsequent Annual Budgets. Thus, the extent of high-level ownership of the MTEF, involving approval and evaluating progress, is as yet very limited.

Some of the elements of a more strategic and operational MTEF are not yet in place or are based on insufficient analysis. These include: (i) limited sectoral coverage for analysis of expenditure prioritization *within* sector programs; (ii) limited analysis of expenditures plans *across* sectors, including limited costing of resources required to meet current sectoral policies; (iii) little analysis of the main economic items of expenditure (e.g. salaries, operations and maintenance spending, transfers, subsidies and investment); and (iv) no analysis of cross-sectoral expenditure issues, such as the budgetary implications of public sector reform.

Finally, the MTEF has had limited circulation outside of Government. It has not been provided systematically to aid agencies as part of the donor dialogue process in order to facilitate joint planning of future assistance. The MTEF has not been published nor made available to civil society organizations and the general public. At the same time, no explicit link is made between budget priorities and strategic Government objectives in the areas of growth and poverty reduction.

Recommendations on MTEF

The Government has undertaken a number of important steps to build the foundations for a more strategic MTEF. Most notably, a Government-level oversight co-ordination committee has been established to guide the process. These initial steps will be built on over the next few years, and this section identifies the highest priority areas for the MTEF.

The underlying objective of the MTEF is to improve the forward planning of budgetary resources and to the MTEF as a tool to guide the Annual Budget. In the short term, the MTEF for 2004–2006 should be prepared and presented to Government *during the first half of 2003* in order to provide guidance for the preparation of the 2004 Annual Budget. This should project the total budgetary framework for the medium term and identify sectoral priorities for current and capital expenditures. Consistent with the 2004–2006 macro/fiscal framework, realistic sector resource ceilings should be set, within which sector ministries can develop their expenditure plans for the 2004 Budget.

At the same time, the Ministry of Finance and Economy should progressively introduce improvements in its MTEF to ensure that it can be used as a strategic tool for targeting resources towards Government priority areas. In particular, the MTEF should be supported by a new department or unit in MOFE which would be in charge of MTEF co-ordination and provide methodological support for the process – this unit would need to work closely with (and have the appropriate institutional authority to do so) the Macroeconomic Department, the Budget Department (covering both recurrent and capital budgets) and the sector expenditure departments. This department or unit could also take over responsibility for co-ordination of donor assistance.

Annex 2 sets out a proposed timetable and methodology for strengthening the MTEF over the next three years. The proposed approach to strengthening the MTEF includes:

- Preparation of a more strategic document for the Government to make decisions on the overall resource framework and resource allocations across sectors, in line with the PRSP;
- Preparation of initial sector expenditure strategies and medium-term expenditure plans, perhaps initially concentrating on pilot sectors;
- Convening of a workshop for MOFE and sector ministry officials to review options for resource allocations for the expenditure framework;
- MTEF to be presented to a newly-established Government economic/budget policy committee for approval and to Parliament for information afterwards;
- MTEF to be presented to the donor community at its next donor co-ordination meeting, and
- publication of summary MTEF to be considered.

Budget Execution

More sophisticated planning of expenditures is futile if there are not also mechanisms to ensure that budget implementation is in line with plans, and that good information is available on budget performance. Much progress has been made in strengthening the budget execution system since the mid-1990s. Achievements from the first round of reforms include:[72]

- Creation of Treasury Single Account (TSA) and amalgamation of bank accounts previously held by budgetary institutions into TSA;
- Establishment of Central Treasury and field Treasury branches;
- Enactment of Treasury System Law, setting out the legislative framework behind the Treasury system;
- Development of procedures to concentrate government revenues into the TSA and handle all government payments through the TSA;
- Deployment of computer hardware and software to perform budget control, payment, accounting and reporting functions;
- Development of a set of accounts to handle inter-treasury, intra-treasury and treasury-CBA transactions;
- Development of a budget execution reporting system that is essentially cash-based and is supplemented with monthly reports on arrears and quarterly reports on receivables and payables; and
- Remittance of government revenues to the TSA with minimum delay and payments from the TSA at the last possible moment.

For efficient and effective budget execution, the execution system should allow for effective commitment control and accountability. Expenditure arrears should not be significant, and there should be active and effective internal audit. Fiscal and monetary accounts should be able to be reconciled to verify actual expenditures.

Weaknesses in budget execution mean that some of these objectives are not yet being met. Firstly, when available cash is below the level of appropriations, sector ministries do not adjust their spending plans; thus when revenues are less than expected, a cash flow problem results. Budgetary allocations

---

72. Summarised in Ramachandran (2001).

are viewed by sector ministries as the target for spending, rather than as an expenditure ceiling or maximum; thus, if there is a shortfall of resources, sector ministries do not identify expenditure areas to cut. Spending ministries take the view that their budget represents a guaranteed level of expenditures rather than an upper limit and thus find it hard to make expenditure reductions when revenues are less than expected. This is a rational response to the belief that, if sector ministries do not use their appropriated allocations, then allocations in the following year will be reduced accordingly. This lack of adherence to cash limits is further exacerbated by poor cash planning and forecasting.

To address these problems, the Treasury should accelerate the establishment of a capable internal audit unit[73] to carry out a regular audit of the expenditure execution process. The establishment of such a unit should take place simultaneously with sorting out responsibilities and functions among various existing auditing units in the Government structure, including the Audit Department, which is a part of the Prime Minister Office, and the Department of Control and Inspections in the Ministry of Finance and Economy, both of which perform functions of external audit. The internal audit unit in the Treasury should have a narrower set of responsibilities, primarily related to monitoring of compliance of budget spending with the budget legislation as well as adequacy of other aspects of its internal control system.

Secondly, the build-up of arrears reflects an incomplete system of commitment controls.[74] Spending units have in the past taken on commitments beyond their annual budget appropriations as a result of weak fiscal discipline and the low credibility of the budget preparation process. Monthly payment limits in treasury ledgers are lower than budget appropriations, but budgetary legislation does not permit MOFE to contain ministries'/spending units' expenditure commitments at a lower level. Since actual payment limits are below appropriations, field treasuries will not authorize payment orders beyond these monthly limits, leading to accumulation of unpaid invoices. These weaknesses are exacerbated by the paper-based systems used for accounting and reporting in sector ministries, leading to delays in information flows to the Central Treasury.

Thirdly, timely reporting on budget implementation is currently weak. The series of quarterly and annual budget reports provide a good framework for supervision and monitoring of budget implementation; however, without accurate information being included on total commitments or its being associated with comprehensive and detailed financial planning, its usefulness is limited. Similarly, the paper basis of data compilation for these reports means that the reports are circulated following a significant delay after the end of the reporting period, further limiting their usefulness for Government to make financial management decisions.

Finally, whilst the current amount of control exercised by the Government and Treasury over external funds appears to be appropriate, the smoothing of disbursements of these funds will need to be addressed. Transparent information and regular analysis of disbursement patterns and likely projections of these flows will assist the Government to address bottlenecks.

Recommendations for the Budget Execution System

Further modernization and institutional development of the Treasury is a priority for the Ministry of Finance and Economy. The recent report prepared by the resident IMF advisor has made extensive recommendations on improvements to all aspects of the budget execution system;[75] it is not intended to reproduce that report here, but instead to focus on a few key issues that relate to the credibility of the budget. These recommendations focus on designing and implementing the second generation Treasury reforms, which will concentrate on consolidating the gains made to date and designing and implementing an integrated FMIS database (for field treasuries, line ministries, budgetary institutions) to enable the Central Treasury to have a consolidated view of total Treasury operations, including the recording of commitments. This is expected to have an important impact

---

73. The IMF has been providing assistance to the MOFE with establishing internal audit in all line ministries and their subordinate organizations. The US Treasury is planning to provide assistance with training.

74. The Treasury started the introduction of the system of contract registration in early 2002.

75. Zohrab (2002).

on the generation and availability of data for external reporting. Complementary activities will include further development of the current classification chart, including the development of a simple program classification (see above), a longer budget calendar, and improved formats for budget requests, in line with improvements to the MTEF.

Within this framework particular emphasis should be placed on improving information systems, covering both classification and reporting, since such information is crucial both to the planning, monitoring and evaluation of expenditures. In the long run, a better information environment may allow less emphasis on rigid central controls of expenditure, which can impair the efficiency of resource use, and facilitate moves towards more decentralized systems that simultaneously give managers more discretion and hold them more accountable for results. This view underlines the principle of first getting the basics right before trying to adopt the more sophisticated approaches of modern public sector management.

Regarding measures to discourage the build-up of arrears, it is worth considering amendments to the Budget System Law to stipulate, the Budget Systems Law should be amended to stipulate what cannot be re-appropriated without the approval of Parliament and any other restrictions on virement (e.g. reassignment from wages to other economic items or from capital to recurrent). In addition, the 2004 Annual Budget Law and subsequent Annual Budget Laws should contain provisions: (i) to require the Government to specify commitment ceilings for budgetary institutions and expenditure categories by a certain percentage below the available budgeted expenditure authorizations until the last month of the year; and (ii) to give the Government and MOFE the ability to reduce, by decree at any time during a budget year, total budgeted expenditure by up to a certain percentage without being required to initiate a sequestration law, to protect any expenditure category or to reduce expenditure uniformly across expenditure categories.[76] In addition, measures to strengthen internal audit and the use of well-targeted sanctions will assist in reducing the tolerance of spending beyond budget appropriations.

The virement rules should be re-formulated to permit reallocations on an unrestricted basis, and should not be restricted by the idea that appropriations must be executed unless identified expenditure programs can be executed without using all the corresponding appropriations.

Finally, in order to assist in the efficient provision of resources to meet payment obligations, Treasury should examine ways to improve cash planning and management. In particular, Treasury could: (i) introduce incentive measures to encourage revenue agencies to improve their receipt forecasts; and (ii) introduce incentive measures for spending agencies to meet spending profile targets set by Treasury.

Procurement

The Government has made significant progress in establishing an appropriate procurement system. An appropriate legislative framework underlying the procurement system has been put in place. The Public Procurement Agency has been established and is operational, and the Agency has been working with Treasury to develop detailed regulations for approving, recording and controlling commitments.

The main weakness relating to public procurement is significant delays in payment for procured goods and services, which are caused by revenue shortfalls and cash flow problems. One consequence of this is a reluctance of private companies to participate in public tenders, leading tenders to be cancelled or delayed due to insufficient numbers of bidders to comply with the legislation. Other weaknesses include too low a ceiling on the value of tenders before open tender procedures must be used, a lack of clarity by ministries/agencies procuring goods and services in specifying their requirements adequately, and the too-centralized nature of the procurement system, which places sole responsibility for public procurement on the Central Procurement Agency.

In order to strengthen procurement, it is recommended that the minimum ceiling above which open tender procedures are required be raised and options for moves to a less-centralized system be investigated.

---

76. Ibid.

CHAPTER 5

PUBLIC EXPENDITURE IN THE EDUCATION SECTOR

This Chapter assesses how much Armenia is spending on education, including public and private financing, and evaluates how public financing is being allocated among the levels of education and among the inputs required to provide education. It also analyses the efficiency with which different levels of the system are using inputs, as measured against international norms on input levels and student learning outcomes. It asks whether public financing is being used to minimize the downstream poverty that results from a lack of access to education.

Financing of Education

Table 5.1 shows that Armenia's public expenditures on education are moving in the right direction. They increased as a percent of GDP between 1997 and 2001 by 45 percent—from 2.0 to 2.9 percent of GDP. Given a noticeable expansion of real GDP (by third) in this period, this constitutes a considerable increase in education financing. However, the current level is still very low by international standards, and it is significantly below the average public expenditure in OECD countries of 5.3 percent of GDP in 1998.

As a share of general budget, public expenditure on education in 1998 was below the OECD 1998 average—8.3 percent versus 12.9 percent. However, by 2001 Armenia's public expenditure for education as a percent of total public expenditure, relative to the 1998 percent for the average OECD country, had narrowed significantly, the share of total public expenditures going to education increased from 8.3 to 10.5 percent in the 1997–2001 time period. Education's low share of Armenia's GDP is partly attributable to the fact that Armenia's total government expenditure is very low (about 25 percent of GDP): the Government of Armenia (GOA) gives a share of a small pie to education at rates that approach, although they are still below, the average share for OECD countries.

As footnote 2 for Table 5.1 states, public reports of education expenditures are incomplete. In 2001 these omitted expenditures amounted to 17.3 percent of the reported education expenditures, 2 percent of total public expenditures, and more than 0.5 percent of GDP. Whether to include these expenditures in evaluating the total fiscal effort in education is not clear. On the

TABLE 5.1: PUBLIC AND TOTAL EDUCATION EXPENDITURES AS PERCENT OF GDP AND OF TOTAL PUBLIC EXPENDITURES

Year	Public[1] and Private Expenditure on Education as a Percent of GDP			Public Education Expenditure as Percent of Total Public Expenditure (TPE) [4]
	Public Expenditure[2]	Private Expenditure[3]	Total	
1997	2.2			7.9
1998	2.3			8.3
1999	2.5			8.0
2000	3.0			11.3
2001	2.8	0.9	3.7	10.5
OECD (1998)	5.3	0.7	6.0	12.9

Notes:

[1] These numbers are the consolidated general budget for education (includes employer contributions to health and pension funds), including local budgets for education.

[2] These numbers under-estimate public expenditures in the sector. They exclude repayments of budget arrears and investments in education under the World Bank-funded Armenia Social Investment Fund (ASIF). ASIF investments range between 250–500 million drams per year each year since the late 1990s. They also exclude off-budget foreign grant assistance to the education sector. It has been estimated that these grants amount to US$6.1 million in 1999, US$9.7 million in 2000, and US$9.8 million in 2001. See also Chapter 3.

[3] Private expenditures are expenditures for fees in public or private institutions only. They do not include other family expenses for education, such as textbooks.

[4] The percents in this column represent the consolidated general budget for education divided by the consolidated general budget expenditures.

Source for Armenia figures: Ministry of Finance and Economy, Republic of Armenia.

Source for OECD data: Tables B2.1a and 4.1 OECD, 2001.

one hand, money is fungible and in this sense external grants and credits may substitute for Government fiscal effort. On the other hand, these resources do not arise out of taxes and can be seen as "one-time" or less predictable funding for the sector. Private expenditures are also under-estimated: Table 5.1 reports private fee costs only, not other private costs of education, such as e.g. textbook costs.

Cost Effects of Armenia's Demographic Structure and Enrolment Rates

Public education expenditures are importantly affected by a country's demographic structure and enrolment rates. Relative to the average for OECD countries, Armenia has more school-age students and only modestly lower enrolment rates. At Armenia's average unit cost[77] for students enrolled at all levels, the cost of its demographic structure relative to the average OECD age structure is 0.9 percent of GDP, 3.2 percent of total public expenditure, and 37.3 percent of total education expenditures. If Armenia had both the same age structure and enrolments rates as the averages for OECD countries, the joint effect of these two assumptions on Armenia's 1999 public education expenditures would be to reduce total education expenditures as a percent of GDP from 2.3 to 1.9. It means that because the Armenian population is young, Armenia has to spend relatively more public money to ensure the same level of educational achievements compare to countries with older population.

---

77. Unit costs were calculated net of local and central ministry administrative costs and for slots at all levels that are publicly financed. In 1999, an additional 65,650 students were enrolled in public and private colleges and universities as fee-paying students. As privately financed enrolments, they do not affect Armenia's public expenditures for education and were excluded from the analysis.

Allocations by Level of Education

Armenia has distributions of public financing by educational levels that are comparable to those for the OECD (Table 5.2). In 1998 the average OECD public share of education financing going to different levels was 7.5 percent for preschool, 67.9 percent to primary and secondary education, and 24.5 percent to tertiary education. However, the tertiary share includes 6.4 percent for R&D at universities, the share going to instructional and ancillary tertiary education being 18.3 percent.

Armenia's local budgets for education as a percent of total public education expenditures varied between 8 percent in 2000 and 15 percent in the unadjusted 2002 budget, with 13 percent being the median budget share. However, since local budgets included the financing of extra-curricular activities, not just preschools, shares at this level seem relatively comparable to the OECD share for preschool.

Including general education boarding schools, Armenia's share for primary and secondary education are almost identical to the OECD share: 64.2 percent in 1998 and 66.3 percent in 2002. The tertiary share, including the retraining institutions, is also almost identical: 18.8 in 1998 and, reflecting the increase in fee-based tertiary enrolments, 16 percent in 2002.

Enrolment shares for general education schools, extra-curricular programs, and retraining institutions exceeded budget shares across all years, upper secondary vocational education, boarding schools, colleges, and universities having budget shares that significantly exceeded enrolment shares. Across the time period unit costs of colleges and universities were five to six times the unit cost of general education, in contrast to the 1998 average for OECD countries of a 1.8 ratio of the average unit cost for a tertiary student to the average unit cost for primary, lower secondary, and upper secondary education.

In general, expenditure allocations between major budget categories are not distorted. Relative to the average for OECD countries, Armenia's education system as a whole allocates more to recurrent and less to capital costs. Its allocations between staff and non-staff expenses are comparable to the average for the OECD. However, detailed analyses of recurrent expenditures for the different levels and types of education paint a picture of consistent under-funding: deferred maintenance, under-funding of utilities, and virtually no allocations for the resources associated with improving the quality of educational services, such as teacher training or libraries and other learning resources.

TABLE 5.2: DISTRIBUTION OF PUBLIC EDUCATION EXPENDITURE AMONG LEVELS AND TYPES OF EDUCATION
percent

Level of Education	1997 actual	1998 actual	1999 actual	2000 actual	2001 adjusted	2002 unadjusted
MoES administration	0.6	0.5	0.3	0.2	0.3	0.3
Local budgets for preschools + local share of extra-curricular schools	13.8	13.3	10.9	8.0	13.2	15.2
General education (primary, lower secondary, upper secondary academic)	52.4	55.2	61.4	69.0	63.3	58.9
Upper secondary VET	3.3	2.3	2.0	1.5	1.5	1.2
Boarding schools for general education	6.0	6.7	5.6	4.4	5.5	6.2
Tertiary education	19.7	18.8	17.2	14.3	13.6	15.1
Colleges	7.3	5.8	4.9	3.8	3.4	3.6
Universities	12.4	13.0	12.3	10.5	10.2	11.5
State share of extra-curricular schools	3.0	2.3	1.8	1.8	1.9	2.2
Retraining institutions	0.9	0.9	0.9	0.9	0.8	0.9

Source: MOFE.

What are Armenia's Private Expenditures on Education?

Between 1995 and 2001 the number of private institutions almost quadrupled, although the net gain in students was only about 40 percent. Table 5.3 shows that private payments, predictably, vary by household consumption quintile, but that all quintiles pay something. On average, the richest households spend almost six times as much on education as the poorest households. As a percent of their total household expenditures, the richest spend 66 percent more than the poorest households. For households with children of primary school age, the richest households on average spend about twice as much on education as the poorest households.

State colleges and universities also significantly depend on private fees. Essentially the state tertiary system is becoming privatized. The state institutions divide their numbers of places into "state order" places—places publicly financed—and "fee"—privately financed—places. Table 5.4 shows that the share of fee-based places steadily increased across the 1997–2001 time period for both colleges and universities, reaching 76 percent and 63 percent, respectively, by 2001.

The trend in private funding (fees and donor contributions) as a percent of total funding for tertiary education is positive, having increased from 53 percent in 1997 to 65 percent in 2001. For

TABLE 5.3: AVERAGE PRIVATE HOUSEHOLD EXPENDITURES ON EDUCATION BY CONSUMPTION QUINTILE
Drams per month

| Education level | Consumption Quintile: All Households | | | | | |
	1	2	3	4	5	Total
Basic education	1,293	1,997	2,972	4,371	7,670	3,695
Higher education[1]	53	56	252	190	747	264
Percent in tertiary technical education	72.0	53.9	45.9	28.5	46.9	45.4
Other education	3	4	16	33	628	140
Total	1,349	2,056	3,240	4,593	9,045	4,099
Education as percent of total HH expenditures	4.5	4.9	6.2	6.6	7.5	6.5
Consumption Quintile: Households with Children of Primary School Age Only						
Percent of primary school age children[1]	12.4	17.8	21.8	22.8	25.2	100.0
Average expenditure per child in basic education	2,311	2,526	3,214	4,334	7,139	4,224

[1] Expenditures at the tertiary level are low because not that many households have children of university age that are also enrolled. It was not possible to compute tertiary expenditures for those households with tertiary-age children because the cell sizes were too small.
Source: Integrated Survey of Living Standards (ISLS), 98/99.

TABLE 5.4: TRENDS IN FEE-BASED PLACES IN STATE COLLEGES AND UNIVERSITIES

| Year | Number of State Order Places | | Number of Fee-Based Places | | Fee-Based Places as Percent of Total Places | |
	Colleges	Universities	Colleges	Universities	Colleges	Universities
1997	N.A.	18,927	N.A.	16,997	N.A.	47.3
1998	10,885	18,483	16,292	20,646	60.0	52.8
1999	8,763	17,469	19,285	22,301	68.8	56.1
2000	7,123	17,110	19,747	26,505	73.5	60.1
2001	6,875	17,740	21,848	30,905	76.1	63.5

Source: National Statistical Service.

colleges there is no clear trend, although private funding as a percent of total funding has been increasing since 1999. Trend or not, about 50 percent of college resources come from private payments. Universities show a steady upward trend, with 65 percent of their resources coming from fees and contributions by 2001.

The Budgeting Process
In most years, the executed budgets for the system's core services (general and tertiary) approximated their adjusted budgets, but executed budgets for other levels and types of education were between 60 and 90 percent of their adjusted budgets. A bigger problem is the nature of public accounting and reporting:

- As already discussed in other Chapters, the sector lacks a comprehensive accounting and reporting system for public finances available to the sector, including off-budget grants and credits spent at local levels.
- Local levels of government receive block grants from the central government, but do not report how these grants were spent. A simple example is that local budgets are spent for preschools and extracurricular activities. It is not known how the total is allocated between these two activities, what inputs are purchased for each, or how many children are served by each.
- Private financing needs to be properly measured and reported for all levels of education, but especially at the tertiary level.
- Tertiary institutions have three sources of funds: state funding, student fees, and donor and private contributions. How this money is spent is known publicly only for state funding. However, to evaluate the fiscal health of this level of education, how total funding is allocated needs to be known.

Is the Current System Fiscally Sustainable?
Arrears, although not a large percent of 1999 or 2000 expenditures, is still at about 8–9 percent of annual spending and has to be taken as prima facie evidence that the system is not fiscally sustainable for these time periods.

As of January 1, 2000, the budget arrears in education were 0.18 percent of 1999 GDP. The stock of debt increased in 2000 to 0.25 percent of GDP. There were arrears in all economic categories for both time periods, but they were especially high for utilities, transportation and communication, and other expenses. Growth in debt was greatest for scholarships/ stipends, student meals, and transportation and communication.

Efficiency of Education
In general, Armenia does not use labor or physical capital efficiently in its educational sector. Although earlier studies flagged the system's efficiency problems, data for 1997–2001 show little, if any, progress in terms of a more efficient use of inputs. This record is very troubling when read against an impending decline of 43 percent in the number of 7–16 year olds between 2000 and 2015. As mentioned above, moving toward OECD's demographic structure would, all else equal, lower costs. However, realizing these savings requires Government to develop an aggressive strategy to adjust the size of its labor force and to close and consolidate schools. These actions carry both political costs and opportunities to use savings to increase educational access and quality.

How Efficient is the Use of Labor Inputs?
The efficiency with which labor is used in the sector is evaluated in terms of student/staffing ratios, teaching loads relative to comparator countries, and price, measured by teacher salaries.

Student/labor ratios. The use of labor in Armenia's education system is seriously inefficient. Tables 5.5–5.7 show the 1997–2002 trends in the ratios of students to teachers, non-teaching staff

TABLE 5.5: STUDENT/TEACHER RATIOS BY LEVEL AND TYPE OF EDUCATION

		LEVEL AND TYPE OF EDUCATION						
		Secondary VET		Boarding	Extra-			
Year	General	Up to 2002	Start 2001	(General)	Curricular	Colleges	Universities	Retraining
1997	10.8	6.0	N.A.	6.1	75.4	6.2	6.0	33.1
1998	11.1	5.0	N.A.	6.2	43.1	6.2	6.1	66.7
1999	11.6	4.5	N.A.	4.6	21.3	6.5	6.3	84.0
2000	11.3	4.6	N.A.	4.7	22.5	6.2	5.9	67.6
2001	11.3	4.3	10.3	4.6	20.5	6.7	6.5	92.1
2002	11.2	5.5	7.2	4.6	21.1	N.A.	N.A.	92.0
OECD Country Mean (1999)	Primary: 18 Lower secondary: 15.2 Upper secondary: 14.1					Tertiary: 15.7		

[1] Student/teacher ratios for preschool are based on fulltime teachers only.
Sources for Armenia data: NSS, MOFE.
Source for OECD data: Table D5.1, OECD, 2001.

to teachers, students to non-teaching staff, and students to total staff (teachers and non-teaching staff). All ratios use full-time equivalents (FTEs) for teachers and non-teaching staff. In general, all three tables paint a picture of significant overstaffing.

As Table 5.5 shows, except for the retraining institutions, student/teacher ratios are very low even relative to OECD standards, let alone relative to those for non-ECA low and lower-middle income countries. OECD's Program for International Student Assessment (PISA) shows that the relationship between student/teacher ratios and students' learning outcomes is non-linear. Learning increases as student/teacher ratios increase, but it is declining above ratios of 25:1 (OECD 2001a, figure 8.5).[78] PISA measures the achievements of 15 year old students, an age in most OECD countries that corresponds to enrolment in upper secondary education where the average student/teacher ratio is 14.1. Thus, OECD countries, on average, have inefficient student/staff ratios; Armenia—a country with much more limited resources—has appallingly inefficient ratios.

Although enrolments increased in the state colleges and universities by 28 percent between 1997 and 2002, student/teacher ratios stayed dismally low for state (and private) institutions. These ratios partly reflect high numbers of weekly instruction for students—around 30 hours per week. Students in American universities take about 15 hours of instruction per week, with heavy loads of independent work in libraries, laboratories, and in communities. This mix of classroom and independent study requires that institutions have rich educational resources.

Ratios of non-teaching staff to teachers were high and either flat or increasing across the time period (Table 5.6). Student/non-teaching staff ratios were reasonable for general education[79] and markedly increased in the retraining institutions. However, other levels and types of education had

---

78. These data need to be interpreted carefully. It is possible that countries with higher student/teacher ratios also have generally weaker quality that reduces student learning. Only one OECD country (Mexico) seems to fit this profile. Although students in ECA countries that belong to OECD do not perform well on PISA, these countries also have low student/teacher ratios.

79. In 2001 more than half (56 percent) of the non-teaching staff at this level of education was lower-skilled labor (electricians, cleaners, guards, etc.); 24 percent, professional non-teaching staff (e.g., organizers of cultural and recreational activities); and 20 percent, managers at the school level, such as principals or accountants.

low and either flat or decreasing student/non-teaching staff ratios (Table 5.6). Although private colleges and universities had even slightly lower student/teacher ratios that their public counterparts, their student/non-teaching staff ratios were significantly higher: in 2001, about 26:1, as opposed to 8:1 for state universities and 3:1 for state colleges. Except for the extra-curricular institutions at the beginning of the period and the retraining institutions at its end, student/total staff ratios were very low and declined or were flat across the period. Colleges are strikingly over-manned—one employee for about every two students.

Teaching loads. At the primary and secondary level fulltime teachers have an average annual load of 612 instructional hours—34 instructional weeks of 18 hours a week. This load is below the average load in 1999 for the OECD countries, which varied by level: 801 hours for primary education, 716 hours for lower secondary education, 662 hours for academic secondary education, and 692 hours for secondary VET.

Price of labor. Between 2000 and 2002 average monthly wages in the education sector were below the average monthly public sector wage. However, the average monthly *teacher* salary slightly exceeded the average monthly public sector wage. Teachers work 18 instructional hours/week for 34 instructional weeks, plus perhaps 30–50 percent above classroom time in preparation and other duties for a total in the range of 23.4 to 27 hours/week. By contrast, OECD countries average 38 hours/week at primary, lower secondary, and upper secondary level education (OECD, 2001a, table D3.2).

TABLE 5.6: NON-TEACHING AND TOTAL STAFF RATIOS BY LEVEL AND TYPE OF EDUCATION

Level and Type of Education	Non-Teaching Staff/Teacher Ratio		Student/Non-teaching Staff Ratio		Student/Total Staff Ratio	
	1997	2002	1997	2002	1997	2002
General	0.6	0.6	19.4	18.7	6.9	7.0
Secondary VET (up to 2002)	1.7	6.7	3.6	0.8	2.2	0.7
Secondary VET (started in 2001)	N.A.	1.0	N.A.	7.4	NA	3.6
General boarding schools	1.6	1.0	3.7	4.7	2.3	2.3
Extra-curricular institutions	1.4	1.4	55.7	15.0	32.0	8.8
Colleges	2.0	2.2[1]	3.1	3.1[1]	2.1	2.1[1]
Universities	0.6	0.7[1]	9.4	9.6[1]	3.7	3.9[1]
Retraining institutions	2.0	2.3	16.8	40.2	11.1	28.0

[1] Based on data for 2001.

Sources: NSS, MOFE.

Annual hours worked are not comparable between teachers and other public sector employees. In addition to instructional weeks, teachers work another 7 weeks for an annual total of 41 weeks. Public sector employees, including non-teaching staff in the education sector, work 40 hours/week for 46 weeks per year. The difference between the two groups in work performed is, at the upper range, 1,107 hours annually for teachers and 1,840 hours for other public servants, a difference of 733 hours per year. Current salaries for all public sector employees, including teachers, are extremely low. However, as they rise, the smaller working hours of teachers will become quite costly.

Another way to judge teacher salaries is as a percent of per capita GDP. Table 5.7 shows teacher salaries as a percent of per capita GDP for Armenia in 2001 and for the OECD, on average, in 1999. Clearly, teacher salaries (and those of the public sector in general) in Armenia are seriously below per capita GDP and significantly below averages for the OECD countries. As the economy growths and unemployment declines in Armenia, the sector will not be able to attract or retain

Country		Level of Education		
	Primary	Lower Secondary	Upper Secondary Academic	Upper Secondary VET
Armenia				
Ratio of starting salary to GDP per capita (2001)[1] Ratio of salary after 15 years' experience to GDP per capita (2001)[1]	The minimum salary—presumably the salary paid to new entrants—is 0.37 percent of per capita GDP, independent of qualifications. The salary paid to those with 15 or more years of experience is 0.39 of GDP per capita, independent of qualifications. Salaries do not seem to vary by the level of education taught.			
OECD				
Ratio of starting salary to GDP per capita (1999)	0.97	1.01	1.05	1.06
Ratio of salary after 15 years' experience to GDP per capita (1999)	1.32	1.36	1.46	1.38

TABLE 5.7: TEACHERS' SALARIES AS A PERCENT OF PER CAPITA GDP FOR ARMENIA AND OECD

Sources: MOFE; tables D1.1a-1d, OECD (2001a).
[1] Calculations of salary as a percent of per capita GDP assume that teachers are paid for 12 months.

teachers of quality without raising salaries significantly. To prepare for this future, the sector must start reducing the size of the teaching force and increasing the salaries of those who remain.

To the extent that expected increases in pay affect retention, the vertical compression ratio can be used to assess incentives to stay. The vertical compression ratio is defined as the ratio of the average salary for the highest ranking members of a career (e.g., teachers or principals) to the average salary for entry-level members. Higher compression ratios suggest greater opportunity for salary growth over the individual's career and, ceteris paribus, represent greater incentives to stay in the sector. The vertical compression ratio for Armenia's teachers in 2001 was low: 1.08. In other words, more experience, education, and better examination scores buy a teacher, on average, only 8 percent more than those with less experience and education. By contrast, after 15 years of experience the average OECD teacher can expect a salary that is 36 percent higher than the one received at entry to the occupation.

How Efficient is Physical Capital?
School buildings (infrastructure) raise three main efficiency issues. Is the need for costly school replacement or major rehabilitation being minimized through preventive maintenance? Do average student/classroom ratios and student/school ratios allow for reasonable economies of scale? Is the sector altering the supply of premises to conform to changes in enrolments?

Maintenance. As already discussed, the detailed budgets for different levels and types of schooling show no resources for maintenance. Although even OECD countries often defer maintenance, it is a costly practice. Neglecting school maintenance amounts to borrowing from the future at exorbitant interest rates because it will cost much more to repair (or replace) schools or equipment in the future than it would to repair them in the present.

Economies of scale. Armenia is not using its physical plant efficiently as indicated by measures of the intensity of the use of its schools and school sizes.

Class sizes[80] in general education schools are fairly reasonable, even in rural schools, although they certainly could be larger without endangering learning. Average class sizes in general educa-

---

80. A class is defined as a group of students that study together in a classroom.

tion and boarding schools do not vary across time, and class sizes for secondary VET programs that started in 2001 approximate those for the VET programs in the earlier part of the time period. Their stability signals the use of norms for organizing instruction and budgeting. Colleges have relatively low class sizes—around 13 and dipping as low as 9 in 1999.

Since some classes meet in double or triple shifts, the number of *classes* is not equivalent to the number of *classrooms*. However, in 2000 the vast majority of classes (89 percent) were single shift, 10.3 percent being double shift and 0.6 percent triple shift. Although triple shift classes are pedagogically bad practice, the evidence is that Armenia is not using its classrooms intensively. The percent of students in small communities and isolated areas defines the limits to more intensive use of classrooms, but Government should use its urban classrooms more intensively. Double shifts raise maintenance costs because the school is being used more intensively. However, it reduces other overhead costs as well as the need to build new schools as Armenia experiences what the economics of location predicts it will experience: the gradual emptying of small villages and a greater aggregation of its population in urban centers.

About a fifth of Armenia's general education schools are very small (less than 100 students), and about 50 percent have fewer than 300 students enrolled and serve only about 16 percent of the total students. Small schools are less efficient in terms of student learning. PISA shows a nonlinear relationship between student learning performance and school size (OECD 2001b). It shows increasing student performance as school size *increases* up to 1000 students, performance declining above 1000 students. The basis for this relationship is not clear. However, it can be plausibly hypothesized that on average small schools are less able to attract higher quality teachers and have fewer educational resources available for students. PISA found that both of these factors affect student learning.

As Table 5.8 shows, small schools are also inefficient in terms of input use. Schools with under 100 students have low economies of scale—very low student/teacher ratios and very low student/non-teaching staff ratios—and average unit costs that are more than double the unit costs of schools with 100–300 students. Although economies of scale continue to increase and unit costs to decrease as school size increases, the rate at which economies of scale improve and unit costs decline slows once school size reaches 300 or more students.

Opportunities to improve economies of scale are affected by the number of schools that are in rural areas. In 2001 over 60 percent of Armenia's general education schools were rural schools. They served about 40 percent of the students enrolled. Although it is not known what share of

TABLE 5.8: DISTRIBUTION OF GENERAL EDUCATION SCHOOLS BY SIZE AND RESOURCE USE IN 2001

School Size	Percent of Total Schools	Percent of Total Students	Average Unit Costs (drams)	Student/Teacher Ratio	Student/Non-Teaching Ratio
<100	19.8	2.9	82,935	4.2	5.5
100–300	27.2	13.4	36,226	9.2	12.9
300–500	18.8	19.5	29,180	11.5	18.4
500–700	16.3	23.3	26,865	12.6	22.8
700–900	10.5	20.0	25,044	13.0	25.0
900–1200	5.2	14.1	23,401	13.3	28.2
>1200	2.3	6.7	23,401	13.3	28.2
Total Percent/ Average	100.0	100.0	37,930	11.3	19.5

Source: Ministry of Finance and Economy.

rural schools can realistically be consolidated, Government should vigorously pursue consolidation wherever possible. On all indicators of resource use, rural schools are significantly less efficient than urban ones.

The state system has a large number of tertiary institutions for such a small country—96 institutions in 2001, 19 of these being universities. As discussed later, the reason seems to be that almost all institutions are restricted to one or two faculties. The student/school ratio is reasonable for universities; but it is bad for colleges—about 373 students per institution.

Resizing the physical plant to accommodate changes in absolute numbers of enrolments. Buildings are "lumpy" capital. The stock of schools cannot shrink and expand rapidly in response to changes in demand. Between 1997 and 2002, different levels and types of education adjusted in different ways to changes in enrolments. Armenia is not resizing the physical plant for *general education* to accommodate changes in enrolment numbers. The number of general schools *increased* while the number of students *decreased*. The number of extra-curricular institutions remained constant, but the number of students in 2002 was about half the number in 1997. Student/school ratios for other types and levels of education show improved ratios because enrolments numbers increased, not because Government reduced the number of institutions.

Is Armenian Education Internally Efficient?

Average time to completion (repetition), rates of non-completion (dropout rates), and absenteeism among enrollees determine the internal efficiency of the system at all of its levels.

Repetition and drop-out rates. Although repetition rates are thought to be low, systematic data on them do not exist.[81] The data on dropouts seem more accurate than in most countries since exit from a school is not equated with exit from education. In 2000 about 5 percent of those enrolled in general education exited their schools, but only about 0.5 percent of the total enrollees seem to have been true dropouts for reasons of illness, disability, poverty, or unspecified reasons. Over 50 percent of the exits changed schools. About 36 percent left the Republic of Armenia and may or may not have enrolled in schools in the countries to which their parents moved.

School attendance. Even if enrolled, students may not attend school. Attendance rates seem to have declined in some ECA countries. In Armenia 1.7 percent of those enrolled across the levels of education had missed a month or more of schooling during the school year. The percent was lowest for primary school (grades 1–8)—1.5 percent and for university—1.9 percent. It was highest for those enrolled in college (6.2 percent). If these data are approximately valid, attendance does not seem to be a major problem for Armenian children.

External Efficiency: How Well is the Sector Building Human Capital?

The external efficiency of an education system is measured by how well it positions its graduates to obtain jobs at wages that support families. Implicit in this statement is that education systems have to adjust to labor supply/demand shifts to become or remain externally efficient. Also implicit is that external efficiency is contextual; it is not a constant under all conditions. The nature of a country's labor demand and its political and civic society define the skills and knowledge—what is often called the "educational quality"—that its educational system needs to deliver. In Armenia's case an education system that positions its graduates to navigate a modern, market-based economy and open society is needed.

Armenia does not know the learning performance of its general education students relative to students in other countries with which Armenia will eventually compete and cooperate. Unlike many of its neighbors in the region, Armenia has not participated in any of several international

---

81. One study reported a repetition rate of 0.02 percent in the primary grades and 2 percent in lower secondary education, but the source of these data is not clear (United Nations Development Program, 2001).

assessments of learning, especially two assessments that measure the skills and knowledge required by modern workplaces: OECD's *Program for International Student Assessment* (PISA)[82] and OECD's *International Adult Literacy Survey* (IALS).[83]

Performance of ECA countries on international assessments. In the absence of international comparative data for Armenia, it is important to examine the performance of those ECA countries that did participate in one or more of the international assessments. Their performances may indicate how Armenian students would have performed on these assessments. Countries of the region started the transition with somewhat similar education systems, even though these are now diverging from one another.

Table 5.9 shows the rank orders of the ECA countries that participated in PISA among all participating 31 OECD, ECA, and other countries. This table shows that on average participating ECA countries scored below the OECD average on all three scales: reading literacy, mathematics, and scientific literacy.

TABLE 5.9: RANK ORDER OF ECA PARTICIPANTS FOR PISA, RELATIVE TO 31 COUNTRIES

Region and Country	Rank on Combined Reading Literacy Scale	Rank on Mathematics Literacy Scale	Rank on Scientific Literacy Scale
Czech Republic	19	18	11
Hungary	23	21	15
Latvia	28	25	27
Poland	24	24	21
Russian Federation	27	22	26

Source: OECD, 2001b.

On the IALS three of the four ECA countries had about 75 percent of 16–65 year old workers who tested at levels 1 and 2 on all three scales.[84] Levels 1 and 2 predict that the individual will have difficulty functioning in a modern workplace. Analyses of IALS data for all participating countries found that achieving the literacy levels required in modern workplaces (level 3 and above) was associated with having completed upper secondary education. However, the differences between the tested skills of adults in Hungary, Poland, and Slovenia versus those of Czech adults and adults

in participating OECD countries cannot be attributed to the quantity of education that low per-
forming ECA populations complete.

The external efficiency of the tertiary system is particularly troubling. In *The Global Competitiveness* Report (2001), Schwab, Porter, and Sachs distinguish three stages of economic
development:

- Factor driven growth: get factor markets working properly to mobilize land, labor, and capital. At this stage the economic focus is natural resource extraction, assembly, labor-intensive
  manufacturing. The primary sector is dominant.
- Investment-driven growth: Attract foreign direct investment and imported technology
  to exploit land, labor, and capital and to begin to link the national economy with the
  global economy. The economic focus is manufacturing and outsourced service exports.
  The secondary sector is dominant.
- Innovation-driven growth: Generate high rate of innovation and adaptation and commer-
  cialization of new technologies. The economic focus is innovative products and services at
  the global technology frontier. The tertiary sector is dominant.

Most of Armenia's economic activity lies in the first two stages of growth. However, its economic future lies in innovation-driven growth. The tertiary sector and its research institutes are
key to spurring this kind of growth. For them to serve this function, *flexibility* for students,
faculty, and researchers is critical. *Quality standards* linked to international standards—especially
in the sciences and social sciences—are critical. The current tertiary system is highly rigid and has
no quality assurance linked to international standards.

The lack of flexibility for students shows up in a number of ways. Entry is not into an institution, but into a faculty within an institution. To enter a university, the applicant can participate in
a competition for up to four free and four fee-based fields of study in one or several universities of
only one city. To enter a college, the applicant can choose only one field of study. If the applicant
fails to gain entry into the chosen field of study, he/she can enter a related program/field of study,
provided that vacant slots are available at the time.

Once enrolled, students are in an intellectual strait-jacket. They cannot take electives. They are
restricted to courses within their faculty, being unable to seek out more relevant or higher quality
courses in other faculties within the institution. Students can change their fields of study within the
same institution if the rector gives permission. Students can change a field of study by transferring
into another institution if the rectors of both institutions agree, but usually a state-financed student
has to shift to the fee-based system.

Most tertiary institutions consist de facto of one or two faculties. Except for Yerevan State
University, most of the 19 universities seem to be narrowly focused—for example, the Yerevan
State Institute of Architecture and Construction, the Yerevan State Institute of Economy, the
Yerevan State Medical University, or the Armenian State Agricultural Academy. Colleges seem seg-
mented into a large number of narrow programs of study that imply a holdover from the days of
the Soviet planned economy.

How Much Time Do Armenian Students Spend in Education?

Trends in gross enrolment rates[85] are a country's early warning system for its human capital.
Table 5.10 shows the estimated gross enrolment rates by level of education. In basic education
(grades 1–8), enrolment rates seem to be trending downwards, although, unlike some other countries in ECA, not dramatically. About 10 percent of the population of basic education ages is

---

85. Gross enrolment rates are defined as total enrolments at a given level of education—for example, secondary education, divided by the population at the ages relevant to that level.

TABLE 5.10: ARMENIA'S GROSS ENROLMENT RATES AND OECD NET ENROLMENT RATES

Grade	1990–91	1996–97	1997–98	1998–99	1999–00	2000–01	2001–02
Primary education							
1	90.2	101.9	96.7	92.5	89.2	92.7	110.2
2	92.6	98.2	100.7	95.9	89.2	83.6	88.7
3	84.9	94.2	98.1	100.8	93.8	83.9	84.1
4	39.2	94.1	94.5	98.4	104.1	87.3	85.7
5	84.6	89.0	93.1	94.5	98.1	91.5	89.2
6	90.6	102.	88.6	93.4	96.8	90.0	94.3
7	94.4	96.5	102.4	88.7	95.3	85.5	91.5
8	92.7	91.8	94.1	100.8	89.7	83.9	88.0
Average (7–14 years of age, grades 1–8)	83.7	96.1	96.0	95.6	94.5	87.3	91.5
OECD (5–14years of age))					97.7		
Secondary education including VET[1] (15–16 years of age)							
9	88.6	71.8	74.7	79.4	80.2	71.9	76.1
10	69.4	63.5	67.3	70.5	70.9	74.8	67.8
Average (15–16 years of age)	79.0	67.6	71.0	75.0	75.5	69.4	72.0
11[2]	66.5						
OECD (15–19 years of age)					76.9		
Tertiary Education[3]							
Without retraining students (17–24 years of age)	N.A.	N.A.	20.1	21.7	21.9	21.0	22.2
With retraining students (17–24 years of age)	N.A.	N.A.	22.3	24.4	25.3	24.1	26.5
OECD (20–29 years of age)					20.7		
Expected years of education: Armenia							
Preschool: 50 percent GER					11.2		
Preschool: 25 percent GER					10.7		
Preschool: 20 percent GER					10.6		
Preschool: 15 percent GER					10.5		
Expected years of education: OECD					16.7		

[1] For most of this time period secondary VET programs were three year programs (grades 9–11); academic secondary programs, only two year programs (grades 9 and 10). VET students in grade 11 were distributed to grades 9 and 10 and the population numbers for the age group 15–16 years used to calculate gross enrolment rates. Using the 15–17 age cohort overlaps with the appropriate tertiary age cohort of 17–24.
[2] Until 1987–1988 general education was 11, not 10, years; 1990–91 was the last year of the 11 year policy.
[3] The 17–24 year old age cohort was used to calculate tertiary gross enrolment rates.
Source: Armenia data: NSS and staff estimates; OECD data: tables C1.1 and C1.2, OECD, 2001a.

apparently not enrolled in school. There are no clear trends for secondary education. Enrolments are not trending up, but neither are they trending down. At the same time, depending on grade, by 2001–02 a quarter to a third of the age relevant cohort was not enrolled at this level. If enrollees in the retraining institutions are excluded, tertiary gross enrolment rates are essentially flat. If students in the retraining institutions are included, tertiary gross enrolment rates are trending upwards.

School expectancy. The school expectancy for the average 5-year-old child is defined as the average duration of formal education in which he/she can expect to enroll over his or her lifetime. As table 5.10 shows, in 1999–2000 the average five year old Armenian child could expect to complete between 10.5 and 11.2 years of education over his/her lifetime, depending on assumptions about preschool enrolment rates. The average OECD five year old in 1999 could expect to complete 16.7 years of formal education over his/her lifetime.[86] In other words, the average five year old Armenian child could expect to complete between 5.5 and 6.2 fewer years of education than the average five year old OECD child. Armenia's school expectancy rates are also below those of selected other countries in the region, such as the Czech Republic (14.4 years), Hungary (13.9 years), or Poland (14.8 years).

In 2001 Armenia increased compulsory basic education from grades 1–8 to grades 1–9, shifting the grades for upper secondary from 9–10 to 10–11. However, for most OECD countries the pre-tertiary grade span is 1–12. Thus, even with the 2001 shift, Armenian students who graduate from upper secondary education will have completed a year less of education. At the same time, Armenia has high gross enrolment rates for its 17–24 year olds—those apt to be in tertiary education, and access to tertiary education, especially to colleges, are not as constrained as in many ECA countries.

Time on task. Relative to the average for OECD countries, Armenian schools have fewer hours of mandatory instructional time[87] per year, although the gaps between Armenia and the OECD countries are not great. At grade 6, Armenia has 765 mandatory instructional hours per year, in contrast to OECD countries that have an average of 902 annual hours. At grade 7 Armenia has 842 annual instructional hours; the OECD, an average of 947 hours. At grade 8 Armenia has 867 annual instructional hours; the OECD, 951 annual hours.

Equity of Education

Unfair learning opportunities matter because individual human capital influences future employment opportunities and wages. Regardless of overall enrolment rates, do children from different groups have equal access to the various levels of education?

Access by Poverty, Location, and Gender

The story on the access of poor children to education is one of good news and bad news. The bad news is that the poorest quintile has noticeably lower total enrolment rates for all age groups than the top four quintiles. (See Table 5.11.) The good news is that for the 7–14 year old age group (primary education, grades 1–8), the top four quintiles have virtually the same enrolment rates. Although the top four quintiles differ in their enrolment rates for upper secondary education (ages 15–17), their tertiary enrolment rates (ages 18–25) are similar except for a jump for the wealthiest quintile. Thus far, Armenia is protecting equity better than some of its regional neighbors.

The data show only a very modest effect of location (urban or rural) on enrolments at the primary level (7–14 years of age), but a significant

TABLE 5.11: GROSS ENROLMENT RATES BY AGE AND CONSUMPTION QUINTILE			
Consumption Quintile	**Age in Years**		
	7–14	**15–17**	**18–25**
Poorest	0.93	0.63	0.11
2	0.98	0.70	0.18
3	0.98	0.73	0.18
4	0.98	0.80	0.19
5	0.98	0.78	0.24

Source: ISLS 1998/99.

86. For OECD countries school expectancy is calculated by adding the net enrolment percentages for each single year of age from the age of five onwards. In the case of Armenia enrolment rates are also gross, not net. Since we do not have preschool enrolment rates, school expectancy is estimated for different assumed rates.

87. An instructional hour is 60 minutes, not a class period.

interaction effect between consumption quintile and residential location (urban or rural) for the age groups in secondary and tertiary education. All consumption quintiles in rural areas are less apt to be enrolled than their quintile counterparts in urban areas at these two levels of education. The effects of location are particularly pronounced at the tertiary level, where enrolment rates in urban areas are anywhere from double to seven times the rates for students from rural areas, depending on consumption quintile.

There are no significant gender differences in enrolments in general education. From grade 5 the gender enrolment ratios slightly favor girls.

Does Government Finance Education in Ways that Protect the Poor?

Is public finance distributed evenly across the country's consumption quintiles? Table 5.12 shows that, in general, consumption quintile and percent of public expenditures spent on education increase together. Except for secondary vocational/technical education, the poor capture less public money at all levels, especially at the tertiary level.

Tables 5.11–12 showed that the poorest quintile has significantly lower tertiary enrolment rates than the other quintiles and only 46 percent of the wealthiest quintile. Although all quintiles in rural areas have much lower tertiary enrolment rates, tertiary enrolment rates of the poorest rural quintile are only 15 percent of those of the wealthiest rural quintile.

Two main factors underlie the low tertiary enrolment rates of the poorest quintile. First, opportunity costs of tertiary education are higher for children from poor families. Second, access to Armenia's tertiary system is quite open legally. Academic secondary graduates, secondary VET graduates, or college graduates can apply to enter a university. Eighth grade graduates, academic secondary graduates, or secondary VET graduates can apply to enter a college, although 8th grade graduates are restricted to a limited number of programs. However, in practice, relative to secondary academic graduates, graduates of secondary VET are much less apt to apply to university and less apt to gain admission if they apply, the success rate for VET graduates being 30 percent in contrast to the 70 percent rate for academic graduates. Since children from poorer families, especially from the poorest quintile, are much more apt to graduate from the secondary VET track than children from the wealthier quintiles, their curricular path at the secondary level reduces their chances of succeeding in the entrance examinations for tertiary education, especially for universities.

TABLE 5.12: DISTRIBUTION OF PUBLIC EXPENDITURES ON EDUCATION BY CONSUMPTION QUINTILES[1]

Level of Education	Percent of public expenditure captured by consumption quintile					Total Budget (billion dram)	Percent
	Poorest	2	3	4	5		
Primary (grades 1–8)	15.1	18.1	21.2	22.9	22.7	10.8	63.2
Secondary (9–10)	15.4	17.3	19.5	22.3	25.5	2.1	12.3
Vocational-Technical	23.7	20.8	26.8	11.6	17.0	1.6	9.1
Higher Education	6.3	27.5	19.0	24.6	225	2.6	15.3
Total	15.2	18.8	21.1	22.3	22.5	17.0	100.0

Note: Per student expenditure was calculated using enrolment data provided by the NSS and budget data provided by the MOFE. For use in this study, the following line items were dropped from the budget: Maintenance of evening and distance education schools, Realization of Olympiads of pupils, Out of school education, and Additional education expenditures related to libraries.

[1] This analysis excludes all students in private schools and in fee-paying public institutions.

Source: ILCS 1998/99.

If poor students enroll, they command a reasonable share of the state-financed "seats"—wealthier quintiles do not monopolize the state-funded slots at the tertiary level.[88] (See Table 5.13.) Relative to the wealthiest quintile, students from the poorest quintile have a slightly larger percent of state-funded slots, with those from the second poorest quintile exceeding all other quintiles in state-funded slots. The fact that significantly less public financing goes to the poorest students at the tertiary level is more a function of their low enrolment rates at this level than of their financing arrangement if enrolled.

TABLE 5.13: TERTIARY ENROLMENTS BY TYPE OF FINANCING ARRANGEMENT AND CONSUMPTION QUINTILE

Quintile	Tertiary Enrolments by Type Financing Arrangement (percent)			
	State Free	State Fee-Paying	Private	Data Not Available
Poorest	41.7	41.7	10.4	6.3
2	58.6	22.9	15.7	2.9
3	44.4	39.7	14.3	1.6
4	47.1	33.8	17.6	1.5
5	37.8	38.9	20.0	3.3

Source: ILCS (1998/99).

Conclusions and Policy Recommendations

The preceding analysis establishes the basis for a number of possible recommendations. However, its focus is on just four recommendations: more money for the sector, significantly improved efficiencies, a major overhaul of the tertiary system, and reducing the costs and increasing the quality of secondary VET. These recommendations implicate a number of players in addition to the MoES: the MoF, stakeholders for the sector, donors, and the international financial institutions, including the IMF and World Bank. The MoES cannot achieve these objectives alone.

Increase Public Financing of Education to Four Percent of GDP in Five Years

Public expenditure on education as a percent of GDP is about half that of the average OECD country and among the lowest in the ECA region. Private expenditures for education already slightly exceed the average for OECD countries. The sector is running arrears and is failing to fund or is under-funding basic inputs to the sector. In addition, education policymakers hope to modernize the education system in response to the economy's emerging demand for different skills. However, although international credits and grants can pay for some of the transition costs associated with modernization, the sector will need additional budget to sustain these initiatives.

The GOA now spends less than three percent of GDP on education. Although the public purse is small, raising this percent to four percent by 2007 should be feasible, particularly if education policymakers aggressively attack the serious inefficiencies in the sector.

The GOA must spend more on education, and the education sector must focus on increasing the sector's efficiency. Improved efficiency targets can be agreed upon in the context of a medium term expenditure framework. Savings accruing from a more efficient use of capital and labor can be used downstream to finance the transition costs of securing greater efficiency and ultimately to help offset increased funding of the sector.

---

88. Of those enrolled at the tertiary level, ISLS asks if the respondent is enrolled free in state institution, pays a fee in a state institution, or is enrolled in a private institution.

Added financing for the sector should be used in some ways and not in others. *Use increased financing* first on: 1) under-funded inputs to grades 1–11 that demonstrably affect learning or reduce future costs (e.g., preventive maintenance), and 2) raising the enrolment rates of children from the poorest quintile in grades 1–11.

The sector is not funding maintenance that prevents future expensive structural problems. It is under-funding or not funding inputs that PISA shows affect student learning, such as the availability of educational resources *that students use*. Children from the poorest consumption quintile enroll at lower rates at each level of education. Five year targets for improving poor children's enrolment rates should be set. How supply and demand factors combine to produce these lower rates is now unknown, but is knowable. These factors should be the basis for targeted interventions to increase enrolment rates.

Do not use additional financing on tertiary education (see discussion below) or to increase teachers' salaries beyond the average of the public sector wage *until* crucial analyses and policies are in place.

The sector's teaching and non-teaching labor force is overstaffed and accounts for the bulk of public costs at all levels of education. Teachers have minimal financial incentives to improve their performance or to stay in the sector. They work significantly fewer hours than other public sector employees and have lower instructional workloads than the average for OECD countries. The sector apparently does not have clear performance standards for hiring and retaining teachers and therefore has no basis for maximizing on quality.[89] These standards should be set relative to what Armenia wants out of its education system, but this public discourse has yet to occur. Apparently the sector does conduct routine supply and demand studies to determine the pay required to attract and keep good teachers. It does not seem to be thinking through optimal uses of complements to teachers that can increase their effectiveness, such as libraries or laboratories.

These realities argue for a revision of the policy framework governing the sector's labor force. For maximum effect, these policies have to reinforce each other relative to selected objectives. Although teachers' salaries should be maintained at the level of the average public sector wage, starting salaries should not be raised to the OECD standards of per capita GDP until a policy framework that rationalizes the management of the labor force is in place.

Aggressively Attack the Serious Inefficiencies in the System

Labor and capital are the major inputs to any education system. In general, Armenia's student/teacher ratios are appalling, even in urban schools. Ratios in general education are *half* what PISA shows to be optimal ratios in terms of learning outcomes, let alone in efficiency terms. Armenia's use of non-teaching staff is excessive. It has more small general education schools that are inefficient and less likely to support quality education than are warranted by any arguments about rural villages and towns. It is under-utilizing its urban schools in terms of double shift possibilities.

The leadership of the sector has to get serious about these inefficiencies *now* and remain serious as enrolments decline. The current inefficiencies will only get worse as the numbers of Armenia's 7–16 year olds decline by a projected 43 percent between 2000 and 2015. It has been shown that moving toward OECD's demographic structure would, all else equal, lower costs. However, realizing these savings requires Government to pursue an aggressive strategy to adjust the size of its labor force and to close and consolidate schools.

---

89. PISA shows that student performance is higher in schools with higher proportions of teachers that have specialized training in the subjects that they teach (OECD 2001b). Again, these data have to be interpreted carefully. Although the analysis of these data controlled for the socio-economic status of the student's family, these controls are always imperfect. It is possible that better educated teachers teach at schools with students from higher socio-economic families. Given the powerful effect of family background on student performance, it may be this factor that accounts at least in part for the correlation between teacher quality and student performance.

The MOFE, donors, and international financial institutions also have to get serious about inefficiencies, linking financing to efficiency gains and giving the MoES "cover" in implementing an aggressive efficiency strategy. The MoES bears the political costs of downsizing the labor force and consolidating classes and schools.

In 2001 Perkins and Yemtsov (2001) showed the fiscal implications of alternative efficiency reforms. Those analyses and options are entirely germane today and represent strategies that the MoES can use. The sector needs a current and multivariate school mapping database to identify possibilities for consolidating schools, consolidating classrooms, reducing staffing, and introducing multi-grade teaching. Since it often costs money to save money, the tradeoffs between initial costs and expected savings must be analyzed to see if the strategy ultimately saves money. For example, numerous small rural schools are inefficient. However, relative to the costs of the road infrastructure and transport required to consolidate students into fewer schools with better economies of scale, it may be cheaper to maintain a large number of small schools.

As it prepares an efficiency strategy, the sector has to build consensus among all stakeholders about the need for and payoffs from implementing an efficiency strategy. Unfortunately, inefficiencies in the Armenian system coincide with demographics that argue for shrinking the system, at least over the medium term. The country is also running relatively high levels of unemployment.

Thus, the sector has to attend to the political economy of securing efficiencies. Efficiency reforms usually involve concentrated losses and diffuse benefits. When benefits are diffuse, beneficiaries are unlikely to mobilize for change, and losers are apt to organize against the change. Those likely to bear the costs include teachers' unions, villagers whose schools are being closed, parents who prefer small classes and low student/teacher ratios, and the MOES.

These factors suggest that compensating losers will be key to gaining efficiencies. Even if they cannot prevent the introduction of policies designed to increase efficiencies, uncompensated losers will attempt to circumvent or dissipate them during implementation. This evasiveness is why efficiency gains may be briefly realized, only to vanish with time—eventually losers find ways to minimize their losses. Incentives to pursue or acquiesce in efficiency measures can include:

- Reasonable layoff or early retirement packages for redundant staff;
- In the context of a good labor redeployment program, retraining of teachers who are already well educated and can be retrained for other professional services;
- A phasing in of broad competition for the provision of goods and non-teaching services;
- Free and reliable transport for students whose village schools have been closed;
- Flexibility for policymakers at different levels of government in allocating resources between different inputs; and
- Returning savings to the sector for reinvestment.

Radically Reform the Governance, Financing, and Quality Assurance of Tertiary Education

This paper did not focus on any one level of education. However, its analyses hint at fundamental problems in the tertiary system: its financing, efficiency, equity, and external efficiency. Framing a reform strategy will require a special analysis of tertiary education. Implementing it will require building a consensus among the key stakeholders on the way forward.

Role of the state. Whatever form the strategy takes, clearly the role of the state will have to change. At present tertiary institutions themselves and state seem to share governance of the system, but responsibilities seem tangled and unclear. For example, the ministry under which a university operates authorizes the establishment of a new faculty. It is recommended that the institutions themselves be responsible for their own governance. De facto, the state should get out of the business of providing tertiary education.

The state role should be restricted to financing, regulation, and information. Financing should be used to protect access of the poor to higher education and to provide fiscal incentives for institutions to operate in ways defined through transparent processes as in the national interest—e.g., establishing centers of excellence in interactive technology. Regulation should be as light-handed as possible. Information should focus on disseminating the results of quality assessments of different institutions' faculties and instructional programs in order to give customers of the system a more informed basis for choice.

Financing. Tertiary institutions have three sources of funds: state funding, student fees, and donor and private contributions. Trends indicate that tertiary education is gradually becoming privatized. However, the state still allocates free places to institutions by field of study, a policy that involves some version of manpower planning implemented in non-transparent ways. It is recommended that "seats" at all state institutions become fee-based, with state scholarships being targeted on good students from poor families to defray their tuition costs. A significant share of state money goes to the wealthier quintiles.

It is further recommended that the state get out of the business of allocating free slots to colleges and universities by field of study, with students matching themselves to these slots at an institution and for a given field of study. Students should receive scholarships by virtue of their merit and family income status and make their own selections of institution and field of study.

Although there are public records of estimated total revenues for tertiary institutions, how this money is spent is known only for state funding. It is recommended that tertiary institutions submit to the Ministry and later start publish annual budget reports on their expenditures by source of financing and budget category. Without knowing how each institution's total resources are being spent, it is impossible to judge the fiscal health of this level of education.

Efficiency. A full analysis of the efficiency of the universities and colleges is recommended. What is the etiology of inefficiencies at this level? For example, why are student/teacher and student/non-teaching ratios so appallingly low? Why do institutions seem to be splintered into small units?

In short, in the current system students, faculties, and institutions are organized into intellectual silos. However, the skills and knowledge required to fuel innovation-based growth emerge out of interdisciplinary discourse, exposure, and study. The Armenian tertiary system is now structured to prevent that discourse. It is recommended that:

- institutions merge to support a broader array of faculties;
- students be able to apply to multiple institutions, not to faculties; and
- students be able to take courses from different faculties within the university.

The tertiary system does not have credible quality assurance mechanisms. It is recommended that Armenia establish a small independent quality assurance council that organizes expert reviews of universities, faculties, and programs. Review teams should consist of Armenian experts and, in the sciences and social sciences, international experts. As the director of the R&D unit of a Croatian multi-national pharmaceutical said, "Science is not Croatian. It is international."

Reform Secondary VET to Increase its Market Relevance and Reduce Costs

Secondary VET has small enrolments, and, even with the elimination of scholarships and stipends, relatively high unit costs. Its graduates have very limited access to universities.

PISA shows that separating students into different types of schools and programs results in significant between-school variations in learning outcomes. In Austria discounting the differences between school and program types to which students are assigned reduces the between-school variation from 68 to 8 percent; in Belgium, from 76 to 25 percent; in Germany, from 75 to 10 percent; in Hungary, from 71 to 19 percent; and in Poland, from 67 to 14 percent.

In countries with differentiated program or school types, the clustering of students with particular socio-economic characteristics is greater than in systems where the curriculum does not vary significantly between schools. Students from poorer families tend to choose or be directed to programs or schools with less demanding study programs. This socio-economic clustering effect compounds the effects of less demanding programs. The impact of the overall social background of a school's intake on student performance tends to be greater than the impact of the individual student's socio-economic background. Thus, students from a lower socio-economic background attending schools in which the average socio-economic background is high tend to perform much better than when they are enrolled in a school with a below-average socio-economic intake.

Innovation-based economies cannot afford to discriminate between the head and the hand. Mass production economies accommodate considerable variation in the education and skill levels of workers, but knowledge economies are less tolerant of workers with low skills. To prevent the emergence of a group of youth who as adults will encounter employment and wage difficulties, Armenia will have to assure that all students leave secondary school competent in the foundation skills and higher order cognitive thinking skills.

It is recommended that Armenia rethink its secondary education program structure and content in light of the PISA results and the requirements of innovation-based economies. These results do not mean that all students have to go through academic curricula at the upper secondary levels. Vocational/technical programs can have substantial academic content. For the academically less inclined, instructional programs that *integrate* academic and vocational content are highly effective at achieving a quality education. For example, LaGuardia High School in New York City is organized around the repair of aircraft engines. In the context of learning something that real people do in the real world, students acquire the academic foundation skills and knowledge that position them for adult learning and adaptation. The students have to use mathematics, decode the complex manuals published by the manufacturers of different kinds of engines, and exercise diagnostic and problem-solving skills.

CHAPTER 6

PUBLIC EXPENDITURE IN THE HEALTH SECTOR

This Chapter starts with the description of major health outcomes that present evidence of a significant deterioration of Armenia's health system. It then provides an assessment of the financing of the publicly provided health services, which is followed by a more detailed discussion of the trends in different types of expenditures and budgeting problems. The available data on the level of budget expenditures, the incidence of off-budget public financing as well as out-of-pocket payments (particularly those made through informal mechanisms) are used to assess the potential impact of existing financing arrangements on health equity in Armenia.

Health Sector in Armenia: Outcomes, Resources, and Utilization

After independence in 1991, the Armenian health sector inherited a highly centralized system organized in line with the *Semashko* model. The population was guaranteed free medical assistance regardless of social status and had access to a comprehensive range of secondary and tertiary care. In this context, it has been found that quality did not comply with western standards and that informal gratuity payments were commonly expected in secondary and tertiary care (European Observatory, 2001).

The dramatic economic changes that Armenia went through after independence and during the early 90s had a significant impact on the health sector. As most FSU economies, the Republic of Armenia has experienced a significant decrease in the level of health expenditures, a deterioration of the health system and a worsening of the health status of the population. Budgetary spending on health plunged to close to 1 percent of GDP in the mid 1990s (1.4 percent in 1999), bringing the public health care sector near collapse. In addition, not only did the supply of health services deteriorate in terms of both quantity and quality, but the demand dropped too: the impoverished population increasingly could not afford health care services. Finally, the financial constraints were aggravated by other factors such as the effects of the 1988 earthquake and the influx of refugees due to the Nagorno-Karabakh conflict.

TABLE 6.1: HEALTH INDICATORS FOR ARMENIA AND COMPARABLE COUNTRIES

	GDP per capita PPP$ (current)	Health expenditure per capita (current US$) 1997	Birth crude rate (per 1,000 people)	Death rate, crude (per 1,000 people)	Life expectancy at birth (years) Female	Life expectancy at birth (years) Male	Physicians (per 1,000 people)	Mortality Rates Maternal (per 100,000 live births)	Mortality Rates Infant	Mortality Rates Under 5
Armenia	2,559	7(a)	11.2	6	77	71	3.2	35	15	17
Moldova	2,109	36	10.1	11	72	64	3.5		18	22
Georgia	2,664	16	8.7	9	77	69	4.4	70	17	21
Kyrgyz Republic	2,711	15	20.9	7	72	63	3.0	65	23	35
Azerbaijan	2,936	9	15.2	6	75	68	3.6	43	13	21
Kazakhstan	5,871	62	14.6	10	71	60	3.5	70	21	28
Russian Federation	8,377	133	8.8	15	72	59	4.2	50	16	19
Europe, Central Asia	6,794	123	12.2	11	74	64	3.1		20	25

(a) Per capita expenditures for Armenia were not provided in the WDI 2002 dataset, but estimated from the budgetary data (see Table 6.4 below).

Source: World Development Indicators 2002. Notes: All indicators correspond to the year 2000, unless indicated otherwise.

Health Outcomes

Health indicators for Armenia compare favorably to other countries with similar or even higher levels of income (Table 6.1). Armenia has the longest time expectancy, and infant and children mortality rates lower than their neighbors in the Caucasus (Georgia and Azerbaijan).[90] Maternal mortality remains below the average for the CIS but shows an upward trend since 1992 (WHO, 2002). Immunization rates are almost universal and the number of doctors per 1,000 population is around the regional average. The fact that per capita expenditures in health are the lowest in the region poses a puzzle about the relatively better-off health outcomes. That puzzle is partly explained by looking into two other dimensions over time: the evolution of the incidence of infectious diseases and the incidence of off-budget and private expenditures over time.

The Armenian epidemiological profile indicates that respiratory diseases represent about half of the first diagnosis in Armenia (Ministry of Health, 2000) but mortality due to respiratory diseases has been declining and is only 5 percent of the total mortality. Other chronic diseases—such as cardiovascular, neurological, neoplasm, and kidney illnesses—represent a relatively small fraction of the first health care contacts. Conversely, cardiovascular diseases represent 35 percent of the mortality for the population aged 0 to 64 in 1999. The incidence of infectious and parasitic diseases is less than 8 percent of cases, but evidenced a significant increase during the nineties. The increased incidence of malaria and tuberculosis in Armenia reflects—among other factors—the poorly funded health services during the nineties, particularly in preventive care (See Figures 6.1 and 6.2). Similar evidence was observed in other countries in the region such as Georgia, where the incidence of infectious and parasitic diseases increased dramatically to wipe out any gains before 1991 (World Bank, 2001e).

On the reproductive area, Armenia evidenced a relatively high abortion rate, inher-

---

90. Mortality rates based on the Demographic and Health Survey shows much higher infant and under 5 mortality rates for 1996–2000: 36 infants

FIGURE 6.1: INCIDENCE OF MALARIA

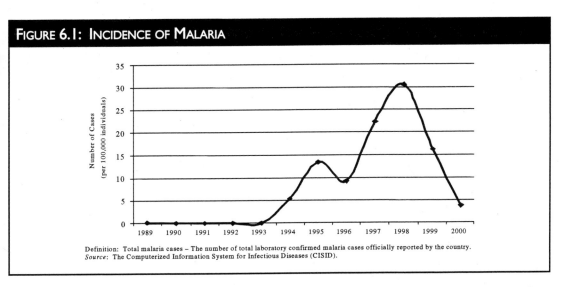

Definition: Total malaria cases – The number of total laboratory confirmed malaria cases officially reported by the country.
Source: The Computerized Information System for Infectious Diseases (CISID).

FIGURE 6.2: NUMBER OF TB CASES NOTIFIED

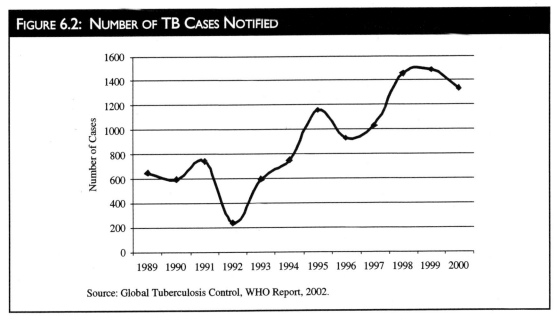

Source: Global Tuberculosis Control, WHO Report, 2002.

ited from the Soviet era when induced abortion was the main fertility control instrument (Abrahamyan and Avagyan, 2001). The abortion rate in Armenia is about 81 per 1,000 women and about 55 percent of the pregnancies ended up in induced abortions (although the registered number of abortions in 1999 was 395 per 1000 live births). Induced abortions in Armenia account for a significant proportion of maternal deaths (between 10 and 20 percent), representing a public health policy problem.

Health Resources and Utilization
The health system in Armenia evidenced a significant oversupply of staff and infrastructure in the past. The official health indicators on resources and utilization suffer from serious biases due to the distorted demographic estimates for Armenia. According to official estimates (collected by

per 1,000 and 39 children under 5 per 1,000. These estimates, however, represent improvements over the first part of the nineties (1991–1995) when infant and children mortality reached peaks of 50.5 and 55 per 1,000, respectively (National Statistical Service, Ministry of Health and ORC Macro, 2001).

the WHO, for instance), the number of doctors per 1,000 population is about 3.3 while adjusted estimates according to more realistic population data indicate about 4 (Table 6.2). Moreover, the trends are reversed: while the number of doctors (per thousand population) was declining according to official figures, it was actually increasing during the nineties. Even though there has been a decline in the absolute number of doctors over the nineties, the impact of emigration was relatively larger. The decline in the number of doctors, however, has been unequal across regions. Between 1997 and 1999, the decline in the overall number of doctors (a 3 percent drop) was mainly explained by the decline of doctors in Yerevan (by about 10 percent) compared to other cities (and regions) where no significant changes were observed. The existing oversupply of doctors during the early nineties, then, has not been reduced at all.

TABLE 6.2: ARMENIA: INPATIENT UTILIZATION AND HEALTH CARE PERSONNEL

	1990	1991	1992	1993	1994	1995	1996	1997	1998	1999
Official estimates										
Physicians per 1,000 pop.	3.9	3.7	3.6	3.4	3.1	3.0	3.1	3.4	3.4	3.3
Outpatient visits per 1,000 pop.	6.9	6.5	5.3	4.8	4.4	4.2	4.6	3.2	2.4	2.3
Hospital beds per 1,000 pop	9.1	8.5	8.4	8.2	7.8	7.6	7.1	6.8	6.7	6.2
Admissions per 1,000 pop	14.0	12.1	9.6	8.2	7.6	7.5	7.5	6.7	6.2	5.8
Average length of stay (days)	15.6	15.5	15.6	15.9	16.3	15.2	14.6	13.9	12.8	12.8
Occupancy rate (percent)	65.6	59.5	48.6	42.4	42.7	40.1	40.4	38.6	33.7	33.4
Adjusted estimates										
Physicians per 1,000 pop.	3.9	3.7	3.9	3.8	3.7	3.6	3.7	4.1	4.2	4.0
Outpatient visits per 1,000 pop.	6.9	6.6	5.8	5.5	5.2	5.0	5.5	3.9	2.9	2.8
Hospital beds per 1,000 pop	9.1	8.6	9.1	9.4	9.2	9.1	8.6	8.2	8.1	7.5
Admissions per 1,000 pop	14.0	12.1	10.4	9.3	9.0	8.9	9.1	8.0	7.5	7.0
Memo items:										
Official population (thousands)	3,520	3,575	3,649	3,722	3,753	3,763	3,782	3,793	3,798	3,803
Adjusted estimates (thousands)	3,515	3,557	3,368	3,261	3,160	3,147	3,150	3,138	3,127	3,129

Note: Official population estimates are obtained from the Statistical Office Annual Reports. "Adjusted estimates" shows the same indicators using the adjusted population estimates that are closer to the recent findings of the Census in November 2001. Also, see Annex 5.

Source: WHO (2001, 2002).

The supply of physical infrastructure was reduced in the nineties due to lack of maintenance, but compared to the shrink in population the oversupply persisted. The number of hospital beds per 1,000 individuals in 1999 dropped by 12 percent compared to 1991 (non-adjusted estimates), but the even more accurate figures from the Census 2001 would rather suggest a slight increase in the same period (18 percent).

The persistent (relative) oversupply of resources, however, was accompanied by a reduction in health care utilization during the nineties. Hospital admissions and outpatient visits per 1,000 population declined between 40 and 60 percent between 1991 and 1999. The decline, however, was more pronounced for outpatient care (57 percent) than for hospital admissions (42 percent). Since 1993, the decline in utilization rates for outpatient care has been twice the decline for inpatient care.

Out patient care in Armenia has been extremely low and declined during the nineties. In 1999, Armenia reported 2.8 contacts per person per year only, much lower than the CIS average (8.3). Armenia ranks as one of the lowest outpatient levels for all CIS and Central and European countries with the exception of Georgia (1.4) and Albania (1.6).[91] Until the mid-nineties, Armenia experi-

---

91. Although estimates for Georgia may suffer from the same downward biases due to migration as well, but corrected estimates are not likely to change the ranking between Georgia and Armenia.

enced a significant reduction in primary health care expenditures that caused a decrease in quality and an increased incidence of out-of-pocket payments to cover the costs of care. The reduction in quality and increased cost for patients explain part of the observed reduction in utilization. The newly FSU states (see Table 6.3) experienced declines in utilization between 1995 and 1998 (-3.9 percent) but it recovered during 1998–2000 (+3.6 percent). While Armenia did not gain in utilization rates, the decline during the 1998–2000 period was less pronounced than during the mid-nineties, partly reflecting the emphasis on primary health care as part of the ongoing reform (see the next section).

TABLE 6.3: CHANGE IN HEALTH CARE UTILIZATION 1995–2000
(per 1,000 individuals)

	Outpatient Contacts		Inpatient Admissions	
	1995–1998	1998–2000	1995–1998	1998–2000
Armenia	−43.7%	−10.5%	−17.1%	−18.1%
Azerbaijan	−15.5%	−16.7%	−25.6%	−5.3%
Belarus	10.5%	0.9%	16.7%	0.8%
Georgia	−54.4%	16.7%	−4.1%	−21.1%
Kazakhstan	−19.7%	12.3%	−8.9%	−4.3%
Kyrgyz Rep.	14.8%	−16.3%	−5.0%	−1.4%
Moldova	−1.2%	−21.7%	−11.4%	−25.1%
Russia	0.0%	3.3%	−3.0%	5.5%
Tajikistan	−5.6%	8.8%	−21.8%	−10.6%
Ukraine	−12.4%	4.7%	−12.3%	1.1%
Uzbekistan	6.0%	18.3%	−30.7%	3.2%
CEE average	0.9%	−3.7%	0.8%	5.8%
CIS average	−3.9%	3.6%	−6.8%	2.3%

Source: World Bank

Inpatient care (as officially measured) is also very low in Armenia compared to other CIS countries and experienced a rather steadier decline during the late nineties. After the collapse in utilization during the early and mid-nineties, most countries started recovering or slowed the decline in their utilization rates for inpatient care. Armenia_together with Georgia, Moldova and Tajikistan_are the few countries that continued their decline in the late nineties. The lower utilization and the poorer funding for hospital care explain also the decrease in occupancy rates and shorter lengths of stay since patients have to cover part of the costs (sometimes the larger part).

Additional evidence from household surveys indicate that the fraction of sick and injured individuals that sought (and received) health care declined from 37 percent in 1998/99 to 31 percent in 2001, while the fraction reporting sickness and injuries also declined. Overall, the number of surveyed individuals that sought health care declined by 20 percent according to the household surveys, corroborating the decline in the observed administrative utilization rates (Table 6.3). The composition of health care utilization also changed. In 1998/99, about 56 percent of those that sought health care went to a polyclinic while only 53 percent did in 2001. Hospitals, on the other hand, increased their market share from 28.6 percent of patients to 30.8 percent. Both data evidence the overall deterioration in utilization indicators and a slightly worse situation among ambulatory and polyclinic care.

Public Health Policies and the Reform Process
The strong emphasis on hospital care in the past, and the observed decline in utilization (mainly in primary health care) led the GOA to emphasize primary health care services as a means to provide better access to health care at costs consistent with the levels of funding in Armenia. In this context, the GOA has approached the reform process in the health sector with three major

concepts: (i) the optimization of the health care system; (ii) the privatization of health care facilities; and (iii) the introduction of medical insurance. In addition to these strategic guidelines, the GOA has developed a number of programs and policies to target specific health problems. Among these are: the National Environmental Health Action Plan of Armenia (NEHAP), tuberculosis control, malaria control, the Armenian-American ophthalmology program, Family medicine in the Primary Health Care, the National Response to HIV/AIDS, programs and strategies to improve child health and development, and programs and strategies to improve reproductive health.

In order to cover the health care needs of the vulnerable, demographic groups have a fee-waiver program for those individuals that qualify as vulnerable.[92] The program provides a basic health care package free of charge to those eligible individuals and for emergency cases. The basic package does not include drugs, which are to be covered directly by patients. The rest has to be earned from the patients.[93]

The optimization of the health care system was motivated by the oversupply of secondary and tertiary infrastructure and personnel (hospitals) as compared to primary health care resources in a context where health care demand and financing had been significantly reduced.[94] The objectives for the privatization of health care facilities were the improvement of health care financing through additional funds from the private sector (and the expected reduction of unofficial payments), the increase of the efficiency of the services provided, and the expansion of health care choices and quality of services.[95] An important component of the optimization process included the creation of a Basic Benefit Package (BBP), the publicly funded package that includes a list of services covered and populations that are eligible for coverage. The BBP constitutes the key element for contracting and budgeting purposes. Publicly funded services are not allowed to exceed 30 percent of the provider's total annual revenues.

The privatization involved actions regarding the status of health care providers in order to induce management decentralization and privatizations of some of the components of the system. Hospitals and polyclinics were converted into semi-private enterprises and the management of health care providers was decentralized. They were allowed to determine the prices of their services, choose the mix between medical and administrative staff, and accordingly allocate resources. Polyclinics were detached from their corresponding regional hospital. Since 1999, health care providers began to operate under contracting arrangements with the State Health Agency (SHA).[96] The creation of the SHA was part of the reform process where financing and delivery of health services were separated.

As part of the health sector optimization the GOA focused on enhancing primary health care services as a means to reduce the financial burden of the higher-cost hospitals. This process involved both the reorganization (and liquidation) of health care organizations and the gradual introduction of family doctors in primary health care using criteria such as number of beds and utilization rates per region. In 2001, pilot programs for optimization of the health sector were drafted for most regions.[97] In Kotaik, for example, a marz with a population of 325,000, the optimization

---

92. The vulnerable groups were defined following the standards of the Soviet system. In 2000, they included: disabled persons (according to three degrees of disability), war veterans, children under the age of 18 with one parent, orphans under the age of 18, disabled children under the age of 16, families with four or more children under the age of 18, families of war victims, victims of political repression, children of disabled parents, and victims of the Chernobyl disaster.

93. Medical care qualified by medical staff as "urgent." Anecdotal evidence, however, suggests that subjective qualification of "urgency" affects the incidence of health care interventions and subsidies, providing free services to those neither in emergency, nor in vulnerable groups (Kurchiyan, 1999; World Bank, 2000a).

94. *Concept of Optimisation of the Health Care System of the Republic of Armenia.* Ministry of Health website. 2002.

95. *Concept of the Strategy of Privatization of Health Care Facilities.* Ministry of Health. 2002.

96. Some pilot contracts were implemented in the last quarter of 1998.

97. Government Resolutions No. 128, 138, 341, 427, and 432 of 2001 approved the healthcare optimization programs for several regions of Armenia.

plan proposes a reduction in the number of beds from 740 to 485 given the low utilization level (about 30 percent).

Merging of health facilities is intended to reduce the duplication of services (such as pediatrics using X-ray services from the specialists' services). In the process, the number of doctors and other staff would be adjusted according to the needs of the serviced population and the new characteristics of the optimized infrastructure indicators.[98] The merging of the Abovian pediatrics and polyclinic facilities, for example, would reduce the current number of doctors from 73 (by January 2001) to between 25 and 28 family doctors offices. The lack of properly trained family doctors is still a problem for the restructuring process. The optimization plans, however, still do not have a clear proposal on the use of the (currently) idle physical resources.

On the last strategic element, the introduction of mandatory health insurance,[99] a more modest progress has been observed due to the economic conditions of the Armenian economy. Given the limited public resources for health, a mandatory health insurance system is intended to be funded through additional payroll taxes (general revenues) or redistributing from the existing payroll (such as redistributing from pensions). The large informal labor market in Armenia poses serious challenges for increasing the cost of labor and creating additional incentives to arrange informal contracts in labor markets.

Reforms in Organization of the Health Sector

The separation between health care provision and financing was effected through the establishment of the State Health Agency in 1998, responsible for purchasing services from providers through contractual mechanisms. Before this, most health care providers had nominal accountability to the local and regional administrations. The regional governments had a role of third-party payers in the health system, but in practice they only conformed to the planning and resource allocation decisions taken at the central level. Funding for the *marz* governments and their corresponding health expenditures were coming from the Ministry of Finance.

After 1998, the public budget for health care is disbursed to health care providers through contracts between the SHA and the providers (now, joint-stock companies). Those funds are directly transferred from the Ministry of Finance. The main tasks of the SHA are: (i) contracting health care providers for services in accordance with Basic Benefits Package; (ii) ensuring the target use of state financial resources and reimbursement of the health care providers; and, (iii) quality assurance.[100] The contractual arrangements between the SHA and the providers, however, are defined in terms of the health *services* that are provided using state property such as infrastructure and equipment. This represents an unclear arrangement since the SHA has limited ability to supervise the functioning of the contracted enterprises, and can only solve the "problems of the filed within the limits of its jurisdiction without violation of the independence of subordinate enterprises" according to the existing regulation.

Hospitals and other health care providers in Armenia have gone through a long reform process. Three major changes occurred in management and financing. In 1993, state health care institutions became state health enterprises, or semi-independent units that could generate their own revenues parallel to state budget financing. In 1995, hospitals and polyclinics were permitted to provide private services in addition to state funded ones, providing them additional autonomy with self-decision on staffing. These joint-stock companies, however, operate under the regulatory framework of private and commercial firms, representing a supervisory problem for the contracting agency (SHA) and the Ministry of Health.

---

98. Note that health care providers (including the optimised ones) have autonomy in their operational activities, such as staff hiring.

99. Concept of Introducing Medical Insurance in the Republic of Armenia. Ministry of Health, State Health Agency. Yerevan 2000.

100. The objectives are specified in the Government Resolution No. 593, 1998.

Despite the fact that practically all doctors and health institutions are *de facto* heavily involved in commercial delivery of health services, the development of the truly private health sector in Armenia is still underdeveloped. Creation of private hospitals and clinics is still very limited. A major reason for this is the existing regulation that does not allow for the establishment of non-profit health providers, and given the different tax status of profit and non-profit organizations, the private sector does not see for-profit health institutions as economically viable. The decline in demand for health services, and the already existing quasi-privatized market, make this market unattractive for private investment. The market for private doctors (particularly obstetrician/gyne-cologists) has been stable around 6 percent of those seeking health care.

Public Financing of Health Care

Budget allocations to the health sector are relatively low compared to other countries. Less than 2 percent of GDP is publicly budgeted for the health sector, even though it has improved from the dramatically low expenditures in 1997 (1.3 percent of GDP). The average for the CIS is close to 3 percent of GDP and Armenia ranks close to Azerbaijan (1.6) but better than Georgia (0.6).

Public health budgets have also evidenced significant variation during the last five years, reflecting the financing changes and the introduction of the SHA. In 1998, the GOA spent about ADM 13.7 billion (about US$27 million) that increased to a peak of AMD 21.6 billion (US$40 million) in 1999, representing 2.2 percent of GDP. The health sector budget increase in 1999 was explained by the increase in allocations to primary health and hospital care which jointly rose from more than ADM 10 billion in 1998 to almost ADM 18 billion. After the 1999 transition year, public funding returned to its historical levels: about US$30 million or 1.6 percent of GDP.

Budgeted public funding, however, is a relatively small fraction compared to other sources in Armenia, particularly those off-budget expenditures in the public sector. In contrast to the previous system, a range of international nongovernmental organizations work in Armenia to deliver humanitarian assistance and implement health programs. Most of these interventions are targeted to improve the existing infrastructure, provide training or deliver specific programs themselves.

Off budget funding has an increasingly important role in the health sector. Estimates based on a survey of international organizations including NGOs of the Armenian Diaspora (Table 6.4) indicate that off-budget funding in the health sector has been increasing over time from one-fourth

TABLE 6.4: ARMENIA PUBLIC EXPENDITURES IN HEALTH
Million Dram

	1997	1998	1999	2000	2001
Budget expenditures	10,089	13,687	21,555	16,019	17,815
Off-budget (donors)	3,512	4,395	10,616	7,740	16,128
Total	13,601	18,083	32,171	23,759	33,943
Memo item:					
- Off-budget share	25.8%	24.3%	33.0%	32.6%	47.5%
As percent of GDP (percent)					
Budget expenditures	1.3%	1.4%	2.2%	1.6%	1.6%
Off-budget (donors)	0.4%	0.5%	1.1%	0.7%	1.4%
Total	1.7%	1.9%	3.3%	2.3%	3.0%
Per capita US $ expenditures					
Budget expenditures	6.6	8.7	12.9	9.5	10.3
Off-budget (donors)	2.3	2.8	6.3	4.6	9.4
Total (Annual US$ per capita)	8.8	11.5	19.2	14.1	19.7

Note: "Budget expenditures" correspond to the actual expenditures for 1997–2001. "Off-budget (donors)" corresponds to estimates of donor assistance to the health sector and do not include training funds.
Source: MOFE, World Bank.

of total public expenditures in 1997–98 to one-third in 1999–2000, to even one-half in 2001. These estimates are consistent with those provided by other sources, that indicate that the proportion of off-budget funding in the public sector is close to 40 percent (WHO, 2002).

The increasing role of off-budgetary items poses additional difficulties for rationalization of the expenditure policy in the sector since these funds are not included in the budgeting process. If budget allocations are made on a per patient basis and off-budget funding varies significantly across regions and health care providers (because of the managers' different ability to raise these funds) the per capita allocation made on budgetary funds may end up in a very unequal allocation. The same distortions could occur across health programs.

Are government expenditures in health (budgeted and off-budgetary) reflecting the needs of the Armenian population? During the late nineties, Armenia observed an increase in its public health care budget from US$20.6 million in 1997 to US$32 million in 2001 (excluding off-budget items).

The Health Sector reform, the separation of financing and delivery activities and the strategic emphasis on polyclinics can be observed in the changes in budget allocations during the late nineties. The emphasis on polyclinics explicitly mentioned in the official policies has achieved some progress expressed in budgetary policies, but planned allocations indicate that this may not be the case in the future.

The increase in budgetary resources allowed an increase in specific budget lines such as primary and secondary health care. In addition, a slight reallocation towards primary health care was observed according to the policy objectives mentioned before. In 1997, budgetary allocation to primary health care (ambulatories and polyclinics) was about US$2.3 million (ADM 1.1 billion) but by the end of 2001 it was already more than US$7 million (ADM 3.9 bn). This absolute increase in polyclinics budget reflected also a relative increase within the health sector budget. Polyclinics almost doubled their share from 11.3 percent to 22 percent in the same period (Table 6.5).

Budgetary resources to hospitals also increased during the period but relatively less then polyclinics (although some reversal is detected lately). Hospital budget increased from US$12.5 to 17 million between 1997 and 2001, but despite this increase of 37 percent the share devoted to hospital care was reduced from 60 percent (between 1997 and 1999) to slightly more than 50 percent (between 2000 and 2001). Most of the drop in the share of hospital care occurred immediately

TABLE 6.5: BUDGETARY EXPENDITURE IN THE HEALTH SECTOR
Million Dram

	1997	1998	1999	2000	2001
1 State administration in health care	42	40	102	172	78
2 Hospitals	6,123	7,742	12,720	7,870	9,421
3 Polyclinics and Ambulatories	1,136	2,605	4,999	4,440	3,908
4 Other health care institutions and services	1,875	2,284	2,349	2,066	1,364
5 Hygienic antiepidemic service	667	735	702	708	866
6 Other programs	245	281	684	763	2,177
Total	10,089	13,687	21,555	16,019	17,815
Composition (percent)					
1 State administration in health care	0.4	0.3	0.5	1.1	0.4
2 Hospitals	60.7	56.6	59.0	49.1	52.9
3 Polyclinics and Ambulatories	11.3	19.0	23.2	27.7	21.9
4 Other health care institutions and services	18.6	16.7	10.9	12.9	7.7
5 Hygienic antiepidemic service	6.6	5.4	3.3	4.4	4.9
6 Other programs	2.4	2.1	3.2	4.8	12.2
Total	100.0	100.0	100.0	100.0	100.0

Source: MOFE.

after the reform period (1999). In 2000, hospital allocations were only 50 but were increased to 53 percent in 2001 and are planned to be 55 percent in 2002.

Despite the recent increase, the total level of public spending in the sector remains low. The existing reimbursement rates, established by the Government for service providers, do not allow them to recover their actual costs. For instance, it is estimated that in 2000, the reimbursement rate for the Vulnerable Population Program represented only 45 percent of the total cost. As a result, the providers' are basically forced to (informally) charge patients. This has strong implications for both the demand for health care and inequality in access to basic services.

Anomalies in Public Budgeting and Expenditures

Actual public expenditures are the result of a budgeting process that involves planning and approval by the National Assembly, revision of the planned budget, financing and final execution. If public expenditures follow the strategies and policies, the budgeting process should reflect those views and respect the planning stages in order to attain certain objectives. In Armenia, significant differences between planned and financed budgets that generate arrears evidence a substantial problem that breaks the link between policies and budgets (Table 6.6).

The GOA spends a larger fraction on hospital care than on polyclinics, reflecting a mismatch between the policy objective of enhancing polyclinics and the corresponding budget allocation. This relatively lower expenditure in primary care reflects the discrepancy between planned and financed budget and the resulting importance of arrears. Evidence from the budgetary plan, financing, and disbursement for 2000 indicates that a significant gap is observed between planned and financed budget for the whole health sector: only 50 percent of the 2000 health planned budget was financed, and despite a reduction in actual expenditures, the health sector accumulated arrears for 40 percent of the expenditures.

These discrepancies reflected in arrears, however, do not incidence different budgetary groups in the same fashion. Almost 80 percent of the administration budget is financed compared to only 48 percent in hospital care. Even worse, only 40 percent of the polyclinics planned budget is financed and polyclinics accumulated arrears for 61 percent of the actual expenditures in 2000.

TABLE 6.6: INSUFFICIENT FINANCING AND ARREARS, 2000
Thousand Dram

Subgroup N	Subgroups of budgetary expenditures operational classification	Annual Adjusted Plan	Financing	Actual Expenditures	Arrears	Financing as percent of Adjusted Plan	Arrears as percent of Actual Expenditure
01	Public Administration in Health	187,517	146,669	172,297	25,754	78.2%	14.9%
02	Hospital Medical Assistance	9,405,783	4,534,234	7,869,516	3,335,282	48.2%	42.4%
03	Primary medical care	4,350,000	1,729,510	4,440,113	2,710,603	39.8%	61.0%
04	Hygienic-epidemiological service	952,927	682,974	707,539	112,864	71.7%	16.0%
05	Other medical services and programs	4,787,877	2,570,319	2,829,136	288,308	53.7%	10.2%
	TOTAL HEALTH	19,684,104	9,663,705	16,018,601	6,472,811	49.1%	40.4%

Note: Item 05 corresponds to items 4 and 6 in the preceding Table.
Source: MOFE.

Institutional Weaknesses

Since the health care providers operate under the regulatory framework of private and commercial firms (as joint-stock companies), the contracts between the SHA and the providers constitute the key element in translating objectives into delivery (assuming those contracts reflect accurately the objectives and policies of the health sector). Contracts to be effective require regulatory framework and a compliance level that are not yet present in Armenia. If a central component of the contract is the *cost per patient*, the contracting agency (SHA) needs to properly assess the accuracy of such costs figures and the variation across levels of delivery (polyclinics, hospitals). The lack of proper reporting does not enable estimating expenditures by economic type such as payroll costs, recurrent expenditures (drugs, utility and materials), investments (equipment) and other expenditures. This poses further difficulties for expenditure planning and actually weakens a potential impact of the optimization plans.

In addition, health providers are receiving direct off-budget assistance from voluntary institutions and hence reducing their cost per patient. Those savings in the delivery of public programs, however, are not captured by the budget process and hence do not benefit the public budget. Neither the Ministry of Health nor the SHA have legal authority to financially supervise the operation of health care providers, leaving them with enough discretion to assess their own costs and capture the savings derived from off-budget contributions. A similar argument can be proposed regarding informal payments. A recent qualitative study on governance and institutions in the health sector has shown that doctors and providers execute enough discretion in the allocation of public programs that could be distorting for the main objectives of such programs. In particular, programs intended to provide free-of-charge health care for vulnerable population groups may end up funding health care for non-vulnerable groups (Kurchiyan, 1999; World Bank, 2000a).

Another problem mentioned in institutional reviews is the rigid structure of the contracts. The standardized contracting scheme that the SHA designed helped in facilitating the massive number of contracts to be signed. Since contract terms are not negotiated, providers end up with a dichotomous choice: sign or no contract. Moreover, given the low reimbursement rate for services delivered, some providers prefer not to participate in the contracting process. The inability of the SHA to properly reimburse the cost associated with specific treatments for targeted populations has forced providers to actually charge patients fees for services and materials in order to cover the costs.

Equity Impact of Public Health Expenditures: The Role of Out-of-pocket Payments

The combination of extremely limited public resources, poor budgetary practices and general lack of monitoring and evaluation has resulted in poor services, particularly for the poor. The incidence of out-of-pocket payments in the health sector and the spread of informal payments to medical and administrative staff have a strong link with health care utilization. About 91 percent of patients in Armenia reported making informal payments, the highest incidence among the countries surveyed in the Europe and Central Asia Region (Lewis, 2000). In 1998/99, out of pocket payments represented about 55 percent of total health care expenditures in Armenia (Table 6.7), almost twice the public budget for health care.

The relative share of households' contributions, however, has been declining over time. During the 2001 calendar year, it is estimated that Armenians spent about ADM 15 billion (or US$27 million), representing only 30 percent of national health expenditures. The decline in private participation in health care expenditures is partly explained by the persistent decline in health care utilization observed in both the administrative and survey data.

The role of out of pocket payments, however, is clearer from an equity perspective.[101] The patterns of health care utilization indicate that the poor face access and/or cost constraints when seeking

---

101. The following findings are drawn from the Armenia Poverty Update (World Bank, 2002b).

TABLE 6.7: ARMENIA NATIONAL EXPENDITURES IN HEALTH

Million ADM	Average 1998–1999	2001
Public expenditures (budget + off budget)	25,127	33,943
–Budget	17,621	17,815
–Off-budget (donors)	7,506	16,128
Private expenditures (households)	31,241	14,783
Total	56,368	48,726
Memo item: Share of private	55.4%	30.3%
In million US $		
Public expenditures (budget + off budget)	48.0	61.5
Private expenditures (households)	60.1	26.8
Total	108.1	88.2
As percent of GDP (percent)		
Public expenditures (budget + off budget)	2.6%	3.0%
Private expenditures (households)	3.2%	1.3%
Total	5.8%	4.2%
Per capita US $ expenditures		
Public expenditures (budget + off budget)	15.3	19.7
Private expenditures (households)	19.2	8.6
Total	34.6	28.3

Source: MOFE, World Bank.

health care. Only 26 percent of those reporting sickness in the bottom quintile received some type of health care, compared to more than 51 percent among those in the top quintile (Figure 6.3).

The differences in health care utilization are also reflected in the type of health care providers and the costs of services (Figure 6.4). Most of the sick individuals in the poorest quintile that sought health care did so in polyclinics (64 percent) and hospitals (28 percent). A very small fraction of the poor went to private doctors (3 percent). The share of users going to polyclinics decreases among the better-off households, probably reflecting poor quality of health care and access to other (better) facilities. Among the better-off households, about 8 percent of the patients sought health care with private doctors, the largest across all socioeconomic levels.

The poor were choosing polyclinics and hospitals partly because they were less likely to be charged there. The possibility to have the health services fees waived may have affected the patients' choice of providers. About 64 percent of the patients reported having paid for health care in 1998/99. Table 6.8 shows that the poor were less likely to pay for the services (about 40 percent), and the probability of paying was even lower in polyclinics (34 percent). This could be the result of the free-of-charge Basic Benefit Package (BBP). Although not specifically targeted to the poor, the BBP had certainly covered some of the poor (to the extent that "vulnerable" categories overlapped with poverty).[102]

The lower utilization of health care services among the poor and the choice of the cheapest providers result in a regressive incidence of private expenditures on health (as expected). The poorest population quintile spent less than 2 percent of the private health care expenditures in Armenia in 1998/99, while the top quintile was responsible for almost 80 percent. This inequality is reflected in very high concentration indices for different health care categories. This evidence indicates that Armenia has a market for privately provided health services among the better off, but that the poor require more public support.

---

102. A potential leakage of the fee-waiver program has been documented in Kurchiyan (1999) since better-off individuals could also have used the BBP if their cases were (improperly) "assessed" as an emergency.

FIGURE 6.3: HEALTH CARE UTILIZATION

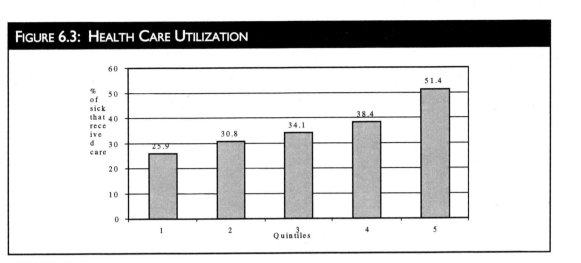

FIGURE 6.4: HEALTH CARE PROVIDERS BY QUINTILES

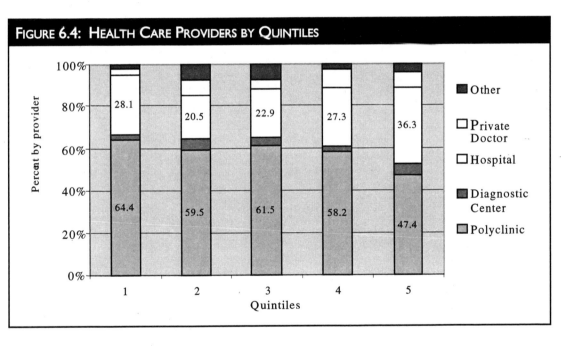

TABLE 6.8: PERCENT OF PATIENTS THAT PAID FOR SERVICES

Consumption Quintiles	Polyclinic	Diagnostic Center	Hospital	Private Doctor	Other	Total
1	34.0	75.0	44.4	80.0	33.3	39.4
2	50.4	18.2	68.3	64.3	40.0	52.5
3	58.5	71.4	66.7	100.0	14.3	59.6
4	75.8	100.0	77.4	76.2	40.0	76.1
5	69.7	100.0	87.5	69.0	6.7	75.3
Total	59.9	75.5	74.8	74.4	23.1	64.1

Source: World Bank (2002b).

Incidence of Public Expenditures

In this context, public expenditures should have a progressive role in terms of improving accessibility of services to the poor, but public spending on health has been regressive because wealthier households have better access and higher utilization of health facilities (Table 6.9). Individuals in the poorest quintile benefited only from 13 percent of total public expenditures, compared to those in the richest quintile that captured almost 40 percent. Even though the individuals in the poorest quintiles were more likely to choose polyclinics as their major health care provider, most of the patients in the polyclinics were from better-off households. This pattern is due to differences in the health care utilization across quintiles, since individuals from better-off households were more likely to seek health care once they were sick (they could afford to pay additional formal and informal charges). In 1999, the government spent about 5,000 billion drams on polyclinics. Patients from the poorest quintile captured only 780 billion compared to those in the richest quintile that captured about twice that amount (1,424 billion). This result is consistent with the observed health care utilization pattern: in the bottom quintile, 25.9 percent of those reporting having been sick went to the doctor, as opposed 51.4 percent in the top quintile. Incidence of public expenditures across health care providers shows that polyclinics are the least regressive intervention. The concentration index for polyclinics (0.114) is less than one-half than that of hospitals and diagnostic centers (0.276).

TABLE 6.9: DISTRIBUTION OF PUBLIC EXPENDITURES ON HEALTH, 1999
Million Dram

	Consumption quintiles					Total	Gini
	1	2	3	4	5		
Hospital	1,699	1,548	1,699	2,340	5,435	12,720	0.276
Polyclinic	780	901	894	1,000	1,424	4,999	0.114
Diag. Centers and other	192	527	336	288	1,007	2,349	0.276
Total	1,699	1,548	1,699	2,340	5,435	12,720	0.180

Conclusions and Recommendations

Although health status indicators in Armenia compare favorably than other CIS economies, there is evidence of a significant decrease of health care utilization (particularly primary health care) and increased vulnerability to infectious diseases. This Chapter found that public expenditures in health in Armenia are relatively low compared to other CIS countries and that despite a persistent oversupply of resources, the quality of and access to such resources is worsening. Armenia needs to increase budget spending on health to at least 2 percent of GDP to stop deterioration in the system and provide better-targeted, higher quality resources. Without significant improvements in the public health budget, the reforms in the sector lack the attribution of a public good that precisely justifies its role.

Government policies in the sector have not been properly reflected in budgetary allocations due to discrepancies between planned, financed and disbursed budgets. In addition, public expenditures in health are segmented in budget and the incidence of off-budget funds is so high that it weakens the budget as a policy tool. Budget segmentation distorts allocations across regions and programs, and makes it much more difficult to pursue equity objectives. It is suggested to move towards consolidation of off-budget grants in the regular budget. It is recommended that donors' contributions to the health sector is accompanied by their inclusion in the budget and the budgetary process. Funds from cost recovery mechanisms (formal fees) should also be reflected in the budget documents.

The current contracting structure between the SHA and the health care providers does not allow the GOA, or the health policy makers, to ensure the accuracy of the health cost estimates and supervise the financial management of the providers (because of their legal status as joint-stock companies). A supervisory and monitoring agency for the health sector should have legal authority to audit the financial management. After some years of contracting the SHA should explore more flexible instruments that incorporate the problems and solutions proposed by providers. Increased flexibility in contracting should be accompanied by increased supervision of those contracts.

Household payments represent at least 30 percent of national health expenditures and have strong implications for equity in health utilization. Programs like the fee-waiver for vulnerable populations have had a small but statistically significant impact on the eligible population (Chaudhury, et al. 2002) and should be strengthened to improve access to health care among the poor. As of January 2001, the Government of Armenia extended the BBP eligibility to the beneficiaries of the poverty family benefit. While the program eligibility expansion (on the extensive margin) is expected to have positive effects on utilization, further refinements of eligibility should improve the targeting of the program. This should be obviously coordinated with the Ministry of Social Security responsible for the eligibility for the poverty benefit.

CHAPTER 7

SOCIAL PROTECTION AND INSURANCE

The social protection and insurance system in Armenia comprises:

- *social insurance* that provides old-age, disability and survivor's pensions, as well as sickness, maternity, and unemployment benefits;
- various *social assistance programs* such as regular monthly cash family poverty benefit; the so-called "social pension" (a regular monthly payment to selected categories of the population—the elderly not qualifying for a labor pension and invalids since childhood);[103] a one time payment for all newborns (a new borne allowance), child care allowance for employed mothers till a child is two years old, and public works (including "food for work" type of programs);
- *social welfare services* to certain categories of the population, including medico-social rehabilitation for veterans and the disabled, services at home for frail elderly and institutional care for vulnerable individuals, such as children deprived of birth parental care, children from destitute and/or dysfunctional families, and children and adults with disabilities;
- *price-discounts* for some groups of the population—this program was substantially reduced in 1999 and currently consists of several privileges mostly for veterans of WW II.

Of the listed programs two are the most important: poverty family benefit and pensions. Approximately 900,000 Armenians or 30 percent of the population receive at least one social

---

103. The "social pension" program was inherited from former Soviet Union. The term pension is confusing, because the program is non-contributory and consists of regular monthly cash benefit paid to certain categories of citizens that supposedly were among the most vulnerable during the Soviet times: those who have never been employed and thus have fallen out of the social insurance coverage or to their descendents incapable of supporting themselves, and invalids since childhood. As such, although administered and funded by the Armenia State Social Insurance Fund, the program essentially belongs to the social assistance, not the social insurance domain of the social protection.

protection benefit. At the same time, according to the 1998/99 Integrated Household Survey, overall poverty incidence in Armenia was estimated at 53.7 percent, while extreme poverty incidence was estimated at 25.4 percent. Based on the same Survey, social transfers (mostly pensions and poverty family benefit) played an important role as a source of family income, particularly for the low income families—they made 13.3 and 15.3 percent of the income of the two bottom quintiles respectively. Their role as a household income source was more important in urban (12.2 percent share on average; 16.6 and 19.6 percent in the case of the first and the second bottom quintile respectively), than in rural households (5.3, 11.0 and 9.1 percent respectively).

The total public spending on social protection accounts for about 5.2 percent of GDP (Table 7.1). In Georgia, for instance in 1999, social protection programs covered about 28 percent of the population, accounting for 4.2 percent of GDP.

Social protection is funded by the state budget (social assistance, except for the social pensions, social welfare services, and military retirement benefits) and by the state Social Insurance Fund (SIF) (labor pensions, unemployment and sick leave benefits, as well as the social pensions) mainly through payroll taxes. There is a significant out-of-budget international donors' participation, particularly in funding of the public works and social assistance programs.

TABLE 7.1: PUBLIC SPENDING ON SOCIAL PROTECTION AND INSURANCE
Million Dram

	1996	1997	1998	1999	2000	2001	2002*
Total Social Protection	31040	41577	47226	59748	53504	60202	66249
As percent of GDP	4.7	5.2	4.96	6.0	5.18	5.11	5.18
State Budget Financed	7578	12614	19957	26100	21952	26108	27029
As percent of State Budget	5.96	8.58	9.75	11.26	9.85	10.88	10.44
Social Insurance Fund **	23461	28962	27269	33648	31552	34094	39219
As percent of Social Protection	75.6	69.6	57.7	56.3	58.9	56.6	59.2

Note: *The data for 2002 is taken from the approved 2002 State Budget of the Republic of Armenia. The GDP for 2002 is calculated assuming 6 percent growth and 2.5 percent inflation.
**State Social Insurance Fund expenditures are shown without transfers from the state budget. These transfers are shown in the budget social expenditures.

Source: Statistical Yearbook of Armenia (1997,1998), pp. 344–353, Yerevan, 2001. Statistical Yearbook of Armenia (1999,2000), pp.369–379, Yerevan, 2001. The Social and Economic Situation in the Republic of Armenia in January–December 2001, pp.107–115, Yerevan, 2002 (in Russian). The 2002 State Budget of the Republic of Armenia. The data on donor participation on social assistance programs is not included.

The review presented below shows that social protection programs in Armenia have played an important role in providing social support to the population and alleviating the extreme poverty, in particular the cash poverty family benefit. However, efficiency and effectiveness of these programs could be enhanced. In the short term, this could be achieved mainly through improved administration, targeting and monitoring. In the medium term, some of the programs would need to be restructured. For example, the pensions system would benefit if stronger links between contributions and benefits were to be established. Also, some new programs, such as cost-effective community-based social work and care services for vulnerable families and individuals need to be introduced in Armenia.

Social Assistance

Social assistance in Armenia comprises several programs, of which the most important one in terms of coverage, resources and poverty impact is the poverty family benefit. Currently it provides regular cash income to 150,000 families with over 550,000 members or 18 percent of the Armenian population. Beneficiary families receive 6,500 drams per month on average. It is a well-administered and targeted program.

The Armenian social assistance system was fundamentally reformed in 1999, when targeted, cash family poverty benefit was introduced. The introduction represents a major reform achievement. The reform made Armenia a leader in the CIS in reforming the social safety net programs.

Prior to 1999, the system comprised 26 small, uncoordinated categorical benefits in cash. The allocation was done at the individual level. The assistance covered 470,905 individuals (December 1998). The benefits were low, ranging from 1,000 to 4,000 dram per individual per month (about US$2 to 8).

In January 1999, the old system was replaced by a cash family poverty benefit targeted at 28 percent of households that were estimated to be extremely poor. The benefit is awarded to eligible households (not individuals) and is significantly higher than any other cash transfer in Armenia. The new system introduced a proxy means-tested targeting mechanism, where households are ranked based on a single-index formula that includes individual and household indicators.[104] The indicators include some of those used in the past (such as disability or orphanhood), but also include additional household-level indicators that are strongly correlated with poverty (such as ownership of a car or characteristics of a dwelling). In addition, the system uses filters such as telephone bills (for international calls), real estate transactions, customs transactions and electricity consumption. The use of the targeting mechanism based on proxies, not income, was motivated by the highly informal nature of the economic activities in Armenia.

Each family that qualifies receives a basic monthly benefit. Initially, it was set at 3,500 drams, then it was decreased to 3,000 drams; currently it is 4,000 drams. In addition, each family member of the eligible household was awarded 1,300 drams. As of the beginning of 2002, in order to adjust the benefit level to the decreased budget allocation, only children up to 18 (approximately 250,000 of them) in eligible families receive the additional benefit (currently set at 1,500 drams).

When the new benefit was introduced at the beginning of 1999, more than 230,000 families were receiving the benefit (28 percent of the estimated total number of families—this percentage was based on the extreme poverty incidence estimates calculated using the 1996 Household Survey). Gradually, due to better screening and improved benefit administration, the number of recipient families was reduced to 217,220 by December 1999, 176,000 by December 2001 and 150,000 by May 2002. The budget allocated to social assistance was increased from 13.4 to 21.1 billion drams in 1999 (i.e. to more than 2 percent of GDP, which is quite a high level), representing an increase of 48 percent in US dollars (Table 7.2). It was then decreased, reflecting

TABLE 7.2: POVERTY FAMILY BENEFIT, 1999–2002

	1999	2000 Planned	2000 Actual	2001 Actual	2002 Planned
Total expenditures, million dram	19,923	16,706	14,378	16,097	14,850
Beneficiary households, thousand	226.5	187.36	187.36	173.3	N/A
Average monthly benefit, dram	7,330	7,430	6,400	7,740	N/A
Spending as percent of the state budget	8.45	7.49	6.45	6.7	5.7
Spending as percent of GDP	2.0	1.62	1.39	1.367	1.16[1]

Notes: The GDP for 2002 was estimated assuming 6 percent growth and 2.5 percent inflation.

Source: The Ministry of Social Security.

---

104. The initial formula was developed by national experts in 1993 and served as a targeting mechanism for humanitarian assistance. Some adjustments were made in 1998 based on the data from the 1996 Household Survey.

the decreased number of beneficiaries and severely constrained public resources (the 2002 allocation is 14 billion drams).[105]

Poverty family benefit administration. The benefit is regulated and supervised by the Ministry
of Social Security (MSS). Direct administration (receipt of applications and eligibility assessment,
including field visits) is performed by 55 territorial centers for social assistance, which are established, funded and directly report to the local administration. The centers which employ 650 people
cover entire Armenia. The benefit administration is computerized, with the centralized data base
managed by the MSS. The data base is linked to other data bases relevant for cross-checking and
application of the "filter" proxies for the benefit eligibility assessment. The draft of the final list of
recipient families is prepared monthly by the centralized data base and sent to the territorial centers
for final decision. The benefit is delivered to the beneficiaries through the post offices. In early
2002, in order to make the territorial centers for social assistance more accountable for decisions
on benefit eligibility, as well as management of the poverty family benefit budget, each center was
allocated fixed yearly benefit budget. The allocations were decided based on the 2001 data, as well
as estimates of the demand for the benefit on the territory covered by each respective center. If
there are savings due to better targeting of the benefit, the center may decide to include new beneficiaries or award a one-time benefit to families that are assessed to be extremely poor (based on the
field visit) but formally do not qualify for the benefit. Currently, one-time assistance can be up to
12,000 drams. At the end of the year, the Ministry is going to evaluate the experience, prior to
deciding whether to continue with the fixed budget allocation practice.

All appeals are addressed to a special commission established at the local government level.
The commissions include representatives of the local government and local NGOs. The commissions are only authorized to give their recommendations to the territorial centers of social assistance, which are vested the power to make a final decision. If a client is not satisfied, he/she can
appeal to the court. Often, clients complain directly to the Ministry.

The MSS has put substantial efforts into improving the family poverty benefit administration,
including provision of clear guidelines (that are promptly adjusted to reflect any changes in the
benefit administration procedures), developing and improving the management information system, training of benefit administrators in the territorial centers for social assistance, and continuous
monitoring and supervision. Particularly important is that the Policy Analysis and Development
Unit in the MSS employs highly qualified staff capable of designing a household survey type
research, as well as conducting sophisticated econometric analysis of household surveys data. This
is important for the assessment of the poverty benefit targeting efficiency and effectiveness and
further development of the targeting mechanism. The Ministry also pays attention to providing the
public with timely and adequate information on changes in the benefit.

Poverty family benefit targeting efficiency. Poverty Update for Armenia (World Bank, 2002b)
estimates that the social assistance reform in Armenia was well justified: the new mechanism indeed
improved targeting efficiency of the social assistance. The Update compares targeting efficiency of
the old and the new social assistance system, based on the 1998/99 Integrated Living Condition
Survey (Table 7.3). Using the consumption aggregate, the Poverty Update finds that the poorest
population quintile received 16 percent of the social assistance benefits before the reform (including child, single mother and other benefits, but excluding pensions). At the same time, the old
system provided an equal share (16 percent) to the richest quintile, evidencing a significant leakage
to the non-poor. After the reform was introduced, the share of the bottom quintile doubled—
it received almost one-third of the transfers, while the richest captured 10 percent. These improvements are reflected in the significant change in the concentration index, from an almost neutral
–0.07 to a very progressive –0.27 after the reform. It suggests that the family poverty benefit was

---

105. The figure includes also the payments due for November and December 2000, which totals 2.328
billion dram, so only 12.5 billion drams were available for current payments of family benefits in 2002.

TABLE 7.3: CHANGES IN DISTRIBUTION OF CASH SOCIAL ASSISTANCE, 1998–1999

	Fraction of the Social Assistance Budget Captured by Each Consumption Quintile					Total Budget (billion dram)	Concentration Index
	1	2	3	4	5		
Before reform	15.6%	30.5%	25.8%	12.4%	15.7%	13.44	−0.071
After reform	31.8%	33.8%	14.6%	9.4%	10.2%	21.10	−0.272

Note: The Survey notion of ìsocial assistance benefitsî includes child benefits, single mother benefits and other benefits. Compensation instead of privileges, unemployment benefits, scholarships, and pensions are not included as social assistance. The survey instrument design was not adjusted to reflect the reform of the social assistance that took place in the middle of the Survey period. However, given that poverty family benefits replaced other social assistance benefits, it is captured properly by adding up the sources indicated above. *Before* denotes the incidence for those households surveyed from July 1998 to December 1998. *After* denotes the incidence for those households surveyed from January 1999 to June 1999.

Source: Armenia, Poverty Update, The World Bank 2002b.

relatively well targeted in 1999, although there was scope for improvements in targeting, since the non-poor (top 40 percent) still captured one-fifth of the transfers.

Unfortunately, there are no household survey data for the second half of 1999 and 2000 that would enable the analysis of the targeting efficiency and effectiveness of the family benefit and its impact on poverty in Armenia. Such analysis would be possible for the year 2001, once the data cleaning is completed and the data base is released by the National Statistical Service.

Developments related to the family poverty benefit in 1999–2002. Since its introduction in January 1999, the following major developments could be observed in relation to the family poverty benefit:

(i) the benefit has been paid regularly, except for a short period in 2000, when it was not paid for two months. The arrears have been cleared at the beginning of 2002 and the payment of the benefit is current;

(ii) the spending on benefit has continuously declined: from 2.0 percent of GDP in 1999 to 1.4 percent of GDP in 2001, and to 1.16% in the 2002 budget. The Government has explained the decrease by poor fiscal performance on the one hand, and high economic growth recorded in Armenia since 1999 on the other, which presumably has resulted in the decrease in both extreme and overall poverty. However, this decrease, as well as changes in other poverty measurement indicators can only be confirmed by the household survey data. While it may be the case that spending 2 percent of GDP on family poverty benefit is unaffordable for a low income country such as Armenia, spending too little may compromise the Government's efforts to alleviate poverty among the extremely poor;

(iii) the Ministry of Social Security has made significant efforts to compensate for the decrease in spending on the family poverty benefit by decreasing the number of households receiving the benefit through: (i) a better screening of the households (so as to decrease the error of inclusion through better and more thorough eligibility checking procedures, including visits paid to the applicant families); (ii) adjustments in the proxy formula (so as to decrease the error of inclusion); and (iii) a decrease in the benefit amount (currently, the average benefit is more than 20 percent lower than in 2001). The adjustments in formula have been based on the analysis of the 1998/99 Integrated Household Survey data, a beneficiary assessment of the poverty benefit (undertaken in Spring 2001), and the new proxy formula piloting experience (Fall 2001 – see Box 7.1).

> **BOX 7.1: RECENT STEPS TO IMPROVE TARGETING OF POVERTY BENEFIT**
>
> In 2000, the Policy Analysis and Development Unit of the Ministry of Social Security developed a new proxy formula using the 1998/99 Household Survey data (that formula was supposed to replace the old formula, defined by experts). The simulations showed that the new formula would improve the targeting of the benefit. However, they also indicated that its implementation would result in substantial changes in the structure of beneficiaries—about 30 percent of the beneficiaries were expected to change: the new formula would include more children and less pensioners, which was more in line with the poverty profile and information from the field from the territorial centers for social assistance. Given this complex political economy of the implementation of the new formula, the Government was hesitant to go ahead with it. Instead, the adjustment was done in the following way: at the beginning of 2002, the average pension in Armenia was increased by about 700 drams. As a result, 18,000 families with pensioners become ineligible for the poverty benefit. At the same time, the Government decided to increase the basic benefit to 4,000 drams and pay additional benefit of 1,500 drams only to children in eligible families. In this way the structure of beneficiaries has moved more towards the structure that would result from the new formula implementation. Also, families with children receive more money than families without children. However, ultimate assessment of actually achieved improvements in targeting efficiency and effectiveness could be drawn only based on the household survey analysis.

Recommendations on Social Protection

Based on: (i) the importance of the poverty family benefit for poverty alleviation among the extremely poor in Armenia; (ii) positive experience in its implementation; and (iii) a high probability that extreme poverty (as well as overall poverty) is going to remain an issue in the medium term, the following is recommended in the short to medium term:

- The cash poverty family benefit program should be maintained as a core of the social assistance system. Also, given that the high share of informal economic activities is likely to persist in the medium term, the targeting mechanism based on welfare proxies should be preserved.
- The Government should refrain from introducing any additional regular monthly programs such as, for instance, a housing allowance or similar.
- Efforts to improve the targeting mechanism should be continued. Based on the 2001 Integrated Living Conditions Survey, a new formula should be developed. Also, the adequacy of the benefit amount should be evaluated based on the 2001 poverty measurement results.
- Efforts to improve the benefit administration should continue through training of the benefit administrators, improved eligibility testing procedures, strengthening the role of the local authorities and communities in benefit delivery, etc. A beneficiary assessment planned for summer of 2002 is expected to provide information that will serve as a basis for improvements in the benefit administration.
- The Government should make efforts to ensure that the Integrated Living Conditions Survey is conducted regularly, since it provides information necessary for poverty monitoring and adjustments in the social assistance programs.

How much should be spent on the poverty family benefit? Table 7.4 provides an assessment of the resources needed to significantly alleviate extreme poverty in Armenia. The key parameters are the extreme poverty incidence, poverty shortfall, and the leakage of the resources to non-targeted population. The estimate is based on the results of the Poverty Update based on the 1998/99 ILCS (World Bank, 2002).

The estimates indicate that the budget for the family poverty benefit has to be kept at the minimum of 1.4 percent of GDP, if significant extreme poverty alleviation is to be achieved.

Child benefits. There are two types of cash benefits targeted at children in Armenia. One is a one time payment to new born babies. It amounts to 5,900 drams and its objective is to help families with the expenses when a new baby is born. The other is a child care allowance, which is paid to

TABLE 7.4: RESOURCES NEEDED FOR THE EXTREME POVERTY ALLEVIATION—THREE SCENARIOS

Extreme poverty incidence	Poverty shortfall	Poverty shortfall in dram	Resources needed (perfect targeting)	Leakage	Resources needed billion dram	Resources Needed, percent of GDP
20%	25%	2,183	15.8	20 percent to the non-poor and 30 percent to other poor	23.7	2.4
15%	25%	2,183	11.9	10 percent to the non-poor and 30 percent to other poor	16.7	1.7
15%	20%	1,745	9.5	40 percent to other poor	13.3	1.35

Memo items: Prices of 1999. Food poverty line per adult equivalent AMD 8,730 (see World Bank, 2002b).

employed mothers after the maternity leave has expired (70 calendar days after the delivery). It is a regular monthly benefit paid until a child is two years old. The benefit ranges between 2,300 and 3,500 drams. In 2000, there were about 20,000 beneficiaries. Both benefits are funded by the state budget and their primary objective is to stimulate families to have more children. There is no information to assess the poverty impact of these two benefits. However, given the fact that: (i) majority of the children in Armenia are born to unemployed mothers; (ii) the families with unemployed members tend to be affected by poverty more than the average; and (iii) the importance of adequate provision for young children for their physical and cognitive development, both benefits should be maintained. Hence, the new born allowance should be increased to provide a meaningful assistance to families with a new born baby. As far as the child care leave is concerned, it is longer than in other countries (in most of the CIS countries it lasts till a child is 18 months old). Given the high poverty rate among children 0–5 years of age, on the one hand, and constrained budget on the other, the Government should consider shortening the benefit duration for 6 months, while increasing its amount.

Social Insurance

Armenia's pension system is mandatory for all economically active individuals, including self-employed in agriculture. It provides labor pensions, based on the payment of social insurance contribution. Benefits comprises old-age, disability and survivors' pensions. The statutory retirement age has been increasing gradually (half a year per calendar year) since 1996 and it is supposed to reach 65 (men) and 63 (women) in 2005 and 2011 respectively.[106] Currently, the retirement age for males is 62.5 years and for females 57.5 years, on condition that they have at least five years of employment history. Although significantly curtailed, early retirement provisions still exist (currently, 19,100 pensioners or 3.9 percent of the total number of the recipients of labor pensions have retired under the privileged conditions). According to the new State Pension Law (passed in Parliament in the first reading on June 4, 2002), most of them will be gradually phased out. Pensioners are allowed to work and continue receiving the pensions. Disability pensions are certified by

---

106. Armenia was among the first countries in the Region to increase the retirement age. The increase for women (8 years) is among the biggest in the Region. In most of the cases, the increase was 5 years for either gender. The pace of increase is similar to other countries in the Region.

TABLE 7.5: PENSIONS, 1996–2001

	1996	1997	1998	1999	2000	2001
The number of pensioners, thousand	**607.0**	**587.7**	**574.7**	**569.3**	**560.2**	**552.9**
Labor pensions (based on payment of contributions)	536.5	526.3	524.7	509.9	501.7	483.6
Old age	435.5	429.1	418.3	414.4	401.3	392.7
–of which under early retirement provisions	18.9	18.2	18.9	18.7	18.9	19.1
Disability	99.8	100.1	100.7	64.4	65.3	66.7
Survivors pensioners	37	26.1	24.7	14.4	14.3	5.0
Social pensions	51.0	50.7	47.9	47.4	46.7	47.0
Old-age	15.9	14.2	12.1	12.0	10.2	9.4
Disability				35.3	26.9	28.2
Of which children up to 16				8.6	8.1	8.1
Military service pensioners	19.5	23.1	22.6	23.0	22.8	22.3
Average monthly pension, dram	3152	3673	3793	4421	4473	4574
Labor pensions	3061	3645	3710	4337	4364	4470
Old-age pension	3164	3718	3824	4457	4581	4586
–of which under early retirement provisions	2843	3491	3520	4103	4088	4109
Disability	3067	3093	3555	3550	3550	3561
Survivors pensioners	3794	4978	5003	4874	4745	4696
Social pensions	2631	2634	2754	3393	3403	3379
Old-age	2631	2634	2754	2964	3174	3200
Military service pensioners	5701	4620	4649	6278	7018	9580
Average monthly wage, dram, current prices	9469	13581	18000	20157	22706	23943
Average pension as percent of the average wage	33.3	27.0	21.1	21.9	19.7	19.1
Total spending on pensions, nominal, billion dram	22.9	25.9	26.2	30.2	30.1	30.4
o/w: On labor pensions	19.7	23.0	23.4	26.5	26.3	25.9
On old-age labor pension	16.5	19.1	19.2	22.2	22.1	21.6
GDP in current prices, billion dram	660.0	798.5	951.9	989.1	1032.0	1177.7
Total Revenues of the SIF, as percent of GDP	3.57	3.96	3.49	3.75	3.62	3.61
o/w: payroll taxes and other mandatory social payments	3.08	3.59	2.67	3.19	3.05	2.97
budget transfers	0.15	0.35	0.81	0.37	0.57	0.62
Total spending on pensions as percent of GDP	3.48	3.24	2.75	3.05	2.91	2.57
o/w: Spending on labor pensions as percent of GDP	2.98	2.88	2.45	2.68	2.55	2.20
Spending on old-age labor pensions	2.5	2.4	2.01	2.24	2.14	1.83
The actual population of Armenia, thousand	3075	3056	3030	3009	2994	3002
All pensioners as percent of the actual population	19.7	19.2	19.0	18.9	18.7	18.4
Old-age pensioners as percent of the actual population	14.2	14.0	13.8	13.8	13.4	13.1
Total pensioners as percent of the population in pensionable age: women 57+, men 62+	159.8	151.8	146.3	143.0	139.0	133.8
Total labor pensioners as percent of the population in pensionable age: women 57+, men 62+	141.2	135.9	133.6	128.1	124.4	119.5
Total old age labor pensioners as percent of the population in pensionable age: women 57+, men 62+	114.6	110.8	106.5	104.1	99.5	97.0
Male population 62 and over (actual)	137.0	141.3	145.1	148.5	151.2	151.7
Female 57 and over (actual)	242.8	245.6	247.6	249.4	251.8	252.6
Total pension age population (actual)	379.8	386.9	392.7	397.9	403.0	404.3

Notes: Actual population estimates are based on the preliminary results of the 2001 Population Census.

Source: State Social Insurance Fund.

special commissions under the Ministry of Social Security. Family members of a deceased pensioner or a person who qualified for a pension before he/she has died, are eligible for a survivor's pension. Individuals with less than five years of working history, invalids since childhood, and other individuals not qualifying for a labor pension are entitled to a social pension.

Old-age labor pension formula consists of two parts: (i) a flat part or basic pension; and (ii) variable part, the size of which depends on the number of years worked. Other types of pensions are calculated as a percentage of the old-age pension. The formula represents an attempt to differentiate pensions by the number of years worked and hence somewhat reflect the length of contribution history. However, the low level of pensions, and small differences in their levels, coupled with high contribution rates and an easy access to the social pension create strong disincentives to participate, especially for farmers and self-employed. Pensions in Armenia are indexed discretionally, based on available resources.

Labor pensions are financed through a payroll tax. The payment is not individualized, that is the tax is paid as a bulk sum on the payroll and hence the payment is difficult to control. The social pensions are also financed from the payroll tax. However, being a social assistance benefit, they should be financed from the general tax revenues.

Military pensions are regulated by a separate law. They are only administered by the state Social Insurance Fund (SIF). Their level is significantly higher than the level of other pensions. They are funded by the state budget.

Social insurance is administered by the state Social Insurance Fund, with local branches covering entire country and the central office in Yerevan. The SIF is responsible for the collection of social insurance contributions as well. It is the largest public sector entity that has its own budget almost entirely separated from the regular Government budget. Total average spending of the SIF in the last five years amounted to about 3.5 percent of GDP, which in 2001 made about 16 percent of total spending of the regular government budget (including expenditures of local governments). The operation of the SIF is governed by its Charter. The government introduced a number of important amendments to the SIF Charter in 2001 to ensure more accountability of the SIF management, as well as more transparency of fund operations. Specifically, the amended charter provides for Parliamentary approval of the SIF budget, maintaining of fund accounts with the Treasury, and streamlined accountability lines for the SIF Board, which has to report to the Ministry of Social Security, the Government and Parliament.

The Government, supported by the World Bank, developed a comprehensive pension reform strategy and approved it in December of 1999. The implementation of the strategy has been progressing well with support from the World Bank, USAID and other donors. It is expected that the new State Pension Law, which would replace the existing Soviet-type of social security system by the individual pension accounts, will become effective before the end of 2002. The Government also adopted a decision to transfer responsibility for funding social pensions from the SIF to the regular budget, starting from January 2003. This decision covers only a part of total SIF liabilities that ultimately will have to be transferred to the budget, but this marks a start of the very important transition process.

Recent Performance of the Pension System

Pensions in Armenia are low. In 2001, the average pension was only 20 percent of the average wage (down from one-third in 1996), or 12.6 percent of the GDP per capita, which is one of the lowest ratios in the Region. In 1999, the average pension made only 50 percent of the food poverty line. The pensions were not indexed at all in the 1999–2000 period. Only as of January 2002, the average pension was increased by about 15.5 percent or 700 drams, reaching 5,400 drams.

Overall, pensioners gained very little from Armenia's economic growth of the past few years. While in 1996–2001 the nominal average wage increased by 153 percent, average pension increased by only 45 percent. Respectively, an average pension to average wage ratio declined from one-third in 1996 to less than 20 percent in 2001. When compared to other CIS states, Armenia has the lowest pension/wage ratio (Table 7.6).

TABLE 7.6: AVERAGE MONTHLY PENSIONS AND WAGES IN CIS COUNTRIES IN 2000 (at current exchange rates)									
	Armenia	Belarus	Georgia	Kazakhstan	Kyrgyz Republic	Moldova	Russia	Ukraine	Azerbaijan
Average pension (Armenia –100 percent)	100	381.5	100	343.2	118.5	85.2	360.5	190.1	195.0
Average wages (Armenia – 100 percent)	100	174.8	79.3 (1999)	228.5	61.5	77.9	187.9	100.5	117.5
Average pensions as percent to average wages	19.2	42	24.5	28.9	37.5	21	36.9	36.4	31.9

Note: Estimated using average annual exchange rates for 2000 based on the data from the NSS.

Another indication of the current distortions in the structure of social protection in Armenia could be seen in a very low ratio between the average labor pension and average family poverty benefit. In Armenia this ratio was below 1.2 in early 2002. For instance in Lithuania, the similar ratio amounts to 1.6, in Serbia — 3.9, and in Bulgaria exceeds 4. Such a disproportion creates a serious incentive distortion for low income population.

However, in contrast to many other countries in the Region, Armenia has managed to pay pensions regularly through most of the 1990s. It avoided accumulating significant arrears in the payment of pensions, except in 2000 when the pension arrears reached almost two month of pension payment (0.35 percent of GDP). Since then, arrears have been cleared and the payment of pensions is current. Although the SIF is allowed to borrow commercially, the Fund policy so far has been to refrain from it.

A failure of the pension system to deliver some of the benefits of the economic growth to pensioners reflects an increasingly weak capacity to collect sufficient revenues for pension financing. As a result, the public spending on pensions as a fraction of GDP has steadily declined: from 3.5 percent in 1996 to 2.6 percent in 2001. In the case of labor pensions that share has declined from 3.0 to 2.2 percent.

There are several factors that are responsible for such a low level of pensions.

Too many pensioners. In Armenia, in 2001, there were 552,900 people receiving pensions, or 18.4 percent of the population (Table 7.5). At the same time, the estimated number of the population in pensionable age was 404,300 or 13.5 percent of the population. Most of the pensioners— 87.5 percent were labor pensioners. Recipients of the social pensions made 8.5 percent. The rest (4.0 percent) were military pensioners. The number of pensioners has been gradually decreasing over 1996–2001, due to the increase in retirement age, cleaning and streamlining of the SIF records, and out migration.[107] The number of pensioners dropped by 10 percent since 1996.

However, although the total number of pensioners relative to the population in pensionable age declined since 1996, it is still excessive—134 percent—down from 160 percent in 1996 (Table 7.5). The number of labor pensioners is still 20 percent higher than the number of the population in pensionable age. This is mostly due to the relatively high share of disability pensions in the total number of labor pensions—14.0 percent in 2001. Although that share declined since 1996 when it was 18 percent, there is still room for its further decline through more strict and more rigorously implemented criteria.

---

107. According to the Armenian pension legislation, pensioners residing abroad cease receiving the pension as long as they stay out of the country.

Too few contributors. Economic developments during the early 1990s have brought about a greatly decreased level of formal employment. According to the 1998/99 Integrated Living Conditions Survey, in 1998/99 there were about 1.24 million labor market participants.[108] About 300,000 were unemployed, 400,000 were salaried workers and the rest—540.000—were self-employed (including farmers). In 2000, according to the SIF data, 490,000 people paid social insurance contributions (17 percent down from 1997). Hence, there were 0.9 contributors per one labor and social pensioner (military pensioners not included, because they are funded by the budget). Most of the self-employed, including farmers, do not contribute at all: although they make more than half of those covered by the social insurance, they contributed only 1.5 percent to the collected amount of contributions. This low (and declining) system support ratio reflects a narrow based economic growth in Armenia, as well as a large scope of informal employment (to which high labor taxation is one of the contributing factors).

Small formal taxable wage bill. In addition to low formal employment, formal wages are low as well: 24,000 dram per month. Moreover, according to the SIF, the average wage on which contributions were paid to the fund was 22,000 dram in 2001. The combination of the low average wage and low number of contributors results in a very low wage bill subject to social insurance contributions payment—about 11 percent of GDP.

Low collection rate and widespread under-reporting. In the 1998/99 Integrated Living Conditions Survey, households reported income from salaried employment of about 168 billion dram or almost 17 percent of GDP.[109] Furthermore, they reported income from self-employment at about 21 billion dram or 2.1 percent of GDP. A comparison with the wage bill on which the social insurance contributions are paid suggests a collection rate of about 58 percent. The remaining 42 percent of the earnings reported in the household survey is not reported for fiscal purposes or/and is under-collected by the SIF. Increasing compliance from 58 to 75 percent would increase the SIF revenues from social insurance contributions from about 2.9 to 3.75 percent of GDP, allowing the average labor and social pension to be increased to about 6,600 Drams.

The potential for collection of contributions looks even better when net household income from farming is included. In the 1998/99 household survey, Armenian households reported average net income from farming at 11,235 drams per month. That income made 10 percent of annual GDP. Assuming that the social insurance contribution rate for farmers was 10 percent, the compliance rate of 70 percent would yield another 0.75 percent of GDP in revenues for the SIF, increasing its potential estimated revenues to 4.5 percent of GDP and consequently potential average monthly labor and social pension to 7,500 dram.[110] If the SIF were responsible only for funding of the labor pensions, this level of its revenues would yield an average labor pension of 8,200 dram (35 percent of the average wage, or 90 percent of the food poverty line).

The low collection rate of social insurance contributions can be explained by: (i) poor enforcement; (ii) weak reporting and monitoring; and (iii) lack of incentives for workers and employers to comply with the payment of the social tax.

▨ *Poor enforcement.* In principle, employers have to pay the social insurance contribution due not later than two days after they have paid out the wages. However, many employers fail to comply with this legal requirement and arrears on the social insurance contributions are accumulated, particularly in the case of large state enterprises. At the beginning of 2002, the arrears on contributions for wages that were paid out were about 9 billion dram (0.8 percent of 2001 GDP, or 22 percent of the total SIF expenditures in 2001).

---

108. In pre-transition Armenia, there were 1.6 million economically active people. All of them were (wage) employed, and social insurance contributions were paid for all of them.

109. See *Armenia Poverty Update*, World Bank 2002.

110. The assumption is that pensions made 90 percent of the SIF expenditures. Military pensions are excluded from this calculations (they are funded by the government budget).

■ *Weak reporting and monitoring.* The payroll is paid in bulk—there are no individualized lists of employees, their wages and social insurance contributions due/paid, which makes control over compliance difficult. Moreover, some enterprises, particularly large, still un-restructured state-owned firms, are implicitly subsidized by the Government by being allowed not to comply with their obligations towards the SIF.

■ *Weak incentives for participation.* Incentives for the employers and employees to comply with the social tax obligation are weak. First, the minimum employment (and presumed contribution) history required is low—anyone who can show 5 years of employment has the right to receive the labor pension. Second, benefits are low and unattractive. Third, the imbalance between the amount of social insurance contributions a regular contributor would put into the system and the amount of benefit he/she would receive effectively dis-courages those covered by social insurance from participating. Roughly speaking, in order to receive an old-age pension of 5,000 dram per month for about 20 years, an average worker needs to contribute monthly 5,000 dram for the same amount of years. Hence, beneficiaries with less than 20 years of contribution history could be considered winners. This imbalance is caused by a redistributive character of the pension system, which derives from universal coverage, almost a flat benefit structure and a low system support ratio. The incentives for participation are further diluted by the social pension, universally available to everyone with less than five years of contribution history at the age of retirement.

More pronounced differentiation in benefits based on contributions paid is expected to improve compliance. The new Law on State Pensions will introduce a contribution-based benefit system through introduction of notional accounts and actuarially fair calculation of pensions, as well as more strict conditions for drawing the benefit. Incentives could be strengthened further if these changes are coupled with a decrease in the social insurance contribution rate.

Overall, the discussion above suggests that the Armenian economy, as it is now, generates enough income to afford and sustain fiscally higher average pensions. It the short to medium term, until the new pension system comes into full effect, the Armenian Government may conduct the pension policy that would aim at an increase in pensions through combined improvements in compliance and a decrease in contribution rates.

High contribution rates. Although lower than in most of the CIS countries, the Armenian social insurance contribution rate is still high. A high contribution rate discourages compliance from both employers and employees and promotes informal sector activities. The SIF main source of revenues is social insurance contribution imposed on a payroll, which the Fund collects on its own, independently from the Ministry of State Revenues. Starting from January 2001, payroll taxa-tion in Armenia is based on a three-tier regressive rate system, according to which employers have to pay (per employee per month) "5,000 drams + 15 percent (of monthly wages from 20,000 to 100,000 dram) + 5 percent (of wages above 100,000 dram)", and employees pay 3 percent of gross wages. It is estimated that in 2001, for the monthly wage of 27,000 dram (about $50) the effective rate for payroll tax was 25 percent, which represents a decline from 31 percent in 2000. Still, the level of payroll taxation seems to be high for Armenia's current income level. This is an important factor to explain low compliance levels in small private businesses (self-employed, farmers): as discussed above, in 2001, total payments made to the SIF by self-employed was insignificant and amounted to about 1.5 percent of total payroll tax collected.

High labor taxation (including income tax) creates strong incentives for both employees and employers not to formalize labor contracts: employees prefer current to future consumption, while employers seek to reduce costs and increase competitiveness.

Links with the state budget. Pensions in Armenia are financed from two principal sources: the social insurance contributions and the general budget. The social insurance contribution finances social insurance benefits: labor pensions (old-age, disability and survivor's), maternity and sick leave benefits, and unemployment benefits. It also finances social pensions. The central budget finances military service related pensions.

In principle, SIF should only be responsible for administering social insurance benefits. All other benefits_including social pensions_should be administered (and financed) by other government bodies. Military pensions should most probably be administered by the Ministry of Defense. Social pensions, as discussed bellow, should be funded by the state budget and administered by the Ministry of Social Security, within the system of poverty targeted benefits.

Efficiency of pension administration. Despite significant efforts, Armenia is yet to establish an efficient social insurance administration. The administration of pensions is in need of better record keeping, modern IT equipment, accounting based on international standards, strong internal and external institutional and financial audits, skilled staff, more efficient organization, improved financial management, modern management information system, etc. Currently, a major effort financed by the USAID to introduce individual accounts and improve management information system in the SIF is under away. This effort is an integral part of the Government's strategy to introduce a system of personal identification numbers (PIN) in Armenia. The distribution of PINs to the population is expected to start in January 2003. Similarly, the system of individualized records for social insurance is expected to start functioning during the course of 2003.

Payment of pensions to beneficiaries is another issue that needs a strategic decision. Currently, most pensions are delivered to beneficiaries through the post system. A small number of pensions in Yerevan (about 20,000) is delivered through the Saving Bank. The rest of the pensions in Yerevan are delivered by the SIF pensions payment department. The delivery of pensions by the SIF itself (which is a very uncommon practice in the Region) is justified by its efforts to prevent leakage of funds at the point of pensions delivery: it is argued that the delivery services provided by the post office are poor and non-transparent, that is the SIF has very limited means to control the process. This is an issue, which needs further analysis and discussion.

Sustainability of the Pension System

A detailed financial and actuarial forecast of the current pension system in Armenia, based on the World Bank's PROST model, was done by PADCO (2001). Its primary conclusion is that the current system is financially sustainable and does not generate any serious risks for the fiscal system in the medium term. But the system fails to generate adequate benefits, and contributions are too high in relation to benefits provided. The "rate of return" on contributions to the SIF is low and therefore creates strong incentives for non-compliance.

With the current low pension levels, the medium-term outlook for the SIF is favorable. The Fund will run surplus even under the most conservative assumptions, such as: (a) no increase in the number of contributors: and (b) no improvement in the payroll tax compliance rates above their actual levels achieved in 1999. It is also assumed that pensions will be indexed only for inflation, but not for real wage growth. This positive outlook is primarily driven by the favorable demographic situation in Armenia, which, assuming that emigration would slow down, is very different from most other transition economies of Central Europe as well as Russia and Ukraine. The Armenian population is still relatively young (the average age for women is now 33.9 and for men 30.7 years), and it is expected to grow over the next 45 years. The number of new retirees is projected to be relatively low over the next 15 years.[111] This is because the cohort that will be retiring in this period was affected by low birth rates during WWII. Also, the retirement age will be increasing till 2011. Overall, the number of pensioners in 2010 is expected to be about 12 percent lower than in 2001.

Given a favorable environment created by the positive demographic outlook, and taking into account the discussion above, the Government of Armenia has an opportunity to radically improve the design of the pension system and implement it successfully. The medium-term objective should be to improve the performance of the pension system so that the average pension is significantly increased (as the new pension system is gradually phased in), as well as to successfully implement the new pension system spelled out in the newly-adopted state pension law that focuses on introduction

---

111. However, the demographic outlook deteriorates after 2015.

on notional accounts and contribution defined benefits (with a redistribution/solidarity component in the form of the basic benefit, so as to allow for equity and better protection against poverty of low wage earners).

Recommendations on Pensions

In the light of the discussion above, the following is recommended:

Pay pensions regularly and raise its level in real terms. In the short to medium term, the Government should give priority to paying pensions regularly and raising their level in real terms (to about 35 but no more than 40 percent ratio between the average nominal pension and the average nominal wage). In order to achieve these, the Government should not resort to increasing the social insurance contribution rates. Instead, it should focus on improving compliance.

Improve payroll tax collection. In order to improve revenue collection, the following specific actions could be taken: (i) the payment of the social insurance contributions should be individualized immediately, that is the contributions should be reported and paid for each employee individually; (ii) the rule that no wage payment should be allowed without prior payment of the payroll tax liabilities should be introduced and strictly enforced (including the court action); (iii) in order to increase the number of participating taxpayers, and given the non-transparent environment for tax collection in general, a separate action plan for each group of taxpayers should be prepared and implemented.

Better enforcement would yield better results only if combined with incentives for participation. These may include: (i) lower social insurance contribution rates; (ii) bigger differentiation of the social and labor pensions levels with the former much lower than the latter. Also, the eligibility conditions for social pensions should be much stricter: for instance, a person should be eligible for an old-age social pension only at the age of 70 (both genders), provided that he/she does not qualify for a labor pension and only if he/she is assessed as living in absolute poverty. Other categories of social pensions could also become conditioned on the economic situation of an applicant; (iii) differentiation of the labor pension based on the contribution history, combined *with* an increase in the minimum eligibility history (as envisaged by the new Law on the State Pensions). Introduction of individual accounts and related distribution of social insurance cards will provide an excellent opportunity for the SIF to register all potential payers of social insurance contributions.

Strictly separate financing of the social insurance benefits from other benefits. The social insurance contributions should finance only labor pensions and other social insurance benefits. In that sense, the administration and financing of military service-related pensions should be moved out of the SIF (for instance, to the Ministry of Defense). Similarly, social pensions should be financed by the state budget and their administration should be transferred to the Ministry of Social Security. As discussed above, social pensions should be evaluated to determine their poverty impact and accordingly reformed.

Maintain tight eligibility criteria. The Government should refrain from introducing any early retirement provisions, or any special retirement benefits (for instance, special pensions for particular categories of government employees such as judges, customs officers, etc., or members of Parliament) outside of the public pension system. Current existing early retirement provisions should be gradually phased out—as envisaged by the new pension legislation. Another area of concern is disability pensions. In order to decrease currently high number of disability pensioners: (i) the approach to disability should be changed from invalidity to functional disability, that is the remaining capacity to work; (ii) the third category disability should be abolished; (iii) decisions to award disability should be regularly audited; (iv) the guidelines for disability certification should be adjusted in line with the international best practice; (v) the staff should receive additional training; and (vi) disability certification for social insurance benefits should be moved back to the SIF following the principle that "who pays, decides."

Improve the administration of the SIF. Further improvements in information and financial management systems and in the benefit delivery mechanism are needed. To that end, the following measures are recommended: (i) conduct an institutional and functional review of the SIF and develop an action plan for improvements, including development of a new business plan, operational manuals and procedures, etc.; (ii) introduce management information system comprising a data base on pensioners, those covered by social insurance (participants) and a data base on employers; introduce individual accounts (currently under preparation); computerize financial information flows; (iii) improve reporting procedures, introduce international accounting standards, and regular internal and external auditing; (iv) review the skill mix of the current staff and adjust it to the needs of the new administration; and (v) develop a plan to minimize cash handling in the delivery mechanism.

Successful implementation of the above measures in the short to medium run would allow Armenia to increase pensions and decrease the rates of payroll taxation, as well as establish an environment supportive for introduction of a new pension system based on much stronger links between individual benefits and contributions paid.

Other Social Insurance and Non-insurance Benefits

Social insurance in Armenia provides the following additional benefits to those covered by insurance: maternity leave compensation, sick leave compensation and unemployment benefits such as unemployment compensation and paid re-training.

Maternity and Sick Leave Benefits

Maternity leave is granted to employed mothers for 70 calendar days prior to delivery and 70 calendar days after the delivery (85 days if the delivery is complicated; 110 days if more than one child is born). The compensation amounts to 100 percent of the average wage in the period of three months preceding the leave. In 2001, approximately 6,000 women were receiving the maternity leave compensation. The cost was about 1.2 percent of the total SIF expenditures. The maternity leave provision in Armenia is typical for most of the countries (both developed and countries in transition). Maternity leave compensation is an important family and child welfare benefit but it is not a social insurance benefit. As such, it should be financed from the state budget.

Sick leave compensation. The employed covered by social insurance are entitled to a wage compensation during temporary incapacity to work due to general or professional illness or injury. The level of compensation varies by the duration of employment history. This benefit makes approximately 2 percent of the total SIF expenditures. In contrast to many other countries, including several economies in transition, where a compensation during temporary incapacity to work is partially covered by the employer (first week or first two weeks), in Armenia, it is entirely funded by social insurance. In the medium term, in order to provide for better control of sick-leave use, the following is recommended: (i) shift funding of the first two weeks of the sick-leave compensation to employers; (ii) streamline the rules for the compensation award, and (iii) strengthen control both of the decision makers (medical doctors) and the users by regular audits.

Unemployment Benefits

Unemployment insurance benefits include unemployment compensation, job search and placement assistance, and re-training. The programs are implemented by a wide network of employment offices covering the entire country (funded by the state budget). The financing of benefits is provided by the SIF from the social insurance contributions revenues. In addition, the state budget provides financing for public works programs and unemployment assistance.

Unemployment compensation. An employed person, covered by social insurance at least for the period of 12 months is entitled to unemployment compensation. The compensation duration depends on the length of employment history and can be up to 12 months. Similarly, the amount of compensation depends on the employment history, but it cannot be higher than 3,500 dram per month. The number of beneficiaries varies during the year. For instance, in March 2001, there were 9,400 people entitled to the benefit; by the end of the year their number was reduced to 5,750. During 2000–2001 the benefit accumulated substantial arrears—16 months of payments. The situation has improved in 2002.

Vocational training. The individuals looking for a job registered with the employment offices as the unemployed are entitled to free-of-charge training. The training is organized and contracted out by the employment offices. In 2001, only 989 unemployed underwent vocational training, of which 855 acquired a new profession. There is no information on how many of the re-trained have found jobs and for how long. At the same time, while the employment offices got information on the total of 520 job vacancies, 7,303 unemployed found the job on their own. The same tendency was observed in the previous years, indicating inefficiency and ineffectiveness of the public vocational training system, as well as the public job search and placement assistance.

Unemployment assistance. After the unemployment compensation has expired, the unemployed are entitled to unemployment assistance for a period of three months. The assistance is equal to 1,300 drams and is funded by the state budget.

Public works program. In 2001, the state budget allocated 500 million drams for the public works program. The objectives of the programs are to provide temporary employment to the unemployed, as well as to job-seeking members of families receiving poverty family benefit, improve social infrastructure, improve sanitary conditions in the regions, and renovate cultural heritage sites. In 2001, 9,051 people benefited from the program. In addition to the budget funded public works program, the international donor community is funding a much larger "food for work" program.

Recommendations on Unemployment Programs and Benefits

Unemployment in Armenia is rampant—it is not an idiosyncratic, insurable risk, related to the business cycle, but a systemic risk affecting a substantial part of the population. Therefore, unemployment insurance in such a situation is difficult to justify from the economic point of view. Accordingly, the Armenian Government should consider the following: (i) abolishing unemployment insurance; (ii) providing the unemployed with at least two years of continuous employment history prior to the unemployment a flat rate unemployment assistance (higher than it is now) for a period not exceeding three months; the assistance should be financed by the state budget; (iii) evaluate the efficiency and effectiveness of the employment offices and plan for their rationalization and focus on job search assistance; (iv) evaluate vocational training programs provided to the unemployed and plan for their restructuring—for instance, they can be organized at the request of and in cooperation with the employers and implemented by private contractors; the funding should be provided by the state budget (as well as employers); and (v) evaluate public works programs, provide for their better planning and implementation at the local level and ensure better coordination with programs funded by the international donor organizations. Overall, the policy focus should be on increasing the "employability" of the unemployed, but in a much more efficient and effective manner than is currently the case.

Price-discounts

The widespread system of privileges and price discounts inherited from the former Soviet Union was abolished almost entirely by 1999. The remaining privileges are few (mostly discounted transport and utility tariffs), as well as their beneficiaries—mostly WWII veterans and the disabled. The major issue related to the privileges is that although supposed to be funded by the state budget, they are effectively financed by the service providers. Therefore, the Government should either honor its obligations or abolish the privileges. In any case, it should refrain from introducing any new privileges.

Donor Support

Many international donors, including the Armenian Diaspora organizations are involved in providing support to vulnerable groups of the population in Armenia. Although valuable, the assistance could be much more efficient if it were: (i) better planned and coordinated; and (ii) agreed and jointly implemented with the Ministry of Social Security, so as to avoid a piecemeal approach in providing assistance and initiating changes in the social welfare system.

CHAPTER 8

MAIN FINANCIAL REQUIREMENTS IN PUBLIC INFRASTRUCTURE

Armenia inherited a relatively developed public infrastructure which has been deteriorating quite rapidly over the previous decade due to chronic budget under-financing, insufficient tariffs in most sectors and governance problems. In addition, a considerable part of the available infrastructure financing was provided from quasi-fiscal sources (public enterprises in the energy sector). As was shown in Chapter 3, such quasi-fiscal subsidies from the energy sector to irrigation, drinking water and public transport exceeded 1 percent of GDP a year in the late 1990s, and proved to be unsustainable. Deterioration in Armenia's infrastructure, if not addressed, would become a significant constraint for economic growth.[112]

Since 1999, the Government has advanced its policies to phase out quasi-fiscal subsidies, reduce the overall level of subsidization, and provide for better budgeting of remaining subsidies. This policy shift is still at the early stage.

This Chapter aims at the development of consolidated estimates for funding requirements in five core sectors of public infrastructure_irrigation, water, roads, railway, and Yerevan metro. Based on the existing sectoral reform plans and investment programs, the Chapter provides some pre-liminary estimates for minimum budgetary funding over the medium-term period (2003–05) that would allow for a radical reduction in quasi-fiscal financing and at the same time would seriously improve financing of necessary maintenance and rehabilitation investments based on the expanded explicit budget support.

Summary of Financial Requirements

Table 8.1 summarizes the future financial burden that the Government will have to assume to finance the operations of these five sectors. The estimates are based on the low case scenario, which requires (under the most optimistic assumptions) annual investments and maintenance at the minimum level necessary to avoid further depletion of assets. The table assumes that all currently agreed

---

112. Already today the situation in water and sewage companies poses a serious risk for public health.

TABLE 8.1: FINANCING REQUIREMENTS FOR ADEQUATE MAINTENANCE AND OPERATIONS IN FIVE INFRASTRUCTURE SECTORS FOR 2003–05
US$ million

	2000 Public Financing Plan	2000 Actual	2001 Public Financing Plan	2001 Actual	2002 Public Financing Plan	2002 Additional financing need	2003 Donors' commitments	2003 Budget financing need	2004 Budget financing need	2005 Budget financing need
	Budget Financing : Planned and Actual					**Future Financing Needs**				
Roads and Streets	9.0	8.3	15.0	17.1	33.6	2.2	23.5	7.5	16.0	20.0
Railway	1.0	0.0	0.0	0.0	5.5	0.6	5.0	1.1	0.7	0.5
Metro	1.4	1.5	1.5	1.5	1.4	0.0	0.0	1.4	1.4	1.4
Municipal Water-YWSC	4.8	4.5	6.0	3.9	6.2	1.8	0.6	4.5	2.8	1.0
Municipal Water-AWSC	3.5	5.7	2.5	1.3	2.8	4.2	3.5	1.3	0.8	0.4
Irrigated Agriculture	18.1	15.3	15.4	19.7	19.5	1.2	6.4	9.3	8.8	7.6
1. Total Public Financing	37.9	35.3	40.4	43.5	69.0					
o/w: - Public investments (mostly donor funded)	25.3	22.7	30.9	34.0	59.2					
–Budget subsidies	12.6	12.6	9.5	9.5	11.4					
2. Total Future Budget Financing Requirements						10.1	39.0	25.1	30.5	30.9

Note: for 2002—extra financing, in addition to what has been budgeted.
for 2003–04—additional financing after taking into account the existing commitments from the donors.
Public financing includes budgeted investment and subsidies, and off-budget sources such as the Lincy Foundation.

Source: Staff estimates based on the data from the MOFE, Ministry of Transport and Communications, and State Water Committee.

major donor projects are implemented as planned, and that the targets for improvements in operating efficiencies agreed for these projects are realized. This covers projects funded by the Lincy Foundation in the road sector and the major IDA Credits such as the Transport Project, the Armenia and Yerevan Water Supply Projects, and the Irrigation Development Project.

The financing requirements summarized in Table 8.1 include the provision of counterpart financing for the donor projects, and the full financing of the operating deficits of the public utility/infrastructure companies. These financing requirements, however, do not cover costs of amortization of accumulated debts in these sectors.

The Table suggests that financial needs of the public companies operating in these five sectors will amount to at least $25 million in 2003 and about $30 million in 2004–05. This represents a significant increase relative to the current level of own budget spending that has been $11–12 million recently. The Table also estimates that the current 2002 government budget assumes a financing gap in the infrastructure sectors of about $11 million (0.5 percent of GDP).

Therefore, to ensure an appropriate level of financing in infrastructure, the budget has to increase it allocations for these sectors by almost 1 percent of GDP in 2004–05. The need for such an increase derives primarily from the existing under-financing but it also reflects the rapid decline in availability of donor funding after 2003. The future closure of the Lincy project will require an additional increase in budgetary contribution for road maintenance.

Realistically speaking, these estimates suggest that the current Government financing strategy is not sustainable. The analysis in this report suggests that it is highly unlikely that even under the most optimistic assumptions about prevailing fiscal constraints the Government would be able to increase allocations for the infrastructure sectors by much more than 0.5 percent of GDP, that is, only by half of what would be needed in 2004–05. The Government has to make additional policy adjustments, which could be summarized as follows:

- Completing a financial performance diagnostics/analysis in drinking water, irrigation, electric, urban transport, and power sectors and based on the results developing and implementing an infrastructure sector financial rehabilitation plan to restore each sector to financial viability in the medium term, including Parliament ratification where needed.
- Identification of additional funding sources for infrastructure, such as e.g. additional user charges for road users.
- Identification of additional cost reduction measures, including politically sensitive decisions on closing down specific elements of the existing infrastructure networks (for example, in irrigation and roads) as currently unaffordable.
- Designing and implementing an appropriate public awareness campaign covering the technical and financial performance of the infrastructure sectors.
- Establishing a single utility regulator, developing and adopting the necessary legal framework, including a law on National Monopoly Regulations and provisions to ensure the regulator's financial autonomy, and adoption of a timetable and action plan to transfer economic regulation of specific sectors, including water and irrigation, to the single utility regulator.
- Advancing the development of legal and regulatory framework and financial incentives to expand management of multi-apartment buildings as condominiums (or other forms of housing management by owners) that would become legally responsible for contracting community services, including water and sanitation.
- Raising additional donor financing for infrastructure.

Roads and Streets

The adequate management of the nation's road and street network is essential for future growth and development. The national road network has benefited from a significant infusion of foreign assistance funds during the past five years, which has kept the main roads in a reasonably good condition. However, the local roads, which connect the rural areas to the main commercial centers, and streets in urban areas, including Yerevan city, are in a very poor condition, having received almost no maintenance funding for the past ten years. A conservative estimate of financing for the maintenance of the national road network (US$20.0 million), the local rural roads (US$5.0 million), and the city streets (US$5.0 million) would be in the order of US$30.0 million annually, whereas the Government is now allotting less than US$3 million for this purpose from its own funds. There are also serious issues regarding who should have the responsibility for the management of the local roads that should be addressed.

The most urgent tasks for roads and streets are:

User Charges. At least a part of the substantial financial gap for maintaining the roads and streets, starting in 2003, could be closed with the introduction of additional road user charges by a further increase in fuel taxes, an upward revision of the vehicle registration fees (and their better enforcement), and a tax schedule for heavy trucks that do a disproportionate amount of damage to the roads. International experience suggests that about 80 percent of the needed revenues would be expected to come from fuel taxes. A brief study would be needed to determine the level and kind of charges that would be appropriate.

Responsibility for local road maintenance. The local roads have been almost completely neglected since 1990 due to lack of funds as well as lack of attention by the authorities. Prior to Independence, the local roads were a responsibility of the National Road Directorate, but now they are in theory the responsibility of the local authorities. However, these authorities lack both funds and institutional capacity to handle the maintenance of these roads. The issue of management responsibility should be addressed without delay. There are at least four options: (i) keep the responsibility with the local authorities but develop some more suitable financing arrangements; (ii) return the responsibility to the Armenia Roads, a public company responsible for maintenance of national roads; (iii) hire an administrator reporting to the Ministry of Transport who would be responsible for setting policies for the local roads, and for contracting out the maintenance works on a piecemeal basis; or (iv) entering into one large contract with a contractor who would be responsible for the maintenance of the entire local road network.

Reclassification of the road network. Clarification of responsibilities should be accompanied by a special study to make: (i) a preliminary reclassification of the entire road network; (ii) a determination of how much of the networks should cease to be public roads and who should have responsibility for them; and (iii) identification of legislation needed for establishing the proper system of responsibilities for road maintenance at all levels.

Road Maintenance Authority. New management arrangements will also be needed to ensure that additional funding raised through road user chargers are properly spent and not diverted for financing of other needs of the public sector. International experience suggests that this could be achieved by setting up an independent manager, who will receive all appropriate incomes and be responsible for their efficient use and adequate maintenance of the country road network. Such arrangements could be set up as the Road Fund or a State Road Maintenance Authority, organized as a Joint Stock Company on a commercial basis but with public ownership. It is important that in either case a new entity is governed by the Board with mostly private sector representation, including representatives of main road users.[113]

Railways

The importance of the Armenia Railways operations has been reduced as the share of road traffic has increased. In part because of the closed borders with Turkey and Azerbaijan, rail operations are now restricted to a single line running from Yerevan to the Georgian border plus some short commuter lines in the outskirts of Yerevan. As haulage distances are relatively short, trucks are competitive for most classes of goods. However, an end in the hostilities in the region (including opening traffic through Abkhazia) would change this, and the rail lines then could provide a competitive service.

There are certain circumstances under which Armenian freight traffic is charged higher railway rates than freight from and to Azerbaijan and some of the Central Asian countries under a special agreement that provides for 50 percent discounts for goods moving through the Pharap-Turkmenbashi-Baku-Poti corridor. While Armenia is a party to the governing Serakhs agreement, traffic from Armenia is not considered to be moving through this corridor and therefore does not qualify for the discount. Armenia does, however, receive a 24 percent discount for oil products and a 17 percent discount for other Armenian cargos moving through Georgia. The Government may want to try to negotiate the inclusion of its cargos as part of the Serakhs agreement so that they qualify for the 50 percent discount.

At present, the railway operations do not receive any budget subsidies. Generally, they break even on a cash flow basis, with virtually no resources available for normal maintenance and necessary investments. Revenues from the freight traffic to Georgia generate a positive cash flow and are used to cross-subsidize commuter operations. It is estimated that current financial requirements of the sector amount to about US$0.5 million per year for subsidizing the losses incurred because of the commuter operations, and US$0.6 million per year for the next two years for counterpart financing for an IDA project aimed at improving railway operations.

---

113. Heggie and Vickers (1998) summarize the best international practice for financing and management of the road network.

Potential future costs of maintaining railway operations are quite large but very difficult to quantify at the moment. The existing infrastructure is old and eventually will need replacement. This includes bridges, some of which are a 100 years old, outdated rolling stock, and rail beds that have had only minimal rehabilitation over the last 20 years.

The main policy issues for the railway operations are the following:

- Should the railway continue to operate the commuter lines? It cannot be justified on a commercial basis, and either should be explicitly subsidized (if it is considered a valuable public service), or closed down. A brief study should provide the information required to make a decision.
- Can the railway operations be able to achieve sufficient profitability to finance the major necessary investments? If not, should the Government shut them down in view of the high future costs of updating the system? While some argue that the railway is vital to national security, it seems likely that truck transport could be able to fill the potential gap in services. It is just too early to make a final decision on this and there is no need to because there is no immediate budget costs involved. The new IDA Transport Project is expected to provide considerable improvements in the operational efficiency of the railways from $12.6 million investments to be undertaken in 2002–04. It also will help to clarify costs of future necessary rehabilitation, and thus it would help justify a later decision on longer term prospects of the system. In addition, there is a hope for opening of the borders that may dramatically improve the entire economics of the sector.
- As a short-term priority, the Armenian Government should intensify its negotiations with the Government of Georgia on railway tariffs for Armenian cargo traveling to Georgian ports.

Yerevan Metro

The Yerevan Metro revenues in 2001 were sufficient to cover only about 40 percent of its operating costs, even with understated depreciation. On this basis, it is not generating enough income to keep the equipment operating in a safe condition, or to reduce the water seeping into the tunnel. If the Metro continues to operate on the present basis, it will require a subsidy of at least US$1.4 million annually in the short term. The need for subsidies will probably increase later as aging equipment requires replacement and safety becomes an increasing concern.

At the same time, there is significant room to reduce current losses by improvements in governance (including accounting and reporting systems) and increased passenger tariffs. At the moment, metro's fare of 7.2 cents per trip is 20 percent lower than those charged by surface transport. In addition, about 20–25 percent of the riders go free because of Government decisions that granted free rides to 13 different categories of the population (including children and military personnel). More opportunity for further fare increases should become available shortly if the Government moves decisively with additional increases in fuel taxes for natural gas.[114] As private buses are mainly using vehicles powered with natural gas, which is very lightly taxed, this creates unfair competition for transport powered by both gasoline and electricity.

The main issues for the Metro are:

- How can the operating losses be reduced? Possibilities include increases in fares to at least equal the cost of surface transportation, elimination of free fares, staff reductions, better fare collection controls, and reducing the cost of electricity by installing a tunnel liner.
- Should the Metro continue to operate at all? The introduction of a private bus service has greatly improved surface transportation, reducing the need for metro operations. If it does

---

114. As discussed above, increases in fuel taxes are needed anyway to improve financing of road maintenance.

continue to operate, it should be explicitly subsidized through the budget. These issues will be illuminated by the Urban Transport Study that is just getting under way with the assistance of the World Bank. Efforts should be made to speed up the completion of this study, now scheduled for early 2003, so that it is available before the 2001 budget preparation process starts.

Municipal Water Systems

The Yerevan Water and Sewage Company (YSWC) and the Armenia Water and Sewage Company (AWSC) operate at substantial losses each year (approximately US$6.5 million annually for YWSC and US$4.0 million for AWSC). The Government finances a small part of their operating losses from subsidies in the Government budget, but most of the losses are financed by arrears owed to the power sector. Water losses are enormous, and collection rates are very low (26 percent of billings for YWSC and 31 percent for AWSC in 2001).

The sector is highly energy dependent, and there is a severe backlog of capital improvements and maintenance. There are chronic shortages of water supply, and in some parts of Yerevan water is available for only a few hours each day with poor pressure and frequent lack of service to the higher floors of buildings, extensive leakage and wastage. Contamination of drinking water from leakage of the sewage system, negative pressures and leaky water pipes represents a considerable health hazard, which can be expected to get worse unless the system is upgraded.

Table 8.2 highlights YWSC's operating deficiencies in several respects. There is a dramatic loss of water between the amount that is given to the system and the amount that is actually delivered to water users, indicating major system losses. The quantity of water of given to the system as well as delivered to the users is not actually measured in the absence of meters, but is calculated on the basis of estimated usage, and actual usage may be higher. This calculated figure is also used for billing purposes. The high level of losses (and/or under-billed usage) results in a use of electricity that is almost four times as high per cubic meter of delivered water as in Budapest.

The principal cause of the operating deficit is the low collection rate. Indeed, an adequate level of collections at the existing tariff would result in a positive cash flow for the sector. In Yerevan, the 2001 collection rates showed that the general population was paying only 10 percent of its billings, the private commercial organizations—73 percent, and the Government entities—86 percent. Securing payments from the general public, where the average billing is US$0.86 per month, was difficult because until recently YWSC did not have the legal right to terminate service for non-payment. There are also technical constraints to the cut-off of individual apartments in multi-apartment buildings, along with a general public disapproval of cutting off water supplies and the widespread acceptance of failure to pay.

TABLE 8.2: EFFICIENCY IN WATER DELIVERY: COMPARISON OF YEREVAN WITH BUDAPEST, 2000

	Yerevan	Budapest
Population	1.3 million	2.0 million
Quantity of Water Given to the System, mln Cm./year	431.2	228.5
Quantity of Water Delivered to Water Users, mln Cm./year	118.9	189.9
Electric Power Used, mln Kw.Hours/year	227.4	96.3
Water per person Given to the System, cm./year	331.7	114.3
Water per person Delivered to Users, cm./year	91.5	95.0
Kw. hr/cm given to the System	0.53	0.42
Kw. Hr/cm delivered to Water Users	1.91	0.51

Source: IBRD.

An IDA project is under way that is intended to improve the operations of YWSC, and another project is under preparation for improving AWSC. If successful, the operating losses are expected to decline gradually and reach a break-even point in about six years. The projects provide for both technical improvements and improved management practices needed to increase efficiency of operations. Specifically, they will finance the installation of additional block and retail meters as well as pump and network rehabilitation during 2002 to 2004 in Yerevan, and the employment of independent water operators to manage the companies under a performance-based contract with incentive payments based on results.

In an attempt to overcome the low collections rates, the Government improved monitoring of cash flows to increase the transparency of the companies. YWSC's sales department was restructured with a view to increasing collection rates and improving customer service. Discounts to privileged customers, which were mainly intended as subsidies for the industrial sector, were eliminated in 1999. However, none of these measures were effective in increasing collection rates as yet.

In November 2001, the Government agreed to revise the legal framework to provide powerful sanctions to support payment for water service. These changes include the right of service termination in the event of non-payment introduced in January 2002 by GOA Decree No. 55. The Government also adopted new procedures regarding multi-apartment buildings and condominiums, with service to be billed through a block meter and contracting for water to be through block representatives who will act for all of the residents of the building. In addition, in May of 2002 the National Assembly has adopted new Laws *On Condominiums* and *On Management of the Multi-Apartment Buildings* that established a legal framework for contracting between utilities and apartment block representatives. Based on these new measures, the Government is committed to a program of gradual improvement of collections, with the objective of reaching a positive cash flow by 2007.

The main issues facing the municipal water operations are:

- Could the Government send a strong signal to the water users so that they know that non-payment would lead to a cutoff of service?
- The Government should further advance institutional and governance reforms in the sector, including the expanding condominium forms of housing managements switching to new contract arrangements for water delivery, and enforcing new contracts.
- YWSC's and AWSC's residual deficits should be financed from the central budget between now and 2007 so that the power sector does not have to subsidize these operations.

Irrigated Agriculture

The extensive irrigation network in Armenia operates at a substantial loss (about US$9.5 million per year) because collections for irrigated water services are only about 20 percent of the cost of operations. The operating loss is financed for the most part by arrears owed to the power sector and by considerable government subsidies.

Irrigation is critical for Armenian agriculture, as nearly 80 percent of the total crop production is produced in the irrigated areas (although it is not economic in all places). Currently, about 33 percent of the arable land is irrigated, of which two-thirds by gravity and the rest by pumping stations. IDA is financing an Irrigated Development Project that is intended to reduce the cost of pumping and introduce a modern institutional framework that would support the Government policy to carry out a gradual increase in irrigation tariffs and collection with the goal of reaching full cost recovery in five to six years.

Water tariffs are currently at 40 percent of the cost recovery level, while less than 55 percent of the tariff is actually collected. On average the irrigated farm pays only about US$20 per year.[115]

---

115. However, this is not an insignificant amount, given that the average annual farm cash income (including remittances from abroad) is only about US$350 per farm.

The Government short term priorities in the irrigation sector include:

- Advancing an implementation of a sectoral action plan, including rationalizing collection arrangements, promoting water user associations, reducing staffing levels, improving governance and accountability, and lowering the system's dependence on energy by converting pump-based irrigation into gravity-based irrigation systems.
- Developing regulations required by the newly adopted (May 2002) Water Code and adopting Water User Associations (WUAs) Law.
- Introducing new institutional arrangements, including fair and transparent Transfer Agreements with WUAs, enforceable water delivery contracts, and new collection sharing arrangements with WUAs.
- Providing adequate budget financing of the remaining losses.
- Reviewing the structure of the irrigation network and closing down those elements that are not economical.

CHAPTER 9

PUBLIC INVESTMENTS: TRENDS, STRUCTURE AND SOURCES OF FINANCING

Under the current arrangements, the GOA develops its investment plans and implementation of the investment programs within annual State Budgets by making appropriations on capital construction and capital repair for the projects in basic and social infrastructure. There is no separate capital budget in Armenia. The approach based on public investment programming (PIP) has not been practiced in Armenia either. In 1995, the GOA did prepare a set of Medium-Term Investment Projections consistent with the overall macro and fiscal framework, but this exercise has never been updated.

The main part of the analysis in this Chapter is based exclusively on the data related to public investments funded from the regular state budget, and thus does not cover all sources of public investment finance. This is because there is no systematic data on non-budget public investments that include investments funded from the extra-budgetary funds of sectoral Ministries, from grants provided by international donors, as well as investments made by public enterprises and by the Central Bank.

Table 9.1 provides estimates for the volumes of non-budget public investment for 1998–2001. It shows that in 1999–2000, more than 20 percent of total public investment expenditures were not reflected in the government budget. This share has dramatically increased in 2001 to 44 percent due primarily to an expansion of the grant program by the Lincy Foundation.

As Table 9.2 shows, in 2001 the officially reported capital expenditure of the consolidated budget represented about 3.5 percent of GDP in Armenia. This reflects a considerable decline compared to the levels of the late 1990s_4.4 percent in 1997 and 4.9 in 1998. The decline in the total Government spending between 1997 and 2001 was largely a result of the decline in capital spending.

Main recent trends in capital budgeting could be summarized as the following:

- The coverage of capital expenditures in the budget has been expanded significantly since 1998, when most donor projects (including investment projects) have been consolidated in the budget.
- In 1999, the GOA prepared a comprehensive three-year program on Utilization of Privatization Proceeds for 2000–02, which provided justifications for additional public investments in transport, education, water sectors and the Earthquake Zone reconstruction.

TABLE 9.1: THE LEVELS AND STRUCTURE OF PUBLIC INVESTMENT FINANCING, 1998–2001
Million Dram

	1998	1999	2000	2001
Total Public Investments	54,221	60,950	50,768	73,092
As percent of GDP	5.66	6.15	4.92	6.21
o/w: by the State Budget	46,766	47,005	39,660	41,158
Non-Budget	7,455	13,94	11,108	31,934
–EBFs	1,500	1,500	2,250	7,712
–External Grants	4,031	7,209	5,461	13,108
–Other projects in the EQZ	1,269	3,787	2,259	9,864
–CBA Investments	655	1,449	1,138	1,250
Memo: Non-budget investments as percent of total	13.7%	22.9%	21.9%	43.7%

Source: MOFE, CBA, NSS data and staff estimates.

TABLE 9.2: CAPITAL EXPENDITURES OF THE CONSOLIDATED BUDGET, 1997–2001
as Percent of GDP

	1997	1998	1999	2000	2001
Total Capital Expenditures, million AMD	35,208	46,766	47,005	39,660	41,158
–share in GDP	4.38%	4.89%	4.76%	3.84%	3.51%
–share in total budget expenditures	17.66%	19.52%	16.56%	15.14%	14.42%

Source: MOFE, SIF, NSS data and staff estimates.

Thus, the share of privatization proceeds in investment funding has increased substantially in 2000–01 (see Tables 9.4 and 9.5 below).

▦ The GOA made an effort to accelerate EQZ rehabilitation and adopted several programs for mobilizing additional funding for these purposes. The most recent program was adopted in 2001 (see Box 9.1).

▦ Despite considerable spending funded from the privatization account, the share of investments funded from domestic sources declined from 46 percent of the total in 1996 to 26 percent in 2001 (with some ups and downs in between). Respectively, the share of foreign funded capital expenditures increased, and it is especially high in the energy (98 percent of total), agriculture (96 percent), and transport (68 percent) sectors.

▦ The share of new investment versus capital repair increased substantially in 1997–2001 (Table 9.3). However, this happened not because of declining demand for capital repair but

TABLE 9.3: CAPITAL CONSTRUCTION AND CAPITAL REPAIR, SHARES OF THE TOTAL BUDGET EXPENDITURES AND GDP, 1997–2001

	1997	1998	1999	2000	2001
Total Capital expenditures, million AMD, o/w:	35,208	46,766	47,005	39,660	41,158
Capital Construction	31,771	38,758	41,365	34,754	38,851
Percent of GDP	3.95	4.06	4.19	3.36	3.3
Percent of total expenditure	15.94	16.17	14.57	13.27	13.61
Capital repair	3,437	8,008	5,640	4,906	2,307
Percent of GDP	0.43	0.84	0.57	0.47	0.2
Percent of total expenditure	1.72	3.34	1.99	1.87	0.81

Source: MOFE, NSS data and staff estimates.

due to continuous under- funding of capital maintenance of existing assets. There is an obvious imbalance between relatively high availability of foreign financing for new construction and major rehabilitation works and constant shortage of local funding for proper daily upkeep of the existing assets.

Sources of Capital Expenditure Financing

State budget capital expenditures are segmented between domestically and externally financed projects. Historically, the lion share of total financing derived from external resources (Table 9.4). Domestic investment financing has three components: regular budget, the Government Reserve Fund, and earmarked privatization proceeds. Subsequently, bilateral and multilateral credits finance the rest of capital projects. Most current donor projects aimed at rehabilitation of the existing infrastructure, which deteriorated due to under-financing over the last 10 years. Those are the IDA Credits in transport, municipal services and irrigation, power transmission, rehabilitation of schools and hospitals; IFAD support for rehabilitation of irrigation, Japanese assistance in the energy sector, KFW involvement in the energy and water/sanitation, etc. However, rehabilitation, which is not complemented by increased current maintenance funding from the regular budget is meaningless. Completion of each of the above mentioned projects displays a huge drop in sectoral budget allocation for the respective year, which clearly signals that there is inadequate domestic substitution for externally provided investment credits.[116]

TABLE 9.4: CAPITAL EXPENDITURES FINANCED FROM DOMESTIC AND EXTERNAL SOURCES, 1997–2001

	Total Capital expenditures, million drams	Funded from privatization receipts, million drams	Funded from other domestic sources, million drams	Funded from foreign borrowings, million drams	Share of total financed domestically, percent	Share of total financed externally, percent
1997	35,208	52	17,434	17,721	49.7	50.3
1998	46,766	9,258	19,177	18,331	61.8	39.2
1999	47,005	9,679	13,294	24,031	48.9	51.1
2000	39,660	12,699	7,363	19,598	50.6	49.4
2001	41,158	5,986	7,560	27,612	22.9	67.1
Total	209,798	37,675	64,829	107,293	48.9	51.1

Source: MOFE data and staff estimates.

Trends in Capital Expenditure

Budget provisions for investment spending cover almost exclusively capital construction and rehabilitation of basic physical and social infrastructure, such as road rehabilitation, acquisition and rehabilitation of capital assets in the energy sector, repair and new construction in the municipal water systems, irrigation networks and dams, repair and construction of schools and public hospitals, and public housing. It is worth noting that in the 90s new construction was concentrated in the Earthquake Zone, where both the public infrastructure and housing stock were heavily destroyed or damaged by the 1988 Earthquake (Box 9.1 and Table 9.5). Major investment programs in the EQZ explain a relatively high share of total budget investments that is traditionally spent on municipal services and housing.

---

116. In 2000, the transport sector's budget allocation amounted to just 41 percent of the previous years' actual spending due to the completion in 1999 of the IDA First Transport Credit.

BOX 9.1: PROGRAMS FOR REHABILITATION OF THE EARTHQUAKE ZONE

For special tasks, the GOA had designed and adopted separate multi-year investment programs. It refers especially to the rehabilitation of the Earthquake Zone. The GOA initiated its first program for the EQZ in 1994,
which was then revised in 1998. By that time, the degree of completion of EQZ rehabilitation was about 45 percent. In late 1999, as a part of the Mid-Term Strategy on Use of Privatization Proceeds, the GOA earmarked
additional resources for the Earthquake Zone.[117] The most recent program for EQZ was adopted in mid-2001
to accelerate resolution of housing, infrastructure, schooling, and health issues in this Zone through consolidation of all available sources of investment funding (both domestic and external) for 2001–03. The required total
amount, according to the program, equals 80 billion AMD (7.5 percent of 2001 GDP), out of which 46 billion
was envisaged for housing. Table 9.5 displays both the actual performance of EQZ program in 1998–2001 and
projections for 2002–03.

TABLE 9.5: DOMESTICALLY FINANCED CAPITAL EXPENDITURES (1999–2001) IN THE EARTHQUAKE ZONE FROM ALL SOURCES, MILLION DRAM – ACTUAL AND 2002–03 PROJECTIONS

	Actual			Total	Planned	
	1999	2000	2001	1999–2001	2002	2003
Total domestically funded capital projects, o/w	22,973	20,062	13,546	56,581		
Investments in EQZ	3,463	8,486.2	4,299.7	16,248.9		
Investments in EQZ as percent of total dom. Investment	15.1%	42.3%	31.7%	28.7%		
Total Investments in EQZ, o/w	7,538	10,939	8,205	26,682	35,619	36,177
State Budget, o/w	3,751	8,680	5,001	17,432	6,798	7,235
PrPr + regular	3,463	8,486	4,300	16,249	2,505	
WB health project				—	200	
WB Judicial project				—	300	
Out-of Budget, o/w	3,787	2,259	3,204	9,250	28,821	28,941
Red-Cross	3,243	1,141	1,200	5,584		
Huntsman	30	512	300	842	500	
WB EQZ Rehabilitation Credit				—		
All Armenia Fund	260	336	663	1,259	596	
Lincy	559	559	19,625			
USAID	270	202	472	8,100		
Others	254		280	534		
Total from all sources (million USD)	14.1	20.3	14.8	51.7	62.5	
Investment in EQZ as percent of GDP	0.76%	1.06%	0.70%			

Source: MOFE, MOUD, NSS, CBA data and staff estimates.

The Figure 9.1 and Table 9.6 suggest that the sectoral break-down of capital projects funded on
expense of the consolidated budget has changed significantly over the last three years. However, agriculture remained the largest recipient of budget investments. Almost 26.4 percent of total capital
provisions in 2001 were targeted to the agriculture sector for rehabilitation of the irrigation system

---

117. The program suggested to utilize 4.5 billion drams per year for 2000–02 on housing construction,
school and hospital repair. Actual spending for 2000–01 totalled 8.5 billion drams (94.4 percent performance
for the first two years).

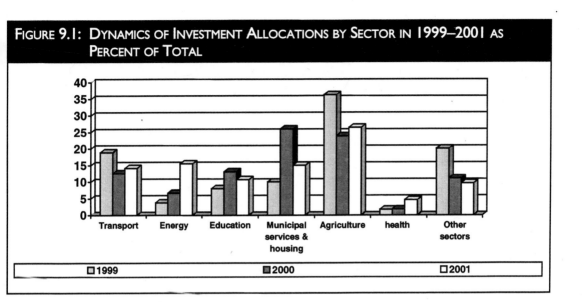

FIGURE 9.1: DYNAMICS OF INVESTMENT ALLOCATIONS BY SECTOR IN 1999–2001 AS PERCENT OF TOTAL

and for improvement of land conditions and mapping. While the sector gets the highest investment share, the recent trend shows a decline from 36.3 percent in 1999 to 26 percent in 2001.

The share of investments in social infrastructure (health, education, culture) has been increased substantially over the last three years: from 10 percent in 1999 to about 16.5 in 2001. This increase can be partially attributed to an increase in the disbursement rate of externally funded credits and to increased allocations from domestic sources (privatization proceeds). Rehabilitation of schools and hospitals is the basic type of investment funded in these sectors.

The energy sector shows a steady expansion of its share of the budget investment envelop. It increased about three times from 1999 to 2001 reaching 15.5 percent of the total. Investments in this sector are almost entirely covered by donor projects (IDA, KFW, EBRD, etc.).

The share of the transport sector has declined from about 19 percent in 1999 to 14 in 2001. This trend derived from two main events:

TABLE 9.6: SECTORAL ALLOCATION OF BUDGET INVESTMENTS IN 1999–2001

Million Dram

	1999	2000	2001
Total capital expenditures	47,005	39,660	41,158
Percent of GDP	4.74	3.84	3.50
Energy	1,790	2,797	6,625
Percent of GDP	0.18	0.27	0.56
Percent of total cap. Exp.	3.8	6.7	15.5
Transport	8,984	5,227	6,089
Percent of GDP	0.91	0.51	0.52
Percent of total cap. Exp.	18.9	12.6	14.2
Education	3,806	5,467	4,598
Percent of GDP	0.38	0.53	0.39
Percent of total cap. Exp.	8.0	13.1	10.7
Health	810	753	1,990
Percent of GDP	0.08	0.07	0.17
Percent of total cap. Exp.	1.7	1.8	4.6
Municipal services and housing	4,771	10,844	6,417
Percent of GDP	0.48	1.05	0.55
Percent of total cap. Exp.	10.0	26.0	15.0
Agriculture	17,262	9,942	11,313
Percent of GDP	1.74	0.96	0.96
Percent of total cap. Exp.	36.3	23.9	26.4
Other	9,582	4,632	4,126
Percent of GDP	0.97	0.45	0.35
Percent of total cap. Exp.	20.1	11.1	9.6

Source: MOFE, NSS data and staff estimates.

completion of the IDA Transport project and a major expansion of road investments funded by the Lincy Foundation that remain outside of the budget.

Investments in the sectors that represent the core public administration (governmental entities, courts, etc.) comprise about 10 percent of total capital budget. They are used for capital repair and reconstruction of administrative buildings, purchasing of office equipment, etc.

Overall Public Sector's Needs in Investment

Table 9.7 provides some illustrative estimates for annual demand in public investment that are based on the analysis in other PER Chapters. As Table 9.7 shows, the current budget provision for capital maintenance of basic public services is only 45 percent of the required amount of annual investments. The ratio is relatively higher for social infrastructure (87 percent) given the GOA efforts to complete school repairs and reconstruction in the EQZ. However, countryside schools are in desperate need of capital investment in order to maintain the basic assets and buildings, improve sanitation (water and sewage systems) and repair/reconstruct the heating supply.[118]

Budget provision for physical infrastructure covers about 68 percent of the annual investment needs in this sector. However, the biggest part of the gap, especially in the road sector, at the moment is covered by out of budget funding (Lincy foundation). The water sector gets only 24 percent of the annually required amount.

The GOA has announced a very ambitious target to complete the housing program in the EQZ by the end of 2003. This will require another US$64 million annual investment in the next two years. So far, the identified financing provided by the State Budget amounts only to 30 percent of the required amount.

TABLE 9.7: PUBLIC SECTORíS NEED IN INVESTMENT AND ACTUAL PROVISION IN FY 2001
US$ Million

	Total demand	Actual capital budget provision in 2001
Total requirement for annual investment, o/w	165.3	74.1
Public Infrastructure*	56.4	38.4
Social infrastructure**	13.6	11.9
EQZ (housing)	64.0	19.3
Others	31.3	4.5

Notes: * Includes municipal water, irrigation, roads/streets, railway and metro. ** Includes health and education sectors (schools, hospitals, ambulatories).
Source: MOFE, NSS, CBA data and staff estimates.

Planning and Budgeting of Public Investments

The lack of general multi-year budgeting in Armenia represents the one single feature that is the most detrimental to the establishment of efficient planning of public investments. Since the implementation of major investment projects takes more than one year, a longer-term budget vision is necessary to assure their sufficient/sustainable financing. A multi-year framework is also important to foresee the future recurrent costs associated with the undertaken investments. As was shown in Chapter 8, the current situation with financing of road maintenance well illustrates this

---

118. According to the Armenia School Boiler Replacement Study, conducted by the USAID contractor in 2000, the total estimated amount for rehabilitation of the heating system of all 1300 basic schools (installation of new boilers, construction of boiler houses and internal distribution network, weatherization of schools) will require an investment of about US$96 million.

problem_while the sector needs about US$30 million a year for current maintenance, the actual domestic financing is just about US$3.0 million per year. In the social sector, recurrent maintenance is also heavily underfinanced, which inflates future demands for capital expenditures.

The fundamental problem of the current investment budgeting relates to the fact that investments are planned and funded based on the residual approach. Capital expenditure is usually the spending category that is the most affected by sudden budget cuts and sequestrations.

However, the existing challenges in capital budgeting are not only related to the level of investment spending, but also, and primarily to the quality of investment budgeting. The GOA has to identify its priorities much more clearly and then adjust resource allocation for capital investments in line with these priorities. So far, there is lack of adequate economic/financial analysis of investment proposals, while tools for efficient inter- and intra-sectoral allocation of the available investment resources remain badly underdeveloped. There is no proper project evaluation and analysis (for example, the impact of current under-financing on project performance). Main budgeting decisions are often driven by a desire to complete unfinished construction or by purely populistic interests. Such decision making suffers from a lack of strategic vision.

At the moment, the Government does not have a real investment strategy, which would be based on realistic estimates of investment needs of the public sector, availability of resources, and clearly spelled out set of priorities. Instead, the investment program is a combination of separated sectoral projects, which are often initiated by donors, prepared by donors, and implemented by sectoral ministries under donor supervision. A separate treatment of domestically and externally financed capital projects does not provide a consolidated vision on the final picture of investment. There is no central oversight of the investment process in the system, which reflects in part the fact that the Government does not have a real Ministry of Economy.

In this respect, the Armenian situation was not much different from the one in most other FSU economies, all of which were affected by a dramatic decline in the overall level of public investments as well as by the residual approach to the investment budgeting. These similarities go well beyond the low level of public investments and also include underdeveloped institutional arrangements for investment budgeting, such as budget segmentation and lack of prioritization.[119]

Weakness of investment planning manifests itself in chronic budget arrears for co-financing of donor investment projects. While co-financing requirements amount on average to 15–20 percent of the total project costs, the budget has been failing regularly to afford this portion. Table 9.8 presents the level of arrears on counterpart funding for 2000–01. As discussed in the earlier World Bank Report (1998a), budget arrears on counterpart funding is among the most traditional indicators of problems in budget management as well as of weak integration between donor programs and the recipient's budget process. It also usually suggests that donor projects fail to establish necessary sustainability mechanisms, which would provide necessary financial support to the

TABLE 9.8: ARREARS ON COUNTERPART FUNDING FOR ONLY IDA FUNDED PROJECTS
Million Dram, Year End

	2000	2001
Arrears on counterpart funding for IDA projects	412.0	943.0
Total arrears on capital expenditures	2,690.0	3,833.0
Counterpart arrears as percent of total domestic budget investment	2.1%	7.0%

Source: MOFE, WB data and staff estimates.

---

119. World Bank's Report "Russia – Towards Improving the Efficiency of Public Investment Expenditures" (2001) provides a comprehensive review of the situation with investment budgeting in Russia, which suggests a number of similarities with the current Armenia's challenges.

project after donors' funds are fully disbursed. In Armenia's circumstances, persistence of arrears on counterpart funding, accompanied by the fact that the Government budget is seriously over-committed, may suggest a need for downsizing the donors' funded investment program, at least till there is tangible progress in budget management and expenditure restructuring.

It is worth noting that the current procedures for capital budget execution and reporting are somewhat different from those that are used for the overall budget expenditures, and which were described in Chapter 4. First, the formal presentation of investment expenditures is based primarily on the administrative (ministries and marzpetarans/regions) classification. This has an advantage of establishing clear institutional responsibility for the execution of respective budget items, but at the same time makes it rather difficult to assess sectoral priorities within the investment program. Secondly, and more importantly, almost all donor assisted investment projects are executed by Project Implementation Units (PIUs), without much involvement from the Treasury. As noted above, the consolidation of these expenditures into the State Budget faces some difficulties because PIUs in most cases have different procedures for procurement, reporting and accounting because by their status they are not budgetary institutions but Joint Stock Companies. This creates additional inconsistencies in reporting, including misunderstanding between the MOFE and donors on the actual level of budget arrears with respect to Government co-financing.

Data Availability and Accuracy

The actual budget execution reports provide for more or less systematic time-series on capital expenditure trends over the last 4–5 years. While the data are classified in both economic and functional categories (broadly consistent with the old GFS classification), there are several cases of mis-classification. For instance, a project that has several different sectoral components is usually reflected in the single sector. Moreover, misclassifications appear to be the most serious for exter-nally financed investment projects. Many such projects are not reflected as part of their respective sectors in the functional classification (ASIF, Lincy, SATAC, etc.). Instead they are shown in "the Non-classified" group of expenditures.

As far as the economic classification is concerned, either the entire amount of foreign financed projects is reflected as capital expenditure, or it is shown in "other expenditures" without separa-tion between recurrent maintenance, operational and capital expenditures. While the MOFE has consolidated foreign financed project expenditures in the regular State Budgets, it is rather a mechanical integration without an accurate classification of these expenses.

In case of domestically financed capital projects one should also take into account expenses made from the GOA Reserve Fund (RF) for investment purposes. In both classifications they are hidden under the RF expenditures. In addition, the program for use of Privatization Proceeds is usually presented separately from the regular budget (as an annex to the State budget) or it is approved by a separate law as an amendment to the annual Budget Law.

The review of expenditures classified as capital expenses in the State budget identified several inconsistencies. The nature of several particular items suggests that they should be removed from the investment part of the budget. Those are spending envisaged for internal audit of the Privatization account, acquisition of driver licenses, recurrent maintenance of roads in the winter season, etc.

ASSESSMENT AND RECOMMENDATIONS ON BUDGET MANAGEMENT SYSTEM

ANNEX 1: ASSESSMENT AND RECOMMENDATIONS ON BUDGET MANAGEMENT SYSTEM[1]

Budget Objectives	Assessment	PER Recommendations
Transparency		
The budget documents should clearly indicate for what purpose funds are being appropriated and who is accountable for those funds.	The high level of detail of the budget documents makes them difficult to analyse and obtain a clear picture of budgetary policy. Appropriations are primarily made by functional classification; functions cross ministries/agencies, leading to difficulties in assigning budgetary responsibility for ministries'/agencies' allocations to single individuals. No justifications (e.g. statements of priority Government policies, strategies) for budgetary allocations.	Reduce the level of detail in the annual budget law – concentrate on administrative classification for appropriation and provide summary and overview of comprehensive budget picture. Provide budget analysis by functional classification in annexes to Annual Budget Law. In the medium term, strengthening of the MTEF will include the preparation of sector strategies to provide the basis for MTEF and Annual Budget allocations.
The basis for budgeting should be well defined.	Basis for budgetary allocations is not transparent. Draft Budgetary allocations are undertaken by MFE on an incremental basis with little recourse to sector ministries nor to planned policies.	Change in the basis of budget estimation from line-items to estimates based on activities needed to undertake broad programmes. Strengthen role of sector ministries in budget preparation process. Annual Budget submissions should be based on MTEF sector strategies. MFE to determine and circulate sector/ministry ceilings, based on the MTEF, to sector ministries prior to beginning of Annual Budget preparation. Changed role for MFE in budget preparation process: more strategic (setting sector/ministry ceilings, co-ordinating MTEF sector submissions, analysing inter-sectoral issues, and analysing and discussing sector budgetary requests with sector ministries)
Budget documents should provide clear linkage between sector objectives and budgets.	No indications of objectives, activities or expected outputs are included in the budget documents.	Preparation of MTEF sector strategies will outline objectives, priorities, activities and expected outputs and expenditure implications for broad programme areas. Introduction of programme area into annual budget presentation/ classification will complete the link between programme activities and budgetary allocations.

Procedures should be clear and well documented. All participants in the budget process should be clear about their roles and responsibilities.	Sector ministry staff in practice have limited role in budget process although according to the Organic Budget Law they should have a more significant role. Role of MFE staff in making budgetary allocations is not clear.	Strengthen role of sector ministries in budget preparation process. Annual Budget submissions should be based on MTEF sector strategies. Role of MFE: to determine and circulate sector/ministry ceilings, based on the MTEF, to sector ministries prior to beginning of Annual Budget preparation. Transfer budget execution role from MFE main departments to Treasury. The roles of sector ministry and MFE staff should be reflected in budget preparation guidelines/instructions.
Expenditure ceilings should be circulated and clearly explained.	No expenditure ceilings set.	As part of MTEF reforms, sector/ministry ceilings will be determined and circulated (on the basis of MTEF macro/fiscal framework) prior to the start of the Annual Budget process.
Legitimacy, Accountability and Credibility		
Budgets should be achievable and relatively close to eventual actual figures.	Unrealistic revenue and cash forecasts have prevented the full execution of recent budgets.	Improvements to estimating revenue projections are an MFE priority.
The budget should be enforceable.	The budget is enforced on a cash basis only. Existing commitments are not always settled, resulting in substantial payment arrears' being carried forward to ensuing accounting periods.	Greater attention needs to be paid to ensuring that arrears do not accumulate, through better commitment controls. Improvements to the accounting methodology for commitments need to be made. These are expected to be fully covered in the second-generation Treasury reforms and a comprehensive FMIS. A system of setting cash limits (e.g. quarterly) below the level of appropriations should be implemented for the 2003 Budget.
Politicians should be involved in the process at an early stage.	Government does not get involved in the annual budget process until it is presented with the draft budget, which is too late for them to have a strategic role.	The political leadership should be involved at a much earlier stage in the budget preparation process, particularly in determining the expenditure ceilings. The chapter sets out a revised calendar, covering preparation of the MTEF and the Annual Budget.
Senior officials in sector ministries must be involved and accountable in each stage of the process.	Sector ministries have little role in budget-setting, thus making functional allocations non-credible, as those expected to implement the budgets are not actively involved in budget setting. The present appropriations (primarily based on functional classification) make it difficult to hold individuals accountable for budgetary allocations.	As part of MTEF reforms, switch away from promulgating budgets on a functional basis; switch to approving budgets according to the administrative classification. . This will give authority to sector ministers and accounting officers to programme and manage their budget to facilitate the achievement of sector policies. The functional allocation will continue to be used for policy and budgetary analysis

(continued)

ANNEX 1: ASSESSMENT AND RECOMMENDATIONS ON BUDGET MANAGEMENT SYSTEM[1] (CONTINUED)

Budget Objectives	Assessment	PER Recommendations
		Sector ministries to be given primary role in programming and implementing sector policies and budgets - moving away from building up detailed budgets in a mechanistic way by cost centres and instead by sector ministries to plan their budgets by broad programme area.
To avoid undermining the budget process, MFE should enforce sector/ministry ceilings; ministries must be aware that budget ceilings will be enforced.	Not applicable, as budgetary ceilings are not set.	As part of MTEF reforms, sector/ministry ceilings will be determined and circulated (on the basis of MTEF macro/fiscal framework) prior to the start of the Annual Budget process.
Comprehensiveness		
Budgets should include all cash transactions, including all external finance and ministries'/agencies' own resources.	State Budget excludes projects funded by external grants and ministries' own resources.	MFE to collect comprehensive data on external projects (grant financed) and reflect realistic expenditure allocations in the Annual Budget. Annual Budget Law should include an annex setting out PIP budgetary allocations by ministry/agency (both domestic and external financing). Budget guidelines to specify that ministry submissions should include ministries'/agencies' resources – both receipts (included in "non-tax revenues") and the use of these resources (included in the allocations for each relevant ministry). A separate annex to the Annual Budget Law could summarise the expected collection of these funds by ministry. Privatisation proceeds should be included in the budget estimates from the 2003 Budget in line with IMF classification conventions.
Link with Government policies		
Annual budget must be consistent with objectives and policies of approved medium and longer-term strategies.	Annual Budgets are not prepared on the basis of the MTEF. Sector/ministry ceilings are not set prior to Annual Budget preparation.	Gradual strengthening of MTEF to ensure that it is strategic and is used to guide Annual Budgets. MTEF and annual allocations should be based on sector strategies setting out short, medium and long-term policies and providing appropriate finance to fulfil these policies.

Robustness and Flexibility

The budget system should be capable of responding to changed circumstances	Revenue shortfalls necessitate expenditure reductions. Such decisions are taken centrally and are arbitrary.	Improved revenue estimation should lessen the risk of shortfalls. Where reductions are unavoidable, spending ministries need to be involved in deciding where cuts can be made and must identify the consequences. Any requests for changes to the budget must be rigidly analysed and justified.
Budget system should be capable of providing budget managers with some discretion over the use of funds in delivering services, provided expenditures do not exceed authorised amounts.	Expenditure budgets are enforced strictly by function and economic items. Little discretion is permitted to sector budget managers to switch funds between items within a function except by formal virement. Budgets and budget reductions are generally imposed from the top down. No sense of ownership of budgets by people responsible for delivering public services (service managers).	Replace line-item budgeting with more flexible arrangements (e.g. budgets appropriated by ministry and broad programme areas). Changes will need to be accompanied by appropriate legislative/ regulation changes, including changes to virement rules and budget presentation. Learn from the experiments on global budgeting being conducted in health and education, particularly with respect to ensuring appropriate accountability and assigning sanctions for budget mismanagement. Training will be needed in financial management for budget managers both in budget centres and in sector ministries.

Strategic

Annual budget allocations should stem from medium-term Government objectives and policy priorities	Annual Budgets are not prepared on the basis of the MTEF since MTEFs to date have been prepared after the annual budget (first year of MTEF) had already been completed. Thus, the MTEF does not inform the annual budget allocations.	
Government should circulate medium-term budget policy framework prior to start of Annual Budget preparation	MTEF policy and framework are not currently circulated.	

Notes: 1. Criteria are described in Chapter 4.

MTEF ACTION PLAN MATRIX

ANNEX 2: MTEF ACTION PLAN MATRIX

	2003	2004	2005
Objective(s)	To prepare and present to Government by June 2003 an initial strategic MTEF covering 2004–2006 which serves to guide the preparation of the 2004 Annual Budget.	To further develop and strengthen the MTEF in order to support the objectives of encouraging strategic reallocation of budgetary resources to meet Government policy objectives.	Complete a comprehensive MTEF for 2006–2008 by June 2005.
Establishment of Process	Implement integrated MTEF-Budget timetable and decision-making process as agreed by MTEF Committees in 2002. MOFE to conduct a seminar for line ministries in January 2003 and issue MTEF Guidelines in March 2003, informing ministries of the process, key dates, core assumptions to be used and the information they must provide. Guidelines should encourage line ministries to align their priorities with the PRSP (once it has been adopted by the Government). Revise the format and content of the 2004 Budget Methodological Instructions to ensure that they communicate to line ministries and other budget organisations MTEF decisions, including indicative expenditure ceilings within which line ministries should prepare their budget submissions. Review the overall MTEF-Budget process and identify any areas where refinement is needed for the 2005–2007 MTEF update.	The indicative expenditure ceilings for 2005 that were agreed during the 2004–2006 MTEF process should be the starting point for line ministries for the 2005–2007 update process. Review the format and content of the 2005 Budget Methodological Instructions to ensure that they communicate to line ministries and other budget organisations MTEF decisions, including indicative expenditure ceilings within which line ministries should prepare their budget submissions. Review the overall MTEF-Budget process and identify any areas where refinement is needed for the 2006–2008 MTEF update.	The indicative expenditure ceilings for 2006 that were agreed during the 2005–2007 MTEF process should be the starting point for line ministries for the 2006–2008 update process. Review the format and content of the 2006 Budget Methodological Instructions to ensure that they communicate to line ministries and other budget organisations MTEF decisions, including indicative expenditure ceilings within which line ministries should prepare their budget submissions. Review the overall MTEF-Budget process and identify any areas where refinement is needed for the 2007–2009 MTEF update.
Institutional aspects	MTEF Committees should be actively involved through the MTEF and Budget decision-making process in reviewing and making decisions on: ▪ Government's fiscal principles and objectives (long and short term) in relation to revenue, expenditure and debt; ▪ Indicative three-year expenditure ceilings for line ministries (existing commitments);	MTEF Committees should be actively involved through the MTEF and Budget decision-making process in reviewing and making decisions on: ▪ Government's fiscal principles and objectives (long and short term) in relation to revenue, expenditure and debt; ▪ Indicative three-year expenditure ceilings for line ministries (existing commitments);	MTEF Committees should be actively involved through the MTEF and Budget decision-making process in reviewing and making decisions on: ▪ Government's fiscal principles and objectives (long and short term) in relation to revenue, expenditure and debt;

	▓ Areas of priority for additional expenditure, should sufficient funds be available at the time the 2004 Budget is being finalised. Government should submit to the National Assembly an amendment to the Budget Systems Law that identifies the MTEF as an annual requirement of the annual budget process and details minimum information disclosure, roles and responsibilities and key dates. During preparation of MTEF 2004–2006, test the preparation arrangements and institutional structure throughout the budgetary cycle. Review the institutional arrangements during preparation of 2004–2006 MTEF to identify any weaknesses to implement for 2005–2007 MTEF. Identify training needs assessment to identify what institutional capacity strengthening will be needed (e.g. macro/fiscal analysis, sector expenditure analysis, etc.)	▓ Areas of priority for additional expenditure, should sufficient funds be available at the time the 2004 Budget is being finalised. Review the institutional arrangements during preparation of 2005–2007 MTEF to identify any weaknesses to implement for 2006–2008 MTEF. Continue to implement MTEF training programme.	▓ Indicative three-year expenditure ceilings for line ministries (existing commitments); ▓ Areas of priority for additional expenditure, should sufficient funds be available at the time the 2004 Budget is being finalised. Continue to review the institutional arrangements during preparation of 2006–2008 MTEF to identify any weaknesses to implement for 2007–2000 MTEF. Continue to implement MTEF training programme.
Consultation and Accountability/ Transparency	2004–2006 MTEF should be presented to the National Assembly in June 2003 for information/debate (for information, not approval). 2004–2006 MTEF (or a summary of it) should be made available to the public (electronically or in hard copy) soon after it is finalised (ideally, by July 2003). Present updated MTEF at donors' conference (September/October).	2005–2007 MTEF should be presented to the National Assembly in June 2004 for information/debate (for information, not approval). 2005–2007 MTEF (or a summary of it) should be made available to the public (electronically or in hard copy) soon after it is finalised (ideally, by July 2004). Present updated MTEF at donors' conference (September/October).	2006–2008 MTEF should be presented to the National Assembly in June 2005 for information/debate (for information, not approval). 2006–2008 MTEF (or a summary of it) should be made available to the public (electronically or in hard copy) soon after it is finalised (ideally, by July 2005). Present updated MTEF at donors' conference (September/October).
MTEF Document	Prepare MTEF 2004–2006 during January to May 2003. Present MTEF to Government in June 2003.	Prepare MTEF 2005–2007 during January to May 2004. Present MTEF to Government in June 2004.	Prepare MTEF 2006–2008 during January to May 2005. Present MTEF to Government in June 2005.

(continued)

ANNEX 2: MTEF ACTION PLAN MATRIX (CONTINUED)

	2003	2004	2005
	The 2004–2006 MTEF should be presented in a format agreed by the MTEF Committees in 2002. This will comprise: ■ Fiscal policy statement, containing the Government's agreed fiscal principles and its long and short-term fiscal objectives. ■ Expenditure Policy Strategy, detailing the policy and expenditure priorities of each sector (built up from line ministry submissions). ■ Revised sector ceilings prior to circulation of Annual Budget guidelines to sector ministries.	The 2005–2007 MTEF should include an assessment of the extent to which the Government is achieving the fiscal objectives set out in the 2004–2006 MTEF. The rationale and factors driving any changes to these fiscal principles and objectives should be explained.	The 2006–2008 MTEF should include an assessment of the extent to which the Government is achieving the fiscal objectives set out in the 2005–2007 MTEF. The rationale and factors driving any changes to these fiscal principles and objectives should be explained.
Macro/fiscal framework	Aim to prepare initial 2004–2006 MTEF macro/fiscal framework by March/April. Present MTEF macro/fiscal scenarios to Government by April. Review macroeconomic policy and prepare updated summary statement of macroeconomic policies. Update macro forecasts and develop two macroeconomic scenarios for preliminary MTEF framework. ■ Identify and analyse weaknesses in macro and fiscal projections. ■ Identify achievable improvements in macro/fiscal projections during 2003. ■ Update PIP projections incorporating all external financing. ■ Ensure consistency between macro and fiscal frameworks. ■ Incorporate PRGF assumptions in macro/fiscal framework. Draft technical note on the 2004–2006 macroeconomic outlook based on updated macroeconomic indicators, an analysis of medium term macroeconomic policy and Government's decision on the macro framework.	Further develop and strengthen macro/fiscal framework. Identify and undertake more detailed analyses of selected macro and fiscal issues, including macro impact of revenue measures.	Further develop and strengthen macro/fiscal framework. Identify and undertake more detailed analyses of selected macro and fiscal issues, including macro impact of revenue measures.

	Update projections for 2004–2006 domestic revenue outlook and incorporate analysis of impact of likely changes in tax policy into medium-term revenue estimates. Present two scenarios for domestic revenues based on the two macro scenarios. Draft technical note on the 2004–2006 domestic revenue outlook based on updated actual revenue data, an analysis of medium term tax/ revenue policy and Government's decision on the revenue framework. Analyse budget deficit financing to include *inter alia* external financing of public investment. Include table of consolidated fiscal operations that includes state and local budgets and Social Insurance Fund.		Include analysis of additional cross-sectoral issues.
Cross-sectoral expenditure issues	Identify cross-sectoral expenditure issues to address for 2004–2006 MTEF. Include analysis of 2–3 key cross-sectoral expenditure issues as annex to MTEF document. Make projections of non-discretionary expenditures (i.e. debt servicing payments) and assess impact of non-discretionary spending on resources available for other expenditures. Analyse trends and develop recommendations and projections for discretionary expenditure by economic items (e.g. wagebill, operations and maintenance, transfers, investment).	Include analysis of additional cross-sectoral issues.	Include analysis of additional cross-sectoral issues.
Sector expenditure strategies	Prepare overall analysis of Government strategic expenditure priorities (based on Government policy statements) Discuss and agree on which sectors will be pilots for sector expenditure strategies. Set out TORs for sector working groups.	Extend sector expenditure strategies to include additional sectors.	Extend sector expenditure strategies to include additional sectors. Include analysis of sector performance?

(continued)

ANNEX 2: MTEF ACTION PLAN MATRIX (CONTINUED)

	2003	2004	2005
	Prepare guidelines for preparation of sector expenditure strategies. If possible, prepare one or more sector expenditure strategies in sectors which are priorities for Government and which are implementing major reform programmes		Review and make any necessary alterations to ensure that the MTEF is comprehensive of all expenditures.
Medium-term expenditure plans	Ministry of Finance to discuss and agree on format (i.e. level of detail and which expenditure categories to include) for medium-term sector ceilings. Set sector and ministry resource ceilings for 2004–2006 at the level of detail agreed during 2002.	Extend resource ceilings to include intra-ministerial programme ceilings. Incorporate ministries' own resources and grants in resource framework.	
Annual Budget process	Revise the format and content of the Annual Budget document/process to enable the linkages between MTEF and the Annual Budget to be made transparent (and any changes between MTEF and the Budget to be explained). In particular, ▪ Discuss necessary changes to the budget classification to enable MTEF to be presented eventually by broad sector programmes. ▪ Ensure necessary changes to budget calendar to enable the 2004–2006 MTEF to be prepared during the first half of 2003. ▪ Include sector and ministry resource ceilings in budget guidelines. Decide on level of detail to present forward budgets for 2005 and 2006 (e.g. at ministry and programme level). ▪ Review virement rules and identify any changes needed to enable strategic intra-sectoral allocations to be made across programmes (rather than across economic items). ▪ Review Treasury rules to identify what changes are needed to enable them to report against the revised budget (e.g. programme) format.	Based on an assessment of the MTEF and Annual Budget process in 2003, make any necessary revisions to the format and content of the Annual Budget document/process.	Based on an assessment of the MTEF and Annual Budget process in 2004, make any necessary further revisions to the format and content of the Annual Budget document/process.

FISCAL AND QUASI-FISCAL SUBSIDIES: SOURCES OF FINANCING AND RECIPIENTS, 1999–2000

ANNEX 3: FISCAL AND QUASI-FISCAL SUBSIDIES: SOURCES OF FINANCING AND RECIPIENTS, 1999
Million Drams

	Total net subsidies received	Total fiscal net	Budget subsidies	Increase in tax arrears	Total quazi-fiscal net	Energy subsidies	Water subsidies	Irrigation subsidies	Heat subsidies	Gas subsidies
Total subsidies, net	**36,713.9**	**36,713.9**	**23,991.2**	**12,722.7**	**0.0**	**0.0**	**0.0**	**0.0**	**0.0**	**0.0**
Net sub./GDP	3.7%	3.7%	2.4%	1.3%						
Net Recipients:										
Transport	573.7	900.2	900.0	0.2	-326.5	-326.5				
Culture	577.8	577.8	577.8		0.0					
Energy	-3,324.5	5,616.2	2,688.0	2,928.2	-8,940.7	-9,698.3				757.6
Drinking water	-1,354.6	5,607.6	5,061.0	546.6	-6,962.2	869.0	-7,831.2			
Irrigation	10,836.3	8,270.2	7,764.4	505.8	2,566.1	3,589.7		-1,023.6		
Heating	-2,207.6	2,289.5	2,600.0	-310.5	-4,497.1				-6,997.6	2,500.5
Gas sector	-8,247.0	165.0		165.0	-8,412.0					-8,412.0
Population	21,762.4	1,300.6		1,300.6	20,461.8	6,771.0	7,803.9	1,023.6	3,590.4	1,272.9
Industry	15,748.1	10,665.7	4,400.0	6,265.7	5,082.4	-1,524.3			3,097.0	3,509.7
o/w: Nairit	9,919.4	4,161.6	4,400.0	-238.4	5,757.8	150.3			3,097.0	2,510.5
Budgetary organiz	1,228.3	0.0			1,228.3	829.7	27.3			371.3
Other	1,120.9	1,321.0		1,321.0	-200.1	-510.3			310.2	
memo: Gross subsidies	70,676.6	36,713.9	23,991.2	12,722.7	33,962.7	9,698.3	7,831.2	1,023.6	6,997.6	8,412.0
Gross sub./GDP	7.1%	3.7%	2.4%	1.3%	3.4%	1.0%	0.8%	0.1%	0.7%	0.8%

memo: Quazi-fiscal financing of subsidies   28,812.0
     as percent of GDP   2.9%
     GDP = 991,549.7

Annex 3: Fiscal and Quazi-fiscal Subsidies: Sources of Financing and Recipient, FY 2000

Million Drams

PUBLIC EXPENDITURE REVIEW OF ARMENIA   171

	Total net subsidies received	Total fiscal net	Budget subsidies	Increase in tax arrears	Total quazi-fiscal net	Energy subsidies	Water subsidies	Irrigation subsidies	Heat subsidies	Gas subsidies
Total subsidies, net	38,335.5	38,335.5	9,741.8	28,593.7	0.0	0.0	0.0	0.0	0.0	0.0
Net sub./GDP	3.7%	3.7%	0.9%	2.8%						
Net Recipients:										
Transport	4,241.2	3,284.7	3,172.5	112.2	956.5	956.5				
Culture	413.6	413.6	413.6		0.0					
Energy	13,043.5	21,758.3		21,758.3	-8,714.8	-20,295.2				11,580.4
Drinking water	223.1	3,347.9	1,277.0	2,070.9	-3,124.8	4,515.8	-7,640.6			
Irrigation	8,540.3	5,206.5	4,760.0	446.5	3,333.8	5,110.5		-1,776.7		
Heating	-4,521.9	0.0			-4,521.9	-28.0			-2,448.8	-2,045.1
Gas sector	-6,894.0	0.0			-6,894.0					-6,894.0
Population	18,204.8	4,627.8	421.9	4,205.9	13,577.0	5,801.4	6,625.5	1,776.7	-114.3	-512.3
Industry	2,647.7	-303.2	-303.2		2,950.9	1,552.6	946.1		2,134.4	-1,682.2
o/w: Nairit	269.7	0.0			269.7	72.2			2,118.2	-1,920.7
Budgetary organiz	1,234.9	0.0			1,234.9	1,311.7	69.0		24.7	-170.5
Other	1,202.4	0.0			1,202.4	1,074.7			404.0	-276.3
memo: Gross subsidies	77,390.8	38,335.5	9,741.8	28,593.7	39,055.3	20,295.2	7,640.6	1,776.7	2,448.8	6,894.0
Gross sub./GDP	7.5%	3.7%	0.9%	2.8%	3.8%	2.0%	0.7%	0.2%	0.2%	0.7%

memo: Quazi-fiscal financing of subsidies   23,255.5
       as % of GDP   2.3%

GDP = 1,032,629.9

DIRECTIONS FOR RE-CLASSIFICATION OF NON-CLASSIFIED BUDGET EXPENDITURES UNDER THE GFS 2001

Annex 4: Directions for Re-classification of Non-Classified Budget Expenditures Under the GFS 2001

NON-CLASSIFIED EXPENDITURES, 2001 State budget, million AMD

		Planned	Actual	Classification under GFS 2001
14	**NON-CLASSIFIED EXPENDITURES**	**45,966.00**	**51,314.97**	
01	**Operations relating to state debt obligations**	17,647.8	12,709.0	01.7.0 General Public Services—Public debt transactions
1	Treasury T-bills service costs (interest rate payment)	8,790.0	6,541.5	01.7.0 General Public Services—Public debt transactions
2	Expenditures on bond-services	28.7	28.7	01.7.0 General Public Services—Public debt transactions
3	Service of credits from foreign countries and international organizations (interest rate payment), o/w	8,829.2	6,138.8	01.7.0 General Public Services—Public debt transactions
02	**Transfers from State Budget to community budgets**	7,641.8	6,801.9	01.8.0 Transfers of a general character
	Financial Equalization Subsidies to community budgets	7,641.8	6,801.9	01.8.0 Transfers of a general character
06	**Other programs**	20,676.4	29,697.0	
1	Issuing passport blank forms	165.0	164.6	01.6.0 Other public services not elsewhere classified
2	Maintenance of Artsvashen community leader's staff	3.0	2.6	01.1.1 Executive and legislative organs, financial and fiscal affairs, external affairs
3	Conducting census in Armenia	92.2	42.7	01.3.2 Over-all planning and statistical services
4	Acquisition of vehicle plate numbers	104.2	100.4	04.5.1 Road transport
5	Reexploitation of Talin's anti-flood system	66.0	17.5	04.2.1 Agriculture
6	GOA counterpart contribution to the ASIF II project	88.0	—	01.6.0 Other public services not elsewhere classified

7	WB-ASIF	1,454.8	1,142.0	01.6.0 Other public services not elsewhere classified
8	Lincy foundation-Culture, Highways, Earthquake area	150.0	143.0	01.6.0 Other public services not elsewhere classified
9	ADA	60.0	60.0	04.1.1 General economic and commercial affairs
10	Clearance of previous budgetary years arrears	4,852.3	6,683.9	01.1.2 Financial and fiscal affairs
11	Reserve fund of RA Government	5,407.0	10,895.9	01.1.2 Financial and fiscal affairs
12	Small and Medium Enterprise Support	20.0	20.0	04.1.1 General economic and commercial affairs
13	Inflows from budgetary loans repayments	(122.9)	—	01.7.0 General Public Services - Public debt transactions
14	Maintenance of seismic services	187.9	181.8	03.5.0 R&D Public order and safety
15	Maintenance of camps	2.2	0.2	10.4.0 Family and children
16	Lincy foundation-Loan project	2,750.0	3,466.7	01.6.0 Other public services not elsewhere classified
17	WB-EDP	825.0	460.4	01.6.0 Other public services not elsewhere classified
18	WB-SATAC II	1,103.9	974.4	01.6.0 Other public services not elsewhere classified
19	Huntsman Fund-Construction of schools and appartments	1,885.4	369.7	06.1.0 Housing development
20	Government's countribution to the Lincy project	19.5	19.4	01.6.0 Other public services not elsewhere classified
21	Other programs	1,203.0	1,203.0	01.6.0 Other public services not elsewhere classified
22	Government investment fund	60.0	33.3	04.1.1 General economic and commercial affairs
23	Application Expenditures	—	3,641.7	03.6.0 Public order and safety not elsewhere classified
24	Measures aimed at effective use of privatization proceeds	300.0	73.8	01.1.2 Financial and fiscal affairs
7	Russia's 73.7 USD debt service	—	2,107.0	01.7.0 General Public Services - Public debt transactions
1	Russia's 73.7 USD debt service	—	2,107.0	01.7.0 General Public Services - Public debt transactions

REVISED DEMOGRAPHIC ESTIMATES[1]

A rmenia has experienced a significant decline in its population due the significant out-migration during the nineties and significant declines in fertility. Biases in population estimates lead into serious biases in basic indicators such as number of beds or doctors per 1,000 population in the health sector. Biases in demographic composition leads also to problems in forecasting sustainability of pension systems or payroll tax related issues. In order to provide a more accurate picture, revised population estimates were computed for Armenia. The estimates are based on the data from a combination of sources, including the Demographic Census, official number of births and deaths, and migration figures.

Different strategies were adopted for developing population estimates between 1990 and 2001, and for those after 2001.

- Population estimates between 1990 and 2001 were based on: (i) 1990 official statistics, (ii) number of births of that year and number of post-neonatal deaths for population under 1 year, (iii) age-specific mortality rates and age-specific net migration for population over 1 year.
- Population estimates after 2001 were based on (i) general fertility rate (own assumptions based on the recent trends), (ii) post-neonatal mortality rate for population under 1 year, and (iii) age-specific mortality rate for population over 1 year.

Sources of the data for year and age specific net migration numbers:

- 2001 population Census: Preliminary results of 2001 Census have been released on Feb 15, 2002 by the NSS. According to Census total number of de facto population in Armenia in 2001 was 3,002,768.

---

1. This Annex is based on estimates and tables developed by Vahram Avanessian, AVAG Consultants.

■ Survey of external migration process in the RoA for 1991–1998, Ministry of SSA and Eurostat, Yerevan 1999, p.25 — Table 5.2.2 Distribution of emigrants by sex and age.
■ Statistical yearbooks 1999, 2000 and 2001.

Methodology

1. Total migration is estimated from Census information for 1990 and 2001 (preliminary).
   Total Net migration = Total population (1990)

   $$+ \text{ Natural growth (1991–2000)}$$
   $$- \text{ Total population (2001 Census)} = -820{,}050$$

2. Year specific net migration (in thousand population):

1991	1992	1993	1994	1995	1996	1997	1998	1999	2000
−83,22	−228,60	−141,10	−127,80	−58,08	−40,97	−42,15	−45,06	−27,36	−25,70

3. Age specific net migration structure:

0–4	5–9	10–14	15–19	20–24	25–29	30–34	35–39	40–44	45–49	50–54	55–59	60–64	65–69	70 and over	Total Population
0,05	0,08	0,09	0,08	0,07	0,11	0,12	0,11	0,10	0,08	0,04	0,02	0,03	0,02	0,01	1,00

4. Age specific mortality rates (deaths per thousand of population of specific age)

1–5	6–10	11–15	16–20	21–25	26–30	31–35	36–40	41–45	46–50	51–55	56–60	61–65	66–70	71 and over
0,8	0,2	0,2	0,7	0,74	0,9	1,2	1,7	2,9	4,5	6,5	11,5	18,4	28,1	

5. General fertility rates (modified: births per 1000 of population in age 20–45) by 5 year average:

1991–1995	1996–2000	2001–2005	2006–2010	2011–2015	2016–2020	2021–2025	2026–2030	2031–2035
Estimated	Estimated	Forecast	Forecast	Forecast	Forecast	Forecast	Forecast	Forecast
53,81	36,5	27,0	31,4	36,4	41,4	46,4	49,4	49,4

Based on the above assumptions population estimates by specific ages were estimated. Age groups and composition are shown in the next tables.

AGE DEMOGRAPHIC COMPOSITION ESTIMATES 1991–2001

	Original 1990	1991	1992	1993	1994	1995	1996	1997	1998	1999	2000	2001
0	2.3%	2.0%	1.9%	1.8%	1.6%	1.6%	1.5%	1.4%	1.3%	1.1%	1.1%	1.1%
1–4	8.8%	8.6%	8.5%	8.3%	8.0%	7.2%	6.8%	6.3%	5.9%	5.6%	5.2%	4.8%
5–9	10.4%	10.6%	10.9%	10.9%	10.9%	11.0%	10.6%	10.3%	9.9%	9.3%	8.6%	8.1%
10–14	8.9%	9.0%	9.2%	9.4%	9.8%	10.2%	10.5%	10.7%	10.7%	10.7%	10.8%	10.5%
15–19	7.9%	8.0%	8.1%	8.3%	8.4%	8.6%	8.7%	8.9%	9.2%	9.6%	10.0%	10.3%
20–24	8.1%	8.0%	7.8%	7.7%	7.6%	7.5%	7.7%	7.8%	8.0%	8.2%	8.4%	8.6%
25–29	9.7%	9.3%	8.7%	8.2%	7.7%	7.4%	7.3%	7.3%	7.3%	7.3%	7.2%	7.5%
30–34	9.1%	9.1%	9.0%	8.9%	8.8%	8.9%	8.5%	8.1%	7.7%	7.3%	7.0%	7.0%
35–39	7.0%	7.3%	7.4%	7.6%	7.9%	8.2%	8.2%	8.3%	8.3%	8.4%	8.5%	8.2%
40–44	4.5%	4.9%	5.0%	5.3%	5.5%	5.9%	6.3%	6.7%	7.0%	7.4%	7.8%	7.9%
45–49	3.5%	3.6%	3.5%	3.5%	3.5%	3.5%	3.9%	4.3%	4.7%	5.2%	5.6%	6.0%
50–54	5.5%	5.0%	4.6%	4.1%	3.6%	3.0%	3.0%	3.1%	3.1%	3.2%	3.3%	3.7%
55–59	4.4%	4.5%	4.9%	5.1%	5.4%	5.5%	5.0%	4.4%	3.9%	3.3%	2.8%	2.8%
60–64	4.2%	4.1%	4.1%	4.1%	4.2%	4.2%	4.4%	4.6%	4.8%	4.9%	5.1%	4.6%
65–69	2.0%	2.3%	2.7%	3.1%	3.5%	3.8%	3.7%	3.7%	3.7%	3.6%	3.7%	3.8%
70 and over	3.6%	3.5%	3.6%	3.6%	3.6%	3.5%	3.8%	4.1%	4.4%	4.6%	4.9%	5.1%
Total	100.0%	100.0%	100.0%	100.0%	100.0%	100.0%	100.0%	100.0%	100.0%	100.0%	100.0%	100.0%

ARMENIA POPULATION 1990–2001, ADJUSTED ESTIMATES FOR 1991–2001

	1990 Original Actual	1991 Adjusted Actual	1992 Adjusted Actual	1993 Adjusted Actual	1994 Adjusted Actual	1995 Adjusted Actual	1996 Adjusted Actual	1997 Adjusted Actual	1998 Adjusted Actual	1999 Adjusted Actual	2000 Adjusted Actual	2001 Adjusted Actual
0	73,716	78,417	76,421	69,245	57,993	50,371	48,263	47,387	43,251	38,786	35,449	34,094
1–4	312,000	300,201	288,077	283,842	278,012	266,863	243,949	218,442	197,793	184,082	173,202	162,233
5–9	366,200	371,007	359,990	354,657	345,522	337,330	334,580	333,826	329,272	315,339	300,018	279,313
10–14	321,800	321,908	311,518	307,518	306,335	312,521	321,308	325,709	328,307	323,438	316,944	317,635
15–19	290,300	290,033	277,671	272,136	266,869	268,984	272,436	277,322	281,200	288,255	297,059	308,074
20–24	286,159	273,701	255,366	247,473	241,205	240,907	243,722	245,481	247,216	249,737	254,279	260,891
25–29	332,700	309,834	275,278	252,090	232,661	222,586	216,584	215,686	216,685	219,503	222,334	229,472
30–34	319,500	326,467	306,984	291,590	272,562	258,828	241,715	228,091	215,692	207,437	201,053	199,761
35–39	238,600	242,151	231,864	231,411	235,630	245,594	257,312	258,850	254,326	246,696	236,678	224,208
40–44	160,600	172,462	162,389	161,281	159,748	168,568	176,397	185,974	195,717	210,486	223,731	239,438
45–49	121,900	101,278	86,195	85,532	92,815	103,624	117,551	123,995	131,385	138,762	150,153	160,908
50–54	191,200	188,032	169,686	143,480	112,672	86,306	66,368	61,980	66,718	79,549	91,670	106,800
55–59	151,600	149,011	152,588	154,954	159,848	167,548	164,186	151,346	128,751	102,120	77,774	59,680
60–64	152,700	158,443	149,078	143,542	134,430	125,120	124,558	132,040	136,418	143,004	150,713	148,530
65–69	73,700	82,506	95,271	108,067	119,229	123,431	128,794	123,949	120,947	114,900	107,231	107,605
70 and over	127,860	121,492	112,319	108,409	106,810	112,710	117,356	126,444	136,873	147,255	155,854	164,037
Total	3,520,535	3,486,942	3,310,697	3,215,226	3,122,343	3,091,291	3,075,077	3,056,521	3,030,551	3,009,348	2,994,142	3,002,678
0–5	464,516	457,959	439,150	423,831	402,084	382,147	362,450	336,492	305,795	277,771	256,387	242,578
6 to 15	669,800	673,654	655,068	648,089	640,950	642,124	642,939	648,780	651,946	644,907	634,381	616,805
6 to 16	729,300	732,836	711,451	704,003	695,525	696,329	699,430	705,355	711,091	703,545	694,960	681,915
16 to 20	286,000	283,455	272,182	266,583	262,079	262,196	265,631	268,990	273,648	278,889	286,067	296,849
21 to 45	1,299,659	1,291,655	1,205,764	1,157,906	1,116,723	1,110,383	1,113,787	1,112,412	1,109,256	1,113,849	1,118,892	1,136,229
46 to 60	479,800	450,689	407,928	388,390	365,630	355,253	349,378	339,971	329,035	320,858	314,832	317,138
16 to 60	2,065,459	2,025,799	1,885,875	1,812,879	1,744,431	1,727,833	1,728,796	1,721,373	1,711,939	1,713,596	1,719,791	1,750,215
61 and over	320,760.00	329,530.11	330,603.91	330,427.58	334,877.42	339,187.13	340,892.62	349,876.66	360,870.87	373,074.15	383,582.81	393,079.95

REFERENCES

Abrahamyan and Avagyan. 2001. "Abortion." In National Statistical Service, Ministry of Health and ORC Macro *Armenia Demographic and Health Survey 2000*. Calverton, Maryland.

Alam, Asad and Mark Sundberg. 2002. "A Decade of Fiscal Transition." Policy Research Working Paper No. 2835. World Bank, Washington, D.C.

Barbone, Luca and Hana Polackova. 1996. "Public Finances and Economic Transition." Policy Research Working Paper No. 1585. World Bank, Washington, D.C.

Chaudhury, N., J. Hammer and E. Murrugarra. 2002. "The Effect of Fee Waivers on Health Care Utilization: Evidence from the Basic Package program in Armenia." World Bank, Washington, D.C.

Cheasty, Adrienne and Jeffrey Davis. 1996. "Fiscal Transition in the Countries of the Former Soviet Union." Working Paper No. 96/61. IMF, Washington, D.C.

Corfmat, François, Allan Firestone and Richard Fulford. 2001. "Armenia Revenue Mobilization." IMF, Washington, D.C.

De Maria, Paolo. 2000. Improving the Budget Process of the Republic of Armenia. USAID Tax and Fiscal Reform Project. Yerevan.

Desai, P., T. Parry, P. Rao and P. Saunders. 1998. *Armenia: Improving Public Expenditure Management*. IMF Fiscal Affairs Department. IMF, Washington, D.C.

Ebrill, Liam, Michael Keen, Jean-Paul Bodin, and Victoria Summers. 2001. *Modern VAT*. IMF, Washington, D.C.

European Observatory on Health Care Systems. 2001. Health Care Systems in Transition. Armenia 2001. Report N. EUR/01/5012669(ARM). Volume 3(11).

Fakin, Barbara and Alain de Crombrugghe. 1997. *Fiscal Adjustments in Transition Economies: Social Transfers and the Efficiency of Public Spending, A Comparison with OECD Countries*. Policy Research Working Paper No. 1803. World Bank, Washington, D.C.

Fontys International. 2000. *Reform Strategy for Higher and Technical Education for the Ministry of Education and Science of the Republic of Armenia*. Final Report. Eindhoven, Netherlands.

Heggie, Ian G. and Piers Vickers. 1998. *Commercial Management and Financing of Roads*. Technical Paper 409. World Bank, Washington, D.C.

Horvath, Balazs, Nita Thacker, and Jiming Ha. 1998. "Achieving Stabilization in Armenia." IMF Working Paper WP-98/38. IMF, Washington, D.C.

IMF. 2001a. "Armenia. Financial System Sustainability Assessment."

IMF. 2001b. "Armenia: Report on Observance of Standards and Codes (ROSC)." Financial Transparency Module.

Kharas, Homi and Deepak Mishra. 2001. "Fiscal Policies, Hidden Deficits, and Currency Crises." In *World Bank Economists' Forum*. Vol. 1. World Bank, Washington, D.C.

Kurkchiyan, M. 1999. "Report on Health Care in Armenia." Mimeo, prepared for the World Bank.

Lewis, Maureen. 2000. "Who is Paying for Health Care in Europe and Central Asia?" World Bank, Washington, D.C.

Martin, Michael O., Ina V.S. Mullis, Albert E. Beaton, Eugenio J. Gonzalez, Teresa A. Smith, and Dana L. Kelly. 1997. *Science Achievement in the Primary School Years*. IEA's Third International Mathematics and Science Study. Chestnut Hill, MA: TIMSS International Study Center, Boston College.

Martin, Michael O., Ina V.S. Mullis, Eugenio J. Gonzalez, Kelvin D. Gregory, Teresa A. Smith, Steven J. Chrostowski, Robert A. Garden, and Kathleen M. O'Connor. 2000. *TIMSS 1999: International Science Report*. Findings from IEA's Repeat of the Third International Mathematics and Science Study at the Eighth Grade. Chestnut Hill, MA: TIMSS International Study Center, Boston College.

McDermott, John C. and Robert F. Wescott. 1996. *Fiscal Reforms that Work*. Economic Issues No. 4. IMF, Washington, D.C.

Ministry of Science and Education, Republic of Armenia. 2000. *State Program for Educational Development (2001–2005)*. Yerevan.

Ministry of Statistics, State Register and Analysis, Republic of Armenia. 2000. *The Socio-Economic Situation of the Republic of Armenia, January–December, 1999*. Yerevan.

Moore, Mick. 1998. "Death without Taxes: Democracy, State Capacity, and Aid Dependence in the Fourth World." In M. Robinson and G. White (eds.) *The Democratic Developmental State: Political and Institutional Design*. Oxford University Press: 84–124. Oxford.

Mullis, Ina V.S., Michael O. Martin, Albert E. Beaton, Eugenio J. Gonzalez, Dana L. Kelly, Teresa A. Smith. 1997. *Mathematics Achievement in the Primary School Years*. IEA's Third International Mathematics and Science Study. Chestnut Hill, MA: TIMSS International Study Center, Boston College.

Mullis, Ina V.S., Michael O. Martin, Albert E. Beaton, Eugenio J. Gonzalez, Dana L. Kelly, Teresa A. Smith. 1998. *Mathematics and Science Achievement in the final Year of Secondary School*. IEA's Third International Mathematics and Science Study. Chestnut Hill, MA: TIMSS International Study Center, Boston College.

Mullis, Ina V.S., Michael O. Martin, Eugenio J. Gonzalez, Kelvin D. Gregory, Robert A. Garden, Kathleen M. O'Connor, Steven J. Chrostowski, and Teresa A. Smith. 2000. *TIMSS 1999: International Mathematics Report*. Findings from IEA's Repeat of the Third International Mathematics and Science Study at the Eighth Grade. Chestnut Hill, MA: TIMSS International Study Center, Boston College.

National Statistical Service, Ministry of Health and ORC Macro. 2001. *Armenia Demographic and Health Survey 2000*. Calverton, Maryland.

OECD (Organization for Economic Cooperation and Development). 2000. *Literacy in the Information Age.* Paris: Organization for Economic Co-operation and Development. Canada: Human Resources Development Canada, and Statistics.

———. 2001a. *Education at a Glance: OECD Indicators.* Paris: Center for Educational Research and Innovation, OECD.

———. 2001b. *Knowledge and Skills for Life.* First Results from PISA 2000. Paris: Organization for Economic Co-operation and Development.

PADCO. 2001. "Financial and Actuarial Analysis of the Armenian Pension System." Armenia Social Transition Program. Report No. 35. Yerevan.

Perkins, Gillian and Ruslan Yemtsov. 2001. *Armenia. Restructuring to Sustain Universal General Education.* World Bank Technical Paper No. 498. Washington, D.C.

Petrossyan, Hayk. 1998. "Public Health Financing and Planning in Armenia." Situational Analysis. TACIS. Yerevan.

Pinto, Brian, Vladimir Drebentsov and Alexander Morozov. 2000. "Give Growth and Macroeconomic Stability in Russia a Chance." World Bank Policy Research Working Paper 2324. Washington, D.C.

Pradhan, Sanjay. 1996. *Evaluating Public Spending: A Framework for Public Expenditure Reviews,* World Bank Discussion Paper No. 323. Washington, D.C.

Preker A., Jakab M., Shneider M. 1999. "Health Financing Systems in Transition: Trends in Eastern Europe and Central Asia." World Bank, Washington, D.C.

Ramachandran, Vijay. 2001. "Treasury Operations in Armenia." Mimeo. Yerevan.

Rutkowski, Jan. J. 2001. *Earnings Inequality in Transition Economies of Central Europe: Trends and Patterns During the 1990s.* World Bank, Washington, D.C.

Schwab, K., M. Porter, and J. Sachs, eds. 2001. *The Global Competitiveness Report, 2001/2001.* The World Economic Forum, Geneva.

State Health Agency. 1998. *Report of Activities.* Yerevan.

Ter-Grigorian, Ara, Karlen Antonyan, Khachatur Kolozyan, and Tatevik Kostanyan. 2000. "The Development of BBP in the Republic of Armenia." TNO Consultants. Yerevan.

Tanzi, Vitto and George Tsibouris. 1999. *Fiscal Reform over Ten Years of Transition.* Paper presented to the Fifth Dubrovnik Conference on Transition Economies, July 23–25.

United Nations Development Program. 2001. *Armenia, Education Sector Review.*

UNICEF. 1998. *Education for All?* The MONEE Project Regional Monitoring Report 5. Florence: UNICEF International Child Development Center.

World Bank. 1997a. *Public Expenditures in Armenia: Strategic Spending for Creditworthiness and Growth,* Report No. 16213-AM. Washington D.C.

———. 1997b. "Staff Appraisal Report: Education and Financing and Management Reform Project for the Republic of Armenia." Washington, D.C.

———. 1998a. "The United Republic of Tanzania: Public Expenditure Review" (In Two Volumes). Washington, D.C.

———. 1998b. *Public Expenditure Management Handbook.* Washington D.C.

———. 1999a. *Armenia: Civil Service Assessment.* Washington D.C.

———. 1999b. *Improving Social Assistance in Armenia.* Report No. 19385-AM (June 8). Washington D.C.

———. 2000a. *Armenia: Institutional and Governance Review.* Washington D.C.

———. 2000b. *Hidden Challenges to Education Systems in Transition Economies.* Washington, D.C.

———. 2001a. *Decentralization in the Transition Economies: Challenges and the Road Ahead.* Washington D.C.

———. 2001b. "Armenia, Georgia, Kyrgyz Republic, Moldova, and Tajikistan: External Debt and Fiscal Sustainability." Board Paper. Washington D.C.

_____. 2001c. *Armenia: Growth Challenges and Government Policies.* Report No. 22854-AM (In Two Volumes). Washington D.C.

_____. 2001d. "Russia: Towards Improving the Efficiency of Public Investment Expenditures." Report No. 22693-RU.

_____. 2001e. "Georgia Public Expenditure Review: The Health Sector." (draft). Washington, D.C.

_____. 2001f. "Ethiopia: Focusing Public Expenditures on Poverty Reduction." Washington, D.C.

_____. 2002a. *Building Institutions for Markets.* World Development Report 2002. Washington, D.C.

_____. 2002b. "Armenia Poverty Update." ECSHD (in process).

World Health Organization. 1996. "Health Care Systems in Transition. Armenia." Copenhagen: World Health Organization. Regional Office for Europe.

Zohrab, John. 2002. "An Assessment of the Current Status of the Treasury of the Republic of Armenia and Scope for Further Enhancement." Mimeo. Yerevan.